DEMOGRAPHY FOR BUSINESS DECISION MAKING

DEMOGRAPHY FOR BUSINESS DECISION MAKING

Louis G. Pol
Richard K. Thomas

Q

QUORUM BOOKS
Westport, Connecticut • London

Library of Congress Cataloging-in-Publication Data

Pol, Louis G.
    Demography for business decision making / Louis G. Pol, Richard K.
Thomas.
        p.   cm.
    Includes bibliographical references and index.
    ISBN 1–56720–014–1 (alk. paper)
    1. Demography.   2. Marketing research.   3. United States—
Population.   4. Decision-making.   I. Thomas, Richard K., 1944–
II. Title.
HB849.41.P633   1997
304.6′024′658—dc20   96–46087

British Library Cataloguing in Publication Data is available.

Library of Congress Catalog Card Number: 96–46087
ISBN: 1–56720–014–1

First published in 1997

Quorum Books, 88 Post Road West, Westport, CT 06881
An imprint of Greenwood Publishing Group Inc.

Printed in the United States of America

The paper used in this book complies with the
Permanent Paper Standard issued by the National
Information Standards Organization (Z39.48–1984).

10 9 8 7 6 5 4 3 2 1

Contents

Preface

Only a decade ago, demography was seen as peripheral to business decision making, and business concerns generally were considered outside the purview of demographers. Several changes over the last ten years, however, have altered these relationships. In particular, many businesses have come to embrace demographic data, methods, and perspectives as important inputs for decision making. There is a growing body of literature—both academic and popular—describing the role of demography in business decision making and an increasing number of demographers are employed as consultants to business organizations.

The role played by demography in business decision making coincides with management's increasingly broader view of information use. Business decisions today are information driven, and owners and managers seek input from a broad range of sources in order to maximize the probability of success. As business/demographic relationships have become clearer, demographic input has come to be more heavily relied on as an important component of the information matrix specific to a given decision. Unlike traditional demography where the focus is on a better understanding of some demographic phenomenon, the emphasis in business demography is on the ways demographic input can contribute to the decision-making process.

Several factors have contributed to changes in the way demography is viewed. As decision making has become more information driven, the use of demographic data has increased. The availability of demographic data in various formats has made its inclusion in the decision-making process routine. Data vendors have repackaged government statistics, and added projections of their own, further advancing the potential for demographic contributions. Most of these data are inexpensive and available at small levels of geography, the level at which most business decisions are made. Enhanced analytical software and improved mapping capabilities have further facilitated the integration of demographic data.

Over the next decade, the relationship between demography and business will evolve even further. The integration of demographic data with business information will be easier and, perhaps more importantly, a larger array of firms will come to view the demographic component of the decision making process as essential.

Acknowledgments

Producing a book involves a team effort, and this book certainly involved assistance from several significant contributors. First, we had important input from eight of our colleagues from across the nation who graciously agreed to write the short biographies included in several chapters. We thank Hallie Kintner, Joan Naymark, Jeffrey Tayman, Thomas Exter, Kenneth Hodges, Peter Morrison, Stanley Smith, and Susan Mott for their contributions. Second, Jackie Lynch, who has now word processed four of our books, was up to her usual high work standards and, frankly, this book never would have been completed without her careful editing, file merging, and patience. Third, Mary Glogowski contributed her editing skills, and, as a result, this book is easier to read. Fourth, three persons assisted us in producing graphics and figures: Cristian Chelariu, Irina Gotcu Mulvey, and Janet Pol. Fifth, we wish to thank Eric Valentine, our editor at Quorum, who provided constant encouragement, while exhibiting considerable patience. Finally, to all of the MBA students who have enrolled in the business demography course at the University of Nebraska at Omaha, thank you for your comments and criticisms of materials that have become part of this book.

The University of Nebraska at Omaha and Medical Services Research Group, our employers, have also been supportive of our efforts. In particular, Denise Smart, Chair of the Department of Marketing at the University of Nebraska at Omaha, and the partners in Medical Services Research Group, provided the kind of environments and encouragement we needed to complete this project.

Finally, while this book is technically not a second edition of Louis Pol's *Business Demography*, published by Quorum in 1987, the current work has been influenced by that effort as well as comments and criticisms of the earlier publication.

DEMOGRAPHY FOR BUSINESS DECISION MAKING

Chapter 1

Business Demography: A Decision-Making Discipline

INTRODUCTION

Over the past 15 years the term *business demography* has appeared with increasing regularity in business articles, the demographic literature, and in presentations and discussions at professional meetings of demographers. Currently, however, there is no widely agreed-upon scope for this developing field of study, but only a loose collection of articles, reports, and cases that involve a demographic/business intersection. This book delineates the nature of this emerging discipline and illustrates how the incorporation of demographic data, methods, theory, and perspectives can improve the decision-making capabilities of individuals and organizations engaged in various fields of commerce.

Business demography is perhaps best defined as the application of the content and methods of demography to business problems and opportunities. *Demography* is the study of human populations. It includes the study of the size, distribution, composition, and change dimensions related to human populations, as well as the associated dynamic factors of migration, fertility, and mortality. Business demography concerns itself with the manner in which such variables as age, income, and occupation influence the business-related behavior of individuals and organizations, and how aggregate characteristics such as the age, income, and occupational structures affect the business environment of markets. Business demographers focus on how current demographic conditions and the projected change generated by the interaction of migration, fertility, and mortality affect the business environment and the strategic decisions required to ensure business success.

Business demography involves the application of the *demographic perspective* to business issues (Weeks 1994, p. 1). The demographic perspective is a manner in which the surrounding world can be viewed. For persons interested in business issues, it means understanding how population processes affect business conditions.

These processes could include the aging or "younging" of populations; the increase, stabilization, or decrease in population size; or the geographic redistribution of people.

Ultimately, this understanding must be applied to the problems and opportunities encountered by the business community. Problems and opportunities are any and all that one has an interest in, and they range from concerns over a decrease in retail sales for a specific store to the identification of market opportunities for a corporation at some point in the future. The key is the link between the demographic processes and the problem or opportunity of interest. When coupled with the knowledge and skills of other disciplines, the demographic perspective becomes a powerful tool for understanding how changes in the size, composition, and distribution of the population affect the business environment.

Demography, demographics, and the demographic perspective are terms often used interchangeably, although they have very different meanings. As noted above, demography refers to the broad-based study of population. *Demographics*, on the other hand, has no agreed-upon definition, and its use varies throughout the academic and nonacademic literature. Most often, demographics is operationalized as the combined static characteristics of a population or a market segment such as average age or median family income. These data are used to describe markets and have intuitive appeal because business-related behavior varies from one demographically defined group to another.

The demographic perspective emphasizes a more in-depth and analytic understanding of the connection between demographic characteristics and processes and business-related behavior. That is, the demographic perspective links ongoing demographic change such as an increase in population size and change in composition with continued alterations in the business environment. This perspective relies on an understanding of the relationship between population processes and alterations in the business environment, and thus facilitates an ability to forecast change in the conditions under which business is conducted. While the distinction between demography, demographics, and the demographic perspective may appear to be unnecessary, by the time the reader has finished this book, the need for distinguishing these three concepts should be clear.

A distinction between demography and business demography is relevant at this point. The focus of most demographic studies as they are conducted by academic or research institution scholars is on one or more demographic phenomena. Researchers wish to predict and explain those phenomena—for example, the unanticipated rise in fertility rates in the late 1980s—by making the understanding of the demographic phenomenon the goal of the inquiry. In business demography, the demographic components are but some of many elements that are drawn together to arrive at a decision. The main focus is the *decision*, and demography is regarded as a tool for guiding the decision-making process.

THE ROOTS OF BUSINESS DEMOGRAPHY

Demography is often subdivided into two broad areas of study. The first is *formal demography*, which refers to the development of models and the advancement of methods specific to demographic studies. This line of inquiry is basic to the advancement of the science of demography and provides the theories, tools, and techniques that business demographers often use. *Social demography*, on the other hand, is the application of demographic methods, data, and theories to social issues. *Applied demography* is a subcategory of social demography and refers to the application of demographic methods, data, and theory to a host of real world problems.

Figure 1.1 depicts applied demography as being composed of three unique components, one of which is business demography. The public/private distinction is made because, while the methods and materials utilized in both types of studies are the same, the unique, profit-oriented, and oftentimes proprietary nature of business demographic work justifies separate consideration. Much of the public sector applied work seen today has a longer history and might have been classified as part of the more general rubric, social demography, at an earlier time.

Figure 1.1
Components of Applied Demography

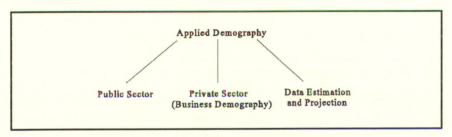

Ford and DeJong (1970, 4–14) were among the first to express social demography as encompassing the relationship between demography and social phenomena. Moreover, social demography involves the intersection of three major analysis systems: demography, social aggregation, and social action. Social action systems include political, health, and economic systems, which comprise the major focus of applied demography today. It is not clear whether or not Ford and DeJong meant to include the private sector dimensions, business demography, as part of their focus on economic systems, but today the linkage between social demography and business demography is clear.

Both public and private sector applications focus on decision making. However, the major goal of those generating estimates and projections is to provide high-quality data for decision making. The estimates and projections category is unique in that it has its own established methodologies and data sets, with a relatively long history of development.

The use of demographic methods, data, and theory in the study of business problems and opportunities can be grouped into a number of categories. These categories include but are not limited to:

- Site analysis;
- Human resources planning;
- Organizational demography;
- Market area assessment;
- Market area financial potential;
- Financial planning;
- Sales forecasting;
- Target marketing;
- Logistics;
- New product introduction.

Business decisions, frequently, have a locational component; that is, the characteristics of a new or existing site must be analyzed and the results integrated into a decision-making process that has several other components. *Site analyses* refer to the processes involved in the selection of new sites and/or the study of the impact of a change in competitors' activities or other environmental change on an existing site. At the same time, planning efforts oftentimes call for labor force analyses that either have an external or internal focus. *Human resources planning* looks at both the impact of external demographic conditions on an area's labor force and an organization's structure (e.g., age, training, and experience) with respect to meeting the demands of its customers. Closely related to human resources planning is *organizational demography*. Organizational demography focuses on the composition (e.g., age and educational structure) of an organization's management and its labor force compared to current and future needs given the present and anticipated competitive environment.

An analysis of the demographic conditions within an already defined market area or a newly developing market comprises a *market area assessment*. This line of inquiry includes both the static and changing characteristics of market areas. A demographic-based analysis of the purchasing ability/preferences of persons or organizations within a new (future) market area can assist in assessing the *financial potential* for that area. Separate from assessing financial potential, *financial planning* for an existing market, including the study of cash flow, return on investment, and capital expenditure strategy, is an area where the input of demographic data can greatly enhance the planning process.

Sales forecasts for particular markets can be improved by tying potential shifts in sales to changing demographic conditions. For example, purchase or usage rates specific to certain demographic characteristics (e.g., age and sex) can be multiplied by age- or sex-specific population projections for a given geographic area to generate overall and/or age-segment-specific sales projections. In the area of *target marketing*, knowledge of the demographic characteristics of one's best customers enables a manager to target this group with some type of promotional material or utilize a direct sales approach to blanket areas that have large concentrations of persons with these same characteristics. For *logistics planning*, population measures of attributes for subgroups such as the senior population are used to determine the transportation patterns appropriate for the delivery of products and services. Once the concentration of persons is determined, simple or sophisticated models can be constructed to efficiently deliver products or services. Finally, demographic input can be important to *new product development*. To the extent that propensities to adopt and purchase new technology and technological updates are tied to demographic characteristics, current and forecasted population size and composition serve as indicators of the potential for new product sales.

The above list is far from exhaustive. As demographically driven analyses increase in number and sophistication, the list will undoubtedly grow. In the remaining chapters, we present a variety of examples that illustrate the wide range of situations in which demographic input can assist business decision making.

One common misconception about business demography is that it is a discipline whose main applications are in marketing and management. While these fields of study have an intuitive connection to business demography and most of the business demographic literature is in these fields, the data, methods, and perspectives of demography are just as valuable to other business fields. Financial planning, including decisions about capital expenditures, cash flow, and resource allocation, has its basis in forecasted financial transactions. Therefore, it is crucial that financial planners base their projections on the best available data, which often include a forecast of sales and other business transactions. To the extent that demographic data, methods, and perspectives can improve the quality of sales forecasts, financial analysts should have more than a passing interest in demographic trends and analyses. Whatever the field of application, business demography is a discipline whose major contribution is in the area of improved decision making.

BUSINESS DEMOGRAPHY AS A DECISION-MAKING SCIENCE

Recently there have been a number of discussions focusing on applied demography as a decision-making science (Swanson, Burch, and Tedrow 1996). In applied demography, the goal of demographic input is to improve the quality of decisions. In business demography, the goal is to apply a demographic perspective and to utilize demographic data, methods, and theory to help decision makers make better choices with respect to commerce-related strategies and the implementation of those strategies.

In order to understand the ways in which demographic input can influence decisions, the decision-making process should be examined in some detail. The steps in this process are identified in Figure 1.2. Before the decision-making process is set in motion, a problem (e.g., declining sales) or an opportunity (e.g., the emergence of new markets) is recognized and regarded as important enough to explore more thoroughly. However, before decision-related activities commence, the resources needed to drive the process are assessed, and, if appropriate, demographic resources in the form of expertise, information, methods, and perspective are identified as requirements. At this point, in-house personnel may be called on to provide the expertise, or a consultant may be secured to assist in the process. Consultants are frequently utilized because few organizations employ personnel with the requisite demographic experience and/or training to perform the desired tasks. The key is to find a consultant with experience in the problem area identified *and* to somehow integrate that person into the decision-making process.

Figure 1.2
Decision Making Process

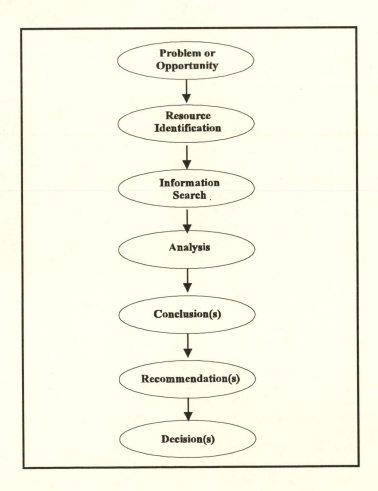

Information search and analysis has a demographic component because a decision has been made *a priori* to include demographic input. An in-house analyst should understand the appropriate methodologies and be able to locate or produce demographic data that are of acceptable quality. Although the analysis often involves traditional statistical techniques (e.g., time series analysis), tools specific to demographic analysis sometimes are applied in order to provide the uniquely demographic information required to arrive at a sound decision.

Business decisions are made in the context of what has been labeled the "triple constraint" (Swanson, Burch, and Tedrow 1996). The components of the triple constraint are (1) performance specification—the level of information accuracy required to drive a decision; (2) time—the speed with which the information needs to be delivered; and (3) resources—the level of resources available to generate the information. Clearly, these constraints are interrelated; for example, a one-week deadline for a specific endeavor may greatly affect information accuracy while minimizing resources expended. These constraints greatly affect the quality of demographic input, and demographers must perform within the context of these constraints as they participate in the decision-making process.

From a management perspective, decisions with regard to performance, time, and resources must be made in the context of the desired outcome and the perceived importance of the information to the decision. When demographic data and analysis are key to a business decision, performance standards rise, the time allocated increases, and resources expended grow, though perhaps not proportionately. In situations where demographic information is less important, appropriate adjustments with respect to the three constraints are made.

All too often demographers have limited input with regard to conclusions and recommendations subsequent to the demographic analysis. Limited input often results because few demographers have training or extensive experience in business decision making. The "best case" scenario is one in which the demographer is also experienced in and knowledgeable about the types of business decisions being made and is therefore qualified to provide input beyond a straightforward demographic analysis. In some areas of analysis, such as health care, in-depth knowledge is essential. Although managers and owners make the final decision, input from a business-qualified demographer can be invaluable.

In addition to identifying steps in the decision-making process, an understanding of current developments affecting contemporary business decisions is important. Several of these developments have demographic dimensions. They include:

- Increasing numbers of competitors;
- Increasing sophistication of competition;
- Internationalization of markets;
- Shifting industry structure;
- Increasing costs of wrong decisions.

Many sectors of the marketplace are becoming more competitive because there has been a significant increase in the number and the source of competition. Competitors are now more sophisticated in the area of strategic planning, with particular emphasis on product development and marketing. Market boundaries have blurred and, with the passage of the North American Free Trade Agreement (NAFTA) and the General Agreement on Tariffs and Trade (GATT) and the solidifying of the European Community (EC), customers and potential customers are found all over the world. Moreover, the developments above, when combined with technological advances and changing consumer preferences, have brought about a radical shift in industry structure. In particular, a shift away from manufacturing and toward service businesses can be seen in many more developed nations. While wrong decisions have always been costly, the implications of poor decisions in the current economic climate are increasingly detrimental.

These developments are forcing organizations to engage in sophisticated high-level decision-making processes. While the processes will always include subjective input such as "gut" feelings, decisions are becoming more data based. Information from a myriad of sources is now being merged into the systems that drive decisions. It is in this environment that a demographic contribution to decision making can be best appreciated. The strong connection between demographic factors and business patterns ensures that the demographic contribution to business decision making will grow stronger and broader over time.

HISTORICAL USE OF THE DEMOGRAPHIC PERSPECTIVE IN BUSINESS

The use of demographic data and methods in business planning has a relatively long history, although there is a shortage of published evidence to this effect. As business strategy in general, and marketing in particular, began to move away from a mass-market approach to new systems of segmenting and targeting populations during the 1960s, demographic data proved useful in the identification of distinct market segments. This tradition continues. There is even a longer history of demographic input into site selection decisions. Late in the last century and early in this one, business owners were interested in the decentralizing pattern of city growth that fostered business opportunities. The availability of demographic data for small geographic units early in this century facilitated the siting of retail outlets and other business establishments. Other examples of early demographic input are found in real estate planning, labor force assessment, and utilities development.

Major advances in business demography began to appear in the 1980s, with three factors primarily responsible for this development. First, demographic data became much easier to access (e.g., on diskette and later on CD-ROM). In fact, an entire industry has developed for distributing demographic data. This development facilitated the increased reliance on data for business decision making. Second, because public and proprietary research had identified clear demographic/business relationships, the business community began to incorporate demographic input into a wider range of planning activities. Currently, it is standard practice to include the "demographics" of markets as part of the informational input to decision making in many industries.

Third, portions of the demographic community began to view business applications as legitimate arenas for research. It was not until 1982 that the Population Association of America (PAA), the largest professional association for demographers in the United States, established an "official" committee that represented business demographers. Today, only 14 years later, approximately 20 percent of the PAA membership identifies applied demography as an area of professional interest. Demographers are now employed by Dayton Hudson Corporation, General Motors, and Nationwide Insurance, among other large organizations. Many other demographers have formed their own consulting firms and their clients include businesses of all sizes across a wide range of industries. In addition, there has been some progress, albeit slow, in the training of demography students in applied techniques. If this trend gains momentum, a much greater level of business involvement can be expected in the future.

ORGANIZATION OF THE BOOK

This book is designed to provide an understanding of demographic processes, methods, and data, documenting how these demographic elements affect business decisions. A brief chapter on contemporary demographic trends is presented initially. This chapter provides the context from which to view the remaining material. Chapter 3 identifies and discusses the sources of the demographic data used in the remainder of the book. Chapters 4 through 9 cover basic demographic processes (migration, fertility, and mortality), along with the three major components of demography (size, distribution, and composition). Because demographic data are typically limited to some unit of geography, a chapter on geographic units and geographic information systems (GIS) are also included. Chapter 10 addresses the rapidly expanding area of study related to estimates and projections of demographic data. Chapter 11 focuses on applications of contemporary business demography.

Some readers of this book already will have had demographic training. Those readers might find it useful to first read the examples and boxed materials in Chapters 4 through 8 and then proceed to Chapters 9 through 11. Those with less demographic training are best served by reading the chapters in order. The boxed material is designed to enliven the presentation and offer contemporary examples of how the principles discussed in the text are applied. Box 1.1 provides a short site selection vignette, while Box 1.2 offers a description of the activities of Hallie J. Kintner, a business demographer at General Motors Corporation.

Box 1.1
Locating Sites for Automatic Teller Machines (ATMs)

One of the many service developments of the 1980s was the introduction of automatic teller machines (ATMs). Once consumers overcame their initial reluctance

Box 1.1 continued

to use these devices to conduct banking transactions, financial institutions rapidly expanded the number of locations having ATMs. One issue initially facing these institutions was the identification of appropriate sites for ATMs.

Preliminary surveys indicated that the ATM market could be segmented into a number of subgroups. This segmentation had implications for the locations that potential customers considered most convenient. Moreover, medium and heavy intended usage was found to be associated with certain demographic characteristics. Some potential customers preferred locations near their residences, much as they preferred some retail stores be close to home; others desired locations near the workplace. The site analyses included a significant demographic component. Neighborhoods and workplace areas that contained concentrations of persons with a "favorable" demographic profile were identified. Once these areas were identified, ATMs were installed in locations within close proximity. Small area census data along with traffic counts and business location figures provided the essential information for preliminary site selection decisions.

The site selection decisions were not complete at this point. Data on ATM usage, shifting traffic patterns, changes in business locations, the development of new residential areas, and changes in consumer preferences were merged to support decisions on closing existing sites and opening new ones. This process continues as ATM location remains an important part of the bank service mix in an increasingly competitive marketplace. Of particular importance is the establishment of a presence in growth areas such as new suburbs, suburban shopping areas, and malls.

More recently, bank consolidation in some markets has resulted in a need to reduce the number of ATMs. ATMs are expensive to construct and operate, and oversaturation of the market carries a heavy financial burden. Moreover, fewer freestanding ATMs are needed as the machines are incorporated into businesses such as grocery stores, convenience marts, airports, and casinos. Again, site analyses incorporating ATM and other bank service use patterns, population growth, and other demographic factors are being conducted. The goal is to reduce costs by closing some existing ATMs, while at the same time provide the best level of service possible. As this ATM "shakeout" proceeds, demographic data and expertise will continue to be important components in the decision-making process.

Box 1.2

A Day in the Work Life of Hallie Kintner

Business Demographer at General Motors Corporation

I am a Research Scientist at the General Motors Research and Development Center. I have a Ph.D. in sociology and demography and an M.S. in biostatistics. I apply demographic and statistical techniques to a wide variety of business issues. I also perform basic research in demography and statistics.

Box 1.2 continued

The Research and Development Center is located in the GM technical park in Warren, Michigan. It is a beautiful setting with a man-made lake and futuristic buildings designed by Saarinen. My office is unusual for GM in that it has walls; most salaried employees are in "bull pens" with desks divided by five foot highpartitions. I am in a department of about 40 persons, including 38 research professionals, most with Ph.D.s.

I try to spend the first two hours of my day doing solitary work that requires thinking and/or writing. I avoid answering the phone and let the voice mail and e-mail accumulate messages. I write papers for both internal and external audiences; some are for professional demographers while others are for lay persons. Later on, I return phone calls, which are usually from people with whom I am collaborating on a project or who are requesting my advice. I frequently provide advice to GM units about various projects related to human resources.

I usually am involved in two or three projects at a time. How do I come to be involved in a project? Sometimes requests come to me from other parts of the corporation through my manager. Other requests come directly to me through personal contacts or people who have become aware of my work. I also initiate some projects on my own, usually in collaboration with others inside or outside GM.

The projects differ in their length and outcomes. Some projects are long term and last a year or more. Others, sometimes called "firefights," last only 1–2 weeks. While most basic research projects have outcomes limited to research papers, project outcomes can vary from brief presentations to management (the most frequent result of a "firefight") to slides for executive presentations to computer programs for other GM units.

I average about two meetings per day. The meetings are usually with 5–10 people with whom I am working on a project. The meetings are usually for communication purposes and for making decisions about technical matters. The initial meetings about a project involve identification of the problem and scoping out the project, including deadlines. Speed of completion is much more important in business than in academic research settings. For firefights, management frequently wants to know the best answer obtainable within a short timeframe.

As an example of a longer term project, I worked with a team to design and carry out a survey of all salaried employees in General Motors. The purpose of the survey was to improve the corporation's ability to identify candidates for positions (jobs) and to plan for the future by collecting information about employees' experiences. The product of the project, the survey results, provided additional employee information to be entered into the human resources management database to augment existing data about employee demographics, educational background, and position history.

The team included representatives from the corporate personnel staff and staff from other parts of the organization, including human resource administration salaried personnel, information management, and EDS, a subsidiary of GM that is responsible for maintaining the human resource management database. I was the only research scientist on the team. The team met as needed, ranging from every two weeks to every two months. Devising the agenda was usually the first item of

Box 1.2 continued

business at every meeting. Each person had been given one or more assignments. We reported back to others about our assignments. Sometimes this involved communicating what happened at another meeting attended by a representative of our team. Other times our assignment was a particular task, e.g., finding out how to post an announcement on employees' paychecks or making arrangements to give a presentation at a meeting. The team was then asked to make a decision about the content and the timing of the announcement. Sometimes we put together a presentation to inform the executives about our progress.

Our team was responsible for the design of the employee survey. For example, we decided not to ask open-ended questions which would permit every employee to describe his or her experiences in great detail. The business reasons for this decision were that planning and selection did not require such detailed information and that an open-ended questionnaire would take more time to complete than a questionnaire allowing only certain responses. We devised tables of terms to describe the type of work activities that the corporation wanted identified for selection and planning. The tables were developed with input from employee focus groups and from managers of particular functions, like communications and legal staff. We held many pre-tests of the questionnaire to examine the tables and the completion of the scanning forms used to record the employee responses.

We were also responsible for designing the system to administer the survey. We decided to require all salaried employees (enforced by supervisors) to respond to the survey rather than to allow voluntary participation with incentives to promote responses. We established a system of contacts through which to pass questionnaires and completed scanning forms. We were very pleased with a response rate exceeding 85 percent, which is very high for a mail-return questionnaire. On the other hand, we were not pleased by the frequent failures of the scanning process, which resulted in unexpected data entry work.

This project took nearly two years to complete but it has had a major impact on the corporation. This survey led to the establishment of an electronic system for posting jobs and sending in resumes.

I enjoy my job because I can often see the results of my work in action. I have worked on several projects that have had major consequences for GM. For instance, I provided analyses which led to decisions on the best ways to downsize the salaried workforce, including which employees were most essential to the future of the corporation and what kinds of personnel tools (window retirement programs and special separation incentive programs) to offer to other employees. I recently won an award from the GM R&D Center for developing a workload model that assists in product planning.

In the future, will business use demography? The future depends on client needs. For instance, I see many opportunities for demographers in business, which is becoming interested in potential customers worldwide as well as in North America. Demographers, however, will face challenges because they are overly dependent on government statistics. As governments shrink in response to budget deficits, they will reduce spending on censuses and surveys. I therefore urge demographers to become more familiar with administrative record systems, which are likely to become a major source of government statistics in the future.

REFERENCES

Ford, Thomas R., and Gordon DeJong (eds.) (1970). *Social Demography*. Englewood Cliffs, NJ: Prentice-Hall.
Swanson, David A., Thomas K. Burch, and Lucky Tedrow (1996). "What is Applied Demography?" *Population Research and Policy Review* (forthcoming).
Weeks, John R. (1994). *Population*. Belmont, CA: Wadsworth.

SUGGESTED READINGS

General

Applied Demography, Newsletter for the State and Local and Business Demography Groups of the Population Association of America.
Farley, Reynolds (ed.) (1995). *State of the Union* (Vol. 1, *Economic Trends*, Vol. 2, *Social Trends*). New York: Sage Publications.
Murdock, Steve H. (1995). *An America Challenged*. Boulder, CO: Westview Press.
Murdock, Steve H., and David R. Ellis (1991). *Applied Demography*. Boulder, CO: Westview Press.
Pol, Louis G., and Richard K. Thomas (1992). *The Demography of Health and Health Care*. New York: Plenum.
Population Research and Policy Review, Special Issue on Applied Demography, Fall 1996.
Rives, Norfleet W. Jr., and William J. Serow (1984). *Introduction to Applied Demography*. Beverly Hills, CA: Sage Publications.
Russell, Cheryl (1987). *100 Predications for the Baby Boom*. New York: Plenum.
Shryock, Henry S., Jacob S. Siegel, and Associates (1976). *The Methods and Materials of Demography* (Condensed version edited by Edward G. Stockwell). Orlando, FL: Academic Press.

Historical Demography

Cippola, Carlo M. (1965). *The Economic History of World Population*. Baltimore: Penguin.
Farley, Reynolds (1996). *The New American Reality*. New York: Russell Sage.
Jones, Landon Y. (1980). *Great Expectations*. New York: Ballantine.
Kahn, E. J., Jr. (1974). *The American People*. New York: E. P. Dutton.
Robey, Bryant (1985). *The American People*. New York: E. P. Dutton.
Wrigley, E. A. (1974). *Population and History*. New York: World University Library.

Chapter 2

Demographic Change in the United States: 1990–2010

INTRODUCTION

The twentieth century has been a period of rapid population growth for the United States, due to large flows of immigrants during the first part of the century and relatively high fertility later in the century. The post–World War II era is noted for annual fluctuations in the number of births and increases in the number of immigrants. Population growth was rapid during the 1950s and 1960s, but has since slowed. By the 1980s, fertility was low, the number of immigrants was increasing, and overall population growth was slowing. Partly as a result of slowing growth, the population was aging, although not as rapidly as will be experienced in the twenty-first century. It is these conditions that shaped demographic reality as the 1980s drew to a close. The early 1990s were marked by 1980s carryover, a small rise in the birth rate, and renewed high levels of immigration. The sections below describe what we consider the four most important demographic trends currently affecting American society.

DEMOGRAPHIC TRENDS

Population Growth and Changing Age Composition
Trend 1: The U.S. Population is Aging and the Rate of Growth is Slowing

Recent fluctuations in the birth rate and increases in the number of immigrants makes forecasting the size and age structure of the U.S. population more difficult than in the recent past.[1] During the mid-1980s, birth rates and immigration flows were generally stable and demographers were relatively confident regarding the accuracy of short-term population projections. Many demographers projected a cessation of population growth, or *zero population growth*, by the middle of the then twenty-first century. That population in 2050 would have been considerably older and more racially/ethnically diverse than today's. However, a legislatively driven increase in immigration volume and an unexpected increase in fertility rates in the late 1980s have made demographers much less confident about these projections (Ahlburg 1993; Ahlburg and Vaupel 1990). Now there is general consensus that the cessation growth scenario is no longer reasonable and that growth will continue into the foreseeable future (Pollard 1994).[2]

Table 2.1 presents population projections by age cohort for 2000 and 2010, with data from the 1990 Census of Population serving as a base for comparison. Although the population is projected to increase by 10.5 and 8.5 percent, respectively, during the 1990s and 2000s, the rate of growth is slowing by historical standards. Growth rates during the 1960s, 1970s, and 1980s, for example, were 13.4, 11.4, and 9.8 percent, respectively.

Variations in the age structure of the population over time are much more marked than changes in population size or the rate of population growth. Currently, population growth at the older ages (age 55 and above), and particularly for the oldest old, is faster than that for younger age groups. At the same time, several younger age groups will experience limited growth or even a net loss in population between 1990 and 2010. In the 20-year period covered, the population age 85 years and over is expected to grow by 2.7 million, or by nearly 89 percent! At the leading

----

[1]An important concern in viewing the tables to follow is the value of looking at both absolute changes and percentage changes in the data presented. While businesses are most often interested in the size of markets, and therefore focus on absolute size, percentage data are useful for ascertaining the relative fluctuation in market segments. The examination of percentage changes across markets provides a way in which to control for size differences and facilitates the identification of the fastest growing segments of the market.

[2]The data used in this chapter are based on the U.S. Census Bureau's most recent middle-series population projections. Although the middle series is regarded as the "most likely" scenario, unforeseen events (e.g., immigration reform legislation) could affect these figures. However, minor fluctuations in birth, death, and/or migration patterns (the only processes that can change the size and age structure of the population) have a relatively small impact in the short run on the national trends being described. In the longer run, small errors are multiplied and minor fluctuations can have a large aggregate effect. At the local level, the impact of any change can be much greater. Today, business owners and managers must be able to make accurate distinctions between local and national trends if local markets are to be clearly understood. Population projection methodology is discussed in more detail in Chapter 10.

Table 2.1
The Population of the United States by Age Group: 1990–2010

Age Group	1990		2000		2010	
Under 5	18,758[a]	(7.5)[b]	18,908	(6.9)	19,730	(6.6)
5-13	31,826	(12.8)	36,051	(13.1)	35,425	(11.9)
14-17	13,340	(5.4)	15,734	(5.7)	16,908	(5.7)
18-24	26,942	(10.8)	26,117	(9.5)	30,007	(10.1)
25-34	43,161	(17.4)	37,416	(13.6)	38,367	(12.9)
35-44	37,435	(15.1)	44,662	(16.3)	38,853	(13.0)
45-54	25,057	(10.0)	37,054	(13.5)	43,737	(14.7)
55-64	21,112	(8.5)	23,988	(8.7)	35,378	(11.9)
65-74	18,045	(7.3)	18,258	(6.6)	21,235	(7.1)
75-84	10,012	(4.0)	12,339	(4.5)	12,767	(4.3)
85 and over	3,021	(1.2)	4,289	(1.6)	5,702	(1.9)
Total	248,710		274,815		298,109	

[a]Numbers in 1,000s.
[b]Percentage of total in parentheses.

Source: Day (1992, Table 2).

edge of the baby boom, persons age 45 to 55 will increase by 18.7 million, or by 75 percent. Absolute losses are projected for the age group 25 to 34, which shows a decline of 4.8 million persons or 11 percent. Little numerical change will be experienced in the age cohorts under 5 years and 35 to 44.

As a result of differential growth rates by age, the age structure in 2010 will be noticeably different from today's. For example, persons age 55 and over made up 21 percent of the population (52 million persons) in 1990. By the year 2010 persons in the same age range will comprise over 25 percent of the population (74 million persons). The key baby boom groups, age 25 to 44 in 1990, comprised 32.5 percent of the population. In 2010, the same age category will make up only 25.9 percent of the population. Focusing on the youngest age groups, those age 17 and younger, the decrease in representation will be from 25.7 to 24.2 percent.

Overall, the U.S. population may well grow by nearly 50 million persons in the two decades examined, and the population in 2010 will be much "older" than the population of 1990. As baby boomers move into the older ages after 2010, the momentum toward an older age structure will be even greater. However, age-group-to-age-group differentials in growth rates will persist as a result of fluctuating fertility rates, the effect of large age groups moving through their childbearing years, and changes in immigration patterns.

Race/Ethnicity
Trend 2:   The United States is Becoming More Racially and Ethnically Diverse

This century has been marked by significant swings in the level of racial and ethnic diversity in the population. Early in the century, mass immigration and the fertility of those immigrants helped form a population rich in cultural variation. The restricted immigration policy in the 1920s and the depression of the 1930s nearly ended immigration and, coupled with the assimilation of the early century immigrants, the population became more homogeneous. However, post–World War II immigration policy, particularly changes in law during the 1980s and beyond, has moved the nation back in the direction of diversity.

Population projection data by race and ethnicity (Anglo, that is, white, non-Hispanic, African-American, Hispanic, and Other) are presented in Table 2.2 utilizing the same age categories as in Table 2.1. Again, these are middle series projections and subject to the same caveats attached to the data in the previous table. The data presented should also be seen in light of the discussion on data by race and ethnicity offered in Box 9.1, which focuses on prospective changes in racial/ethnic classifications in the United States The essence of that discussion is that existing racial/ethnic categories are losing their value because an increasing proportion of the population is of mixed racial/ethnic heritage. In the future, it is likely that the race/ethnic categories utilized by public and private sector analysts will be markedly different.

Instead of providing the raw numbers, Table 2.2 shows percentage breakdowns within each race/ethnicity category along with total population figures. Although Anglos will continue to be the largest population component in 2010, racial and ethnic minority populations are growing at a much faster rate. Between 2000 and 2010, the Anglo, African-American, Hispanic, and Other (mostly Asian) populations are projected to increase by 2.5, 12.9, 28.5, and 38.4 percent, respectively. As a result of this differential growth, the Anglo percentage of the total population will decline from 71.6 to 67.6 percent, while all other groups increase in proportional representation. In 2010, the three minority populations shown in the table will comprise nearly one third of the entire U.S. population, and for certain age cohorts (e.g., the school age population), their representation will exceed 40 percent.

These data also indicate the extent of age variation among the racial/ethnic groups. The Anglo population will be by far the oldest and the Hispanic the youngest, with a difference of over ten years in median age in 2000 (38.4 versus 28.1 years). This differential will widen to nearly 12 years between 2000 and 2010 (40.9 compared to 29.2). About one third of the African-American and Hispanic populations will be under age 18 in 2000, while less than 25 percent of the Anglo population will fall into this category. Although the percentage of population under age 18 will decline for all four groups between 2000 and 2010, the rate of decline for Anglos will be greatest. Conversely, in 2000 over 24 percent of the Anglo population will be age 55 and over compared to 15, 12, and 15 percent for African-Americans, Hispanics, and Others, respectively. By 2010, the age 55 and over differential will widen: Anglo, 29 percent; African-American, 18 percent; Hispanic, 15 percent; and Other, 18 percent. Not only will the Anglo population be the oldest of the four groups, it will be aging at a faster pace than the others.

Table 2.2
Percent of Population by Age and Race/Ethnicity: 2000 and 2010

Age Group	Anglo	African-American	Hispanic	Other	Total
2000					
< 18	23.1	32.0	33.9	29.6	25.7
18-24	8.8	11.1	11.6	10.7	9.5
25-34	12.8	14.3	17.0	16.6	13.6
35-44	16.4	15.7	15.7	16.5	16.3
45-54	14.5	11.6	9.9	12.0	13.5
55-64	9.6	6.9	5.7	7.1	8.7
65-74	7.6	4.8	3.7	4.6	6.6
75-84	5.3	2.6	1.9	2.2	4.5
85+	1.9	1.0	0.6	0.7	1.6
Median Age	38.4	30.1	28.1	30.9	35.6
Total Population	196,701[a] (71.6)[b]	33,834 (12.3)	30,602 (11.1)	13,678 (5.0)	274,815
2010					
< 18	21.0	30.6	32.0	28.4	24.2
18-24	9.4	11.6	11.9	10.8	10.0
25-34	12.1	13.3	14.9	15.3	12.9
35-44	12.7	12.8	14.2	15.1	13.0
45-54	15.6	13.2	12.2	12.6	14.7
55-64	13.4	9.6	7.6	8.9	11.9
65-74	8.3	5.2	4.1	5.2	7.1
75-84	5.1	2.6	2.3	2.7	4.3
85+	2.4	1.1	0.8	1.0	1.9
Median Age	40.9	31.0	29.2	32.0	37.5
Total Population	201,668 (67.6)	38,201 (12.9)	39,312 (13.2)	18,928 (6.3)	298,109

[a]Numbers in 1000s.
[b]Percentage in parentheses.

Source: Day (1992, Table 2).

Households and Families
Trend 3: The Number of Households and Families Will Increase More Rapidly Than Growth in the Overall Population—the Structure of Households and Families Will Continue to be Complex, with a Growing Number of Single-Parent Families.

The latter part of the twentieth century in the United States has seen faster growth in households and families than population and increasing complexity in living arrangements (e.g., more persons living alone and more single-parent families). There is good reason to expect this trend to continue into the twenty-first century, driven by continuing high divorce rates, lower marriage rates, the large number of children born to unwed mothers, and the aging of the population, which leaves many women widows at the older ages of the population (see Chapter 6 for an explanation of this phenomenon).

A household is defined as one or more persons living in a housing unit, while a family is composed of two or more persons who are related by blood, marriage, or adoption living together in a housing unit. Therefore, families are also households, but not all households constitute families. Table 2.3 presents projections of households and families, again based on the middle series population projections. The number of households is expected to increase by 25 million, or about 25 percent, over the 20-year period. However, differential rates of growth are seen among the various household types. Overall, family households will grow faster than nonfamily households, 26 versus 22 percent. The fastest growing household types are family households where either the husband or the wife is not present (DaVanzo and Rahman 1993). Father-only or mother-only families (children present in both) are projected to grow by over 34 percent over the 20-year interval. The absolute increase in mother-only families will be over two million.

By the year 2010, nonfamily households will comprise about 28 percent of all households, down nearly 1 percent from 1990. As might be expected, the largest increase in percentage representation is among male or female only headed households (no spouse present). In 1990, these households made up nearly 15 percent (14 million) of all households. By 2010 this category is projected to make up about 16 percent (18 million) of all households. Although there will be significant growth in the number of households over the 20-year period, the distribution by type of household will not change markedly.

Immigration
Trend 4: The Number of Immigrants Will Continue to be Large and Dominated by Persons from Asia and Parts of the Western Hemisphere.

While the United States was appropriately described as a nation of immigrants early in this century, by the 1950s the statement was no longer true. The peak decade

Table 2.3
Number and Percent of Households by Type: 1990–2010

Household Type	1990	2000	2010	Percent Change (1990-2010)
Family households:	65,330[a]	73,899	82,098	25.7
Married couple:				
With own children	24,512	27,909	31,199	27.3
Without own children	27,156	30,110	32,825	20.9
Male householder with no spouse present:				
With own children	1,331	1,558	1,785	34.1
Without own children	1,729	2,014	2,297	32.9
Female householder with no spouse present:				
With own children	6,031	7,061	8,086	34.1
Without own children	4,570	5,247	5,907	29.3
Nonfamily households:	26,617	29,660	32,487	22.1
Total households:	91,947	103,559	114,585	24.6

[a]Numbers in 1,000s.

Source: Unpublished data supplied by Steven Murdock, Texas A&M University.

for immigration, 1901–1910, was witness to nearly nine million immigrants. These immigrants accounted for 55 percent of total population growth in that decade. During the 1950s (1951–1960) only about one million immigrants were registered, comprising merely nine percent of that decade's population growth. However, since 1960 there has been an upturn in immigration figures, and immigrants now account for about one third of annual population growth.

Table 2.4 provides immigration data on origin by world region for the period 1971 to 1993. Two trends are worthy of note here. First, as already discussed, there has been a substantial increase in total immigration over the time period. In particular, immigration totals rose substantially after 1985 (data not shown in the table) when a series of immigration reform laws were passed by the U.S. Congress. The second highest ten-year immigration total in U.S. history was recorded in the 1980s, with 3.8 million more immigrants than during the 1970s. If the pattern from the first part of the 1990s continues for the entire decade, more than 10 million immigrants will be registered.

The second trend concerns the origin of immigrants. Early in the history of the United States, the vast majority of immigrants came from Europe. For example, between 1901 and 1910, 8.1 out of the 8.8 million immigrants (93 percent) to the U.S. were born in Europe. As European domination ended later in the century, there was a substantial rise in the number of immigrants who originated in Asia and North America. Since 1971, there has been a continuing shift in pattern of origin and, in the period 1991–1993, immigrants from Asia and North America (primarily Mexico) accounted for 80 percent of the total. From 1991 through 1993 Europeans made up only 12 percent of all immigrants to the United States.

Table 2.4
Immigrants by Region of Birth: 1971–1992

	1971–1980	1981–1990	1991–1993
Europe	801.3[a]	705.6	434.9
Asia	1,633.8	2,817.4	1,073.5
North America	1,645.0	3,125.0	1,896.4
South America	284.4	455.9	189.1
Africa	91.5	192.3	91.1
Total	4,493.3	7,338.1	3,705.4

[a]Numbers in 1,000s.

Source: U.S. Department of Justice, Immigration and Naturalization Service, *Statistical Yearbook*, annual reports.

SMALL MARKET ISSUES

National-level trends are played out very differently at the local area, a fact that we cannot overemphasize at this juncture. For example, the age structures of some areas of the United States show little evidence of the post–World War II baby boom. Other areas receive few or no immigrants, and for them the local-level effect of increasing immigration is at most distant and indirect. The next several pages focus on local level differentials starting first with countywide comparisons and then presenting a small market (census tract) analysis. These comparisons illustrate the importance of local area data analysis in understanding the business environment.

Counties

Although national-level demographic trends are important to understand, regional, state, and substate markets such as counties are the geographic areas most often of concern. It is at the substate level of geography that most business decisions are made, with counties and other legal or statistical units frequently used for market area delineation. Also, demographic and business data such as those published in *Sales and Marketing Management* magazine, are available at the county and other substate level of geography.

Table 2.5 provides abridged demographic profiles for San Diego County, California; Shelby County (city of Memphis), Tennessee; and Pinellas County (city of St. Petersburg), Florida. The data for the U.S. total serve as a benchmark. Shelby and Pinellas Counties have populations of similar size, while San Diego County is about three times larger. San Diego County has grown rapidly over the last decade, and Shelby County has experienced little growth, with Pinellas County somewhare in between. However, the comparison of the three is much more complex than simply ascertaining size and growth rate differences. Clearly, these county-level "markets" are not simply a mirror-image of conditions for the United States as a whole. Their age and racial/ethnic compositions not only vary, but none is very much like that of the United States. While one or two income, housing, and health measures may be close to those for the United States, no market is like the United States for all four measures.

Table 2.5
Selected Demographic Characteristics for the United States and San Diego (CA), Shelby (TN), and Pinellas (FL) Counties

	United States	San Diego County	Shelby County	Pinellas County
Population (1990)	248,709,873	2,498,016	826,330	851,659
1980-1990 Growth (%)	9.8	34.2	6.3	16.9
% ≤ Age 14	21.7	19.6	22.9	14.8
% > Age 65	12.5	10.7	9.8	25.8
% White	76.0	65.0	55.1	90.5
% African American	12.1	6.0	43.6	7.1
% Hispanic	9.0	20.4	0.9	2.4
Median Household Income	$30,056	$35,022	$27,132	$25,296
Median Housing Value	$78,500	$186,200	$65,600	$73,500
% Low Birth Weight	6.9	5.8	10.1	6.9
Infant Mortality Rate	10.0	7.1	16.0	10.1

Source: U.S. Bureau of the Census. 1994. *County and City Data Book*. Washington, DC: U.S. Government Printing Office, Table B.

These market-to-market differentials have important business implications. With respect to the market for a variety of products and services, there is substantial variation. For example, the large percentage of persons age 65 and over in Pinellas County (25.8 percent of the total population, or 220,000 persons) indicates a much higher demand for geriatric-related products and services than for Shelby County (9.8 percent or 81,000 persons). Even though San Diego County is three times the size of Shelby County, there are more African-Americans residing in Shelby County (360,000 versus 150,000). There are few Hispanics living in Shelby County; yet over 20 percent (510,000) of the San Diego County population is Hispanic. These racial and ethnic differentials have serious implications for consumer demand when significant consumption differences by race and ethnicity are known or suspected to exist. In addition, median household income is highest in San Diego County, although this figure is somewhat deceiving. Median housing value (one measure of the cost of living) is 2.8 and 2.5 times greater in San Diego than in Shelby and Pinellas Counties, thus eliminating a substantial proportion if not all of the income advantage of San Diego County. As a result of ownership cost differentials, the relative demand for rental housing in San Diego County is greatest.

Finally, the two health indicators noted, percentage of births that are low birth weight ($< 2,500$ grams) and the infant mortality rate, show substantial variation. With respect to low birth weight, the percentage for Shelby County is 1.74 and 1.46 times higher than that for San Diego and Pinellas Counties, respectively. A wider range of infant mortality rates is evident. The rate for Shelby County is 2.3 and 1.6 times as large as that for San Diego and Pinellas Counties, respectively. (See Box 2.1 for an additional discussion of Pinellas County.)

Box 2.1
Market Conditions in Pinellas County, Florida

The table below features data on Pinellas County for the time period 1980 to 1990. Pinellas County grew by nearly 17 percent (123,128 persons) during the 1980s, although growth by age cohort showed wide differentials. The population age 15 to 34 grew fastest, increasing by over 25 percent, and the population age 75 grew slowest, by a little more than 12 percent. The low growth rates at the older ages is not surprising given the high probability of mortality for these populations. The perhaps surprisingly high growth rates for persons 15–34 indicate a substantial rise in the market for a variety of products targeted at that group.

Looking at the components of change (births, deaths and net migrants), it can be seen that without a high level of in-migration, Pinellas County would have lost substantial population during the decade. In fact, without any migration at all the county would have lost 36,000 persons over the ten-year interval, and the momentum for continued decline would have been substantial. Migrants bring with them an entirely different market for a wide range of products and services; for example, they are looking for new providers for a host of services and they change the size and composition of submarkets within the county.

Box 2.1 continued

Demographic Change for Pinellas County: 1980–1990

Total Population 1990	851,659
% < 14	14.8
% 15-34	25.3
% 35-54	23.3
% 55-64	10.5
% 65-74	13.4
% 75+	12.4
Total Population 1980	728,531
% Net Change 1980–1990	123,128
Births	85,167
Deaths	121,446
Net Migrants	159,407
% Change in Households	19.1

Micromarkets

A *micromarket* is defined here as a subcounty market area, although there is no commonly accepted definition for this term throughout the business literature. In principle, micromarkets are highly localized market areas for smaller retailers and service providers. Micromarkets have high potential for rapid population increases or decreases because of their small size and their susceptibility to the types of events (e.g., new housing developments and plant closings) that significantly alter populations over short periods of time. Some micromarkets such as those defined by census tracts, zip codes, and trade areas may be experiencing rapid population growth while others are losing population. These increases or decreases in persons and households are accompanied by changes in population composition.

Tables 2.6 through 2.8 present data on three micromarkets in the Omaha Metropolitan Statistical Area (MSA). Table 2.6 provides information on a shrinking micromarket that is two miles north of the central business district. Tables 2.7 and 2.8 provide data on expanding micromarkets in a part of the metropolitan area where there is intense competition for new business. The variables in the tables represent some of the demographic dimensions that are important to a wide range of business owners and managers. The data are for single census tracts as delineated in 1980 and 1990. The reader is also encouraged to compare these tables with Tables 2.1 through 2.4. Clearly, the national-level trends previously discussed are not mirrored in these micromarket data.

As can be seen in Table 2.6, City Census Tract lost substantial numbers of people and a large proportion of its households during the 1980s, an average of 65 persons and 23 households per year. The age structure, as represented by the percentages of the population under age 5 and the population 65 years old and over, is not very much different in 1990, although changes to other age cohorts during the 1990s are leading to continued population loss. The vast majority of persons in this tract are African-American. Nevertheless, the percentage of African-Americans declined somewhat during the 1980s. About two thirds of the 1980 population age 5 and over lived in the same house as they did in 1975, and this percentage decreased by only about 3 percent during the 1980s. The percentage of working-age persons who were unemployed declined markedly from 1980 to 1990.

Table 2.6
Components of Demographic Change for City Census Tract

	1980	1990	Change (Percent)
Population	4,814	4,161	-650 (-13.5%)
Households	1,658	1,425	-233 (-14.0%)
Percent Population < 5 years	7.5	8.4	(0.9%)
Percent Population ≥ 65 years	18.9	19.0	(0.1%)
Percent Population Age 5 and Above in Same House Five Years Prior to Census	67.4	64.5	(-2.9%)
Percent Unemployed	10.3	5.0	(-5.3%)
Percent African-American	93.8	89.7	(-4.1%)

Source: U.S. Bureau of the Census (1983, 1993b).

Table 2.7, which contains data for Suburban Census Tract I, provides a very different marketplace scenario, including substantial population and household increases. The average annual population/household increase was 160 persons and 61 households, and by 1990 this micromarket had been radically transformed. The population is now somewhat older and has a higher percentage of persons who are African-American. However, the most significant population/household change relates to permanency of residence. Less than one third of the 1980 population age 5 and over had lived in the same house for five years, but in 1990 this figure approached 50 percent. The 1980–1990 growth in this tract was due to in-migration, much of which occurred early in the decade.

Table 2.8 shows an area, Suburban Census Tract II, that has undergone even more change. An increase of 8,001 persons (800 per year) and 2,574 households (257 per year) has fostered the creation of an entirely different micromarket. This

Table 2.7
Components of Demographic Change for Suburban Census Tract I

	1980	1990	Change (Percent)
Population	7,469	9,065	1,596 (21.4%)
Households	2,980	3,595	615 (20.6%)
Percent Population < 5 years	9.0	8.3	(-0.7%)
Percent Population ≥ 65 years	1.9	4.7	(2.8%)
Percent African-American	4.0	5.8	(1.8%)
Percent Population Age 5 and Above in Same House Five Years Prior to Census	29.4	45.6	(16.2%)
Percent Unemployed	3.8	2.0	(-1.8%)

Source: U.S. Bureau of the Census (1983, 1993b).

area has a relatively young age structure, which is conducive to continued population growth. Because there is a great deal of undeveloped land in this area, the prospects for even more growth are considerable. With growth has come increased residential stability, as evidenced by a substantial rise (from 14.9 to 40.9 percent) in the proportion of persons age 5 and over living in the same house from 1985 to 1990.

CONCLUSION

While we regard the trends seen in Tables 2.1 through 2.4 as the most important for the 20–year period covered, other trends will also help shape the business environment. The growing polarization of the income structure involving growth in the number of persons at the income extremes and the shrinkage of the middle class will affect the market's ability to buy goods and services. Shifts in the educational structure with increasing numbers of persons who do not have the requisite skills to compete for good jobs affects labor quality. Shifts in birth rates, when combined with fluctuations in the age structure, determine the number of births and therefore the number of young customers. These trends, along with those presented in Tables 2.1 through 2.4, combine with other factors to shape today and tomorrow's business environment.

The data in Tables 2.5 through 2.8 indicate that national-level trends are not necessarily reflected in local-area observations. They also demonstrate that at subnational levels demographic change can be quite rapid while in other instances little change may occur. At the local level, change can be of such a nature that markets are created, eliminated or restructured in just a few years. Omaha is typical

Table 2.8
Components of Demographic Change for Suburban Census Tract II

	1980	1990	Change (Percent)
Population	6,067	14,068	8,001 (131.9%)
Households	1,956	4,530	2,574 (131.6%)
Percent Population < 5 years	15.3	12.0	(-3.3%)
Percent Population ≥ 65 years	3.1	4.5	(1.4%)
Percent African-American	1.8	1.8	(0%)
Percent Population Age 5 and Above in Same House Five Years Prior to Census	14.9	40.9	(26.0%)
Percent Unemployed	2.4	1.7	(-0.7%)

Source: U.S. Bureau of the Census (1983, 1993b).

of many Metropolitan Statistical Areas in the Midwest with respect to aggregate population change. In states like California, Texas, and Florida, short-run demographic change can be much more substantial and faster than shown here.

Demographic change is a recurrent theme in many of the chapters that follow. Decision making takes place in an environment of change, and an understanding of how and why change is occurring can assist managers and planners in a substantial way. Box 2.2 focuses on how rapid growth of young families in a micromarket drives the market for child care services. Box 2.3 presents another profile of a business demographer.

Box 2.2
Projecting Demand for Child Care Services in a
Rapidly Changing Micromarket

The Omaha Metropolitan Statistical Area (MSA) is no different from most other metropolitan areas. There are substantial intra-area growth differentials, and areas of high growth that present a host of business opportunities. These opportunities are particularly evident in the far-western suburbs, which until a few years ago were corn and soybean fields.

As most often happens, population growth preceded business growth in these suburbs. New residents quickly found themselves "short" of products and services, and most found themselves having to travel relatively long distances for even their most basic shopping needs. The retail business community responded relatively quickly, noting increasing market size and compositional changes, and a whole range of retail stores were built.

Box 2.2 continued

The service industry also responded to this growth, but perhaps in a more cautious manner. Many services are provided in the home (e.g., carpet and house cleaning) and, therefore, the actual location of the business is not very important. For other services—child care in particular—choice is based upon confidence in the quality of service and the location; the site may be near home, work, or on route between home and work. Several child care service providers studied the recent and projected population growth in the western suburbs. They reviewed 1990 census data, observed the growth in the area, and examined the plans of local developers. They learned that most persons in the area lived in single-family dwelling units, and that future growth would be dominated by increases in the number of persons living in single-family units. Population growth was projected to be mostly in the form of families, and, given the age structure of these families, many would have young children. Moreover, these new families were likely to have two wage earners with a subsequent need for child care services. And, the providers expected growth to continue for an extended period of time.

Industry data indicated that quality of care, convenience and price were the three most important concerns for parents in selecting a child care provider. A standard of quality at a fair price could be assured, but convenience was more difficult to implement. Some of the potential providers had the advantage of having established reputations in the community. Others would be new entrants, but they were confident of their ability to quickly gain a positive reputation.

Nearly simultaneously, four major child care service providers chose to locate in one section of the western suburbs. The market responded positively to all four providers, and, at least as long as residential growth continues, there will be a market for their services. However, residential growth will eventually end, families will mature, and the overall size of the market will fall. At that point, these providers will face their next test.

Box 2.3

Joan E. Gentili Naymark—Business Demographer at
Dayton Hudson Corporation

A Day in the Work Life of Joan Naymark

I hold the position of Director, Research and Planning, for Dayton Hudson Corporation (DHC). I have a Master of Arts degree and a Bachelor of Science degree in sociology/demography from Western Washington University in Bellingham, Washington. I apply demographic, geographic, and statistical techniques and concepts to a variety of applications within the site location and strategic planning arenas for the Corporation and its three operating divisions.

Dayton Hudson is the parent corporation for three retail companies: Target, an upscale discount chain with 700 stores throughout the United States; Mervyn's, a promotional family department store with 300 stores primarily in the west and southern United States; and the Department Store division (DSD), which has three traditional department store chains: Dayton's, based in Minnesota; Hudson's, in Michigan; and Marshall Field's, in Illinois.

Box 2.3 continued

The DHC headquarters staff is located in the IDS building, downtown Minneapolis' premier office tower. Target and DSD headquarters are located across the street from DHC, each housing large employee populations. Mervyn's headquarters are in the San Francisco Bay Area. Due to the proximity of company headquarters for Target and DSD, the Research & Planning staff has frequent opportunities to interact and work on projects together with these other corporate bodies.

Research & Planning is a department of 11 professionals and 4 support staff, part of the 200 employees of Dayton Hudson Corporation. Research & Planning is managed by four Team Leaders. Supported by four Research Analysts. All of the Team Leaders and Research Analysts have master's degrees in social science fields such as geography, economics, urban planning, public affairs, and demography. There are four Technical Analysts who hold bachelor's degrees in geography, business, and economics. There are three Secretaries and one Graphics Technician. All of the Team Leaders and Research Analysts work in offices, while the Technical Analysts and Secretaries work in "cubes" with five-foot-high partitions.

The department's primary mission is to provide geographic and site location support to our companies as they build new stores across the United States. For instance, Target recently opened its first stores in Washington, D.C., and Baltimore. Research & Planning was there two years in advance, scouting neighborhoods to find good matches with our customer profile, and evaluating the competition, spending habits and economic health of the various communities in the CMSA.

In order to support the rapid turnaround required for site location studies, Research & Planning places a premium on technology and database systems. The research technicians create, update, and maintain our databases. All staff members work with top-of-the-line PCs connected to the corporate network. The network provides access to internal e-mail, PC software including the Microsoft office suite, GIS software and street files, an external demographic vendor's data package, and all departmental files and databases. Two analysts have SPSS available. A link to the Internet is available on a pilot basis and will be available staffwide in a few months. The corporate library is located on the same floor as the Research & Planning Department. It holds a wide variety of information, including paper, interactive, and CD resources and access to the Internet. The ability to rapidly access and process information is key to Research & Planning's success within the "speed is life" culture at Dayton Hudson Corporation.

I am one of the four Team Leaders in Research & Planning. I started with the company 14 years ago as a Research Analyst, and have worked my way through various positions to assume co-leadership of the department two years ago. I report to the Senior Vice President of Strategic Planning, who reports to the Chief Executive Officer (CEO) of the Corporation. Four people report directly to me, three Research Technicians and a Secretary, with two others reporting through one of my direct reports. In addition, I work with Research Analysts on various projects during the year.

One-third of my projects are my sole responsibility, such as research for the new Super Target prototype store. One-third involve ongoing departmental responsibilities, including managing staff, budgets, and systems, and annual projects conducted with others in a team setting. And one-third involve special, one-time projects conducted in small work groups, typically lasting from two weeks to four months.

I hold weekly meetings with the other Team Leaders to review current projects and departmental issues. I have a bi-weekly "group status" meeting with all members of the

Box 2.3 continued

technical group, with one research analyst or team leader as our guest. We discuss joint projects, finding synergy and better ways to proceed. I have bi-weekly "status" meetings with each person who reports to me to review in greater detail their current projects. And I have bi-monthly "status" meetings with my boss, in which I inform him of departmental issues or provide details of a project I am working on for him. Bi-monthly, our department has a staff meeting, mostly for current awareness and project sharing. Weekly, the Research Analysts and Team Leaders meet to review individual projects from a methodological and conceptual perspective. Monthly, I meet with the other 20 senior/key executives of Corporate staff to review current activities. Quarterly, our department attends a Corporate Staff meeting of all 200 members to be updated on corporate sales performance and special projects underway.

I am responsible for database and systems management, market share tracking, statistical modeling efforts, auditing our record of sales projection accuracy each year, the department budget, and special project work. I also manage occasional site location research in special situations.

Much of my work load is periodic, tied to the corporate calendar. Following the end of the fiscal year January 31st, my group is responsible for year-end database rollover for markets and stores.

- Annual reports on performance for all of our companies and stores including sales, demographic updates, trade area boundary changes, and competitor's activities in our local markets.
- Year-end market share in the largest 100 markets in the country is based on the Department of Commerce Retail Trade reports. I present the rest to the Corporate Operating Committee, a group of the 20 most senior executives of the corporation and operating companies.
- Annual spring Strategy Meetings require significant data preparation and presentation materials. I meet with the Senior Vice President of Target's Property Development to discuss the project's scope and required timetable. I plan the project, delegate and schedule the specific components to staff in my work group, monitor and evaluate the results, and suggest enhancements to the project. I contact staff in other departments to make sure the information is consistent with their parts of the presentation.

During the "back-half" of the year, we plan and implement database enhancements, audit our sales tracking performance, and constantly update our databases with quicker, better information. I am a member of the MIS (Management Information Systems) Steering Committee, which meets every other month. I am responsible for evaluating departmental databases for efficiency, usage, and effectiveness. We often ask the question whether we still need a particular system or database, or if it needs to be in its current form. We constantly evaluate new data and systems products on the market to see if there is a faster, cheaper way to get the same answer.

Projects often originate from my boss on strategic or confidential issues, or from data users in other departments. I have become known as a demographic "expert" within the corporation. I often field questions of interpretation or how-to-access data on demographic issues. Examples:

Box 2.3 continued

- Micromarketing efforts use local neighborhood demographic characteristics to select merchandise, for in-store marketing, and to provide guest services bestmatched to the local area. An example would be to identify all Florida stores which have large numbers of soccer families for the sporting goods buyer.
- Government and private databases identify the names and locations of all K–12 schools. We geocode those records within the GIS system to match stores to all schools within five miles. This is used for local scholarship programs, back-to-school uniforms and backpacks, and other school promotions.
- Neighborhoods with very rapid population growth require searching housing industry permit data and establishing partnerships with outside demographers.
- Tracking the impact of competitors stores' opening or closing near one of our stores requires an updated competition system and monitoring a correct control group of stores.

Currently, we are developing a sales forecasting model for a set of stores. I worked with two research analysts to establish "best practices" at other research departments in the country, and interviewed prospective consultants selling traditional statistical methods as well as neural networks and other artificial intelligence methods. We selected a vendor, detailed the work plan and timetable, negotiated the price, worked with attorneys to draw up contracts, and created the database for the project.

I enjoy the variety of work, and the ability to make a difference in company plans and practices. I am fortunate to work with highly motivated, intelligent, and professional management and staff. I have a great deal of flexibility and discretion to manage projects for the company's benefit. I have excellent resources in equipment, information and staff support. Finding the lowest cost and fastest route to the correct answer, and ensuring that the right questions are being asked are my ongoing challenges. The research paradigm acquired from my demographic and academic training has been a valuable resource in the business setting.

REFERENCES

Ahlburg, Dennis A. (1993). "The Census Bureau's New Projections of the U.S. Population." *Population and Development Review*, 19(1): 159–174.

Ahlburg, Dennis, and J. Vaupel (1990). "Alternative Projections of the U.S. Population." *Demography*, 27(4): 639–652.

DaVanzo, Julie, and Omar Rahman (1993). "American Families: Trends and Correlates." *Population Index*, 59(3): 350–386.

Day, Jennifer C. (1992). "Population Projections of the United States, by Age, Race and Hispanic Origin: 1992–2050." *Current Population Reports*, Series P-25, No. 1092. Washington, DC: U.S. Government Printing Office.

Day, Jennifer C. (1993). "Population Projections of the United States, by Age, Race and Hispanic Origin: 1993–2050." *Current Population Reports*, Series P-25, No. 1104. Washington, DC: U.S. Government Printing Office.

Pollard, Kelvin M. (1994). "Population Stabilization No Longer in Sight for U.S." *Population Today*, Vol. 22, No. 5. Washington, DC: Population Reference Bureau.

U.S. Bureau of the Census (1983). *1980 Census of Population and Housing*, Census Tracts, Omaha Nebraska-Iowa. Washington, DC: U.S. Government Printing Office.

U.S. Bureau of the Census (1993a). *Statistical Abstract of the United States, 1993*. Washington, DC: U.S. Government Printing Office.

U.S. Bureau of the Census (1993b). *1990 Census of the Population and Housing*, Population and Housing Characteristics for Census Tracts and Block Numbering Areas, Omaha Nebraska-Iowa. Washington, DC: U.S. Government Printing Office.

U.S. Department of Justice, Immigration and Naturalization Service. Annual. *Statistical Yearbook of the Immigration and Naturalization Service*. Washington, DC: U.S. Government Printing Office.

SUGGESTED READINGS

Ahlburg, Dennis A., and Carol J. DeVita (1992). "New Realities of the American Family." *Population Bulletin*, Vol. 47, No. 2. Washington, DC: Population Reference Bureau.

Bouvier, Leon F., and Carol J. DeVita (1991). "The Baby Boom—Enterior Midlife." *Population Bulletin*, Vol. 46, No. 3. Washington, DC: Population Reference Bureau.

Martin, Philip, and Elizabeth Midgley (1994). "Immigration to the United States: Journey to an Uncertain Destination." *Population Bulletin*, Vol. 49, No. 2. Washington, DC: Population Reference Bureau.

Murdock, Steve H. (1995). *An America Challenged*. Boulder, CO: Westview Press.

Myers, Dowell (1992). *Analysis with Local Census Data*. New York: Academic Press.

O'Hare, William P. (1992). "America's Minorities—The Demographics of Diversity." *Population Bulletin*, Vol. 47, No. 4. Washington, DC: Population Reference Bureau.

Plane, David A., and Peter Rogerson (1994). *The Geographic Analysis of Population: With Applications to Planning and Business*. New York: John Wiley and Sons, Inc.

Chapter 3

Demographic Data and Business Decision Making

INTRODUCTION

Every time we pick up a newspaper, read a news magazine, or watch a television news report, we are bombarded with demographic information. The media report that Generation X is creating new fads, that the baby boomers are changing the way we do business, or that female-headed households face increasing financial challenges. Virtually every news story and national development, it seems, has a demographic component.

The use of demographic data in news reporting has become so common that we do not consciously label it as "demographic" but as information inherent in the everyday activities of the business world. People often repeat this information at cocktail parties and business gatherings, perhaps not realizing that there is a discrete body of demographic knowledge and a cadre of professional demographers who collectively generate and analyze these demographic facts.

Not only are demographic data of interest to the general public, but the influence of demographic information is increasingly evident in the corporate boardroom. It is difficult to imagine a board meeting in which issues such as product development, marketing initiatives, and the competitive situation are being discussed where demographic factors are not central to the discussion.

There are several reasons why demographic data play such an important role in corporate discussions in all sizes and types of companies and with regard to a wide range of issues. First, most industries today are market driven and demographic data guide many aspects of marketing. The days are long past in most industries when the characteristics of the market can be ignored, and strategy-level deliberations are being driven by the increasingly market-oriented nature of American business. Most of today's products and services, in fact, are made available in direct response to the identified needs of the market.

Second, American consumers as a group have become increasingly diverse. Despite past predictions of growing homogeneity, Americans have become more racially and ethnically diverse, maintaining regional differences, and adapting a variety of lifestyles that would daunt any marketer. Increased levels of immigration and the growing complexity of the American social fabric ensure an American "salad bowl" rather than a "melting pot" for the foreseeable future.

This growing diversity has contributed to the emergence of another trend: changing consumer characteristics. The baby boom generation has rewritten the rules when it comes to consumerism, and this has resulted in reduced predictability of consumer behavior. Marketers do know, however, that today's consumer is going to be well informed, demanding and characterized by high expectations. Box 3.1 presents a discussion of the implications of growing diversity for business planning.

Box 3.1

Demographic Heterogeneity and the End of Mass Marketing

In the 1960s social commentators predicted the complete homogenization of the American population by the turn of the century. Citing the growing influence of the mass media, they predicted that American customs, values and lifestyles would become increasingly uniform and that all Americans would eventually talk like a Midwestern newscaster. These commentators were confident that regional differences would disappear and that behavior patterns—including consumer behavior—would transcend differences in socioeconomic characteristics and cultural background.

Mass marketing, of course, was the order of the day. The market was seen as a homogeneous mass of undifferentiated consumers, with one consumer pretty much the same as any other. National brands were dominant and niche marketing was essentially unheard of. The predicted homogenization would only contribute to the standardization of the American consumer.

Even the most cursory examination of contemporary social trends indicates that these predictions did not materialize. In fact, the opposite has occurred. During the last quarter of this century, America has experienced a resurgence of cultural awareness, the crystallization of regional differences, and the proliferation of diverse lifestyles. This trend has been given impetus by the increasing heterogeneity along a number of dimensions—from socioeconomic characteristics to race and ethnicity to lifestyles. Add to this the growing waves of immigrants (both legal and illegal) and the increasing racial and ethnic diversity of our society and it is obvious why the purveyors of psychographic segmentation systems are drawing an audience.

The growing heterogeneity of the American consumer has led to a revolution in marketing. Mass marketing has given way to *target marketing*—with its foundation in market segmentation. National brands have lost market share to smaller players that have tailored services to targeted segments of the market. Driven by the buying habits of the baby boomers, product developers have produced goods and services geared toward increasingly smaller segments of the market. National brands have been forced to develop regional variations of their products and shift away from one-size-fits-all advertising to target customers in keeping with the specialized characteristics of niche markets.

Box 3.1 continued

Target marketing, in response to ever more refined demographic and psychographic clusters, is now giving way to *micromarketing*, with its ability to focus at the household level. Micromarketing involves the ability to precisely pinpoint very small groups of potential customers and focus directly on their specific buying patterns. Aided by computer technology and ever-improving databases of consumer information, micromarketers can target potential customers down to the block group, the block and even the household. While not all goods and services require this specificity in their marketing, micromarketing offers an advantage in direct mail campaigns and is very useful in identifying potential customers for low-volume, high-cost items.

Other factors also make demographic data an essential ingredient in corporate decision making. A poorly sited facility, a mistimed marketing initiative, a key niche market that is overlooked, or misdirected product development can all incur tremendous costs. The costs involved in building and outfitting a retail outlet, mounting a marketing campaign, and developing a product are all growing, and the losses associated with one bad decision may require ten good ones for the firm to recover.

Perhaps more important in an environment of increasingly scarce resources are the *opportunity costs* linked to a wrong decision. Siting an outlet in one place means there were other, potentially more favorable, sites that were not selected. Money spent on one promotion cannot be spent on another more appropriate one. Product development resources spent on one product cannot be spent on one with more potential. Overlooking a critical niche may mean that a business has been out-positioned by a competitor.

All of these developments underscore an important point: Industry decision makers must go beyond basic demographics and cultivate an in-depth understanding of demographic data concepts and processes. Box 3.2 describes the use of demographic data in database marketing.

Box 3.2

Business Demography and Database Marketing

Database marketing is a form of direct marketing that has received increasing attention as mass marketing has given way to target marketing. Database marketing was pioneered in the financial services industry as it underwent deregulation and the approach has caught on in most other industries. The objective of database marketing is to extract the maximum amount of business from existing customers. Operating on the assumption that it is much more difficult and expensive to acquire a new customer than it is to retain an existing one, database marketing has become popular in an age of shrinking markets in many industries.

Database marketing involves the development of a marketing customer information file (MCIF). This database ideally includes records of all existing customers of the organization. MCIFs may go even farther than that and include information on anyone

Box 3.2 continued

who has responded to a promotional campaign or placed an inquiry concerning a product or service but has never made a purchase. This database can then be utilized for followup sales, for cross-selling, and as the basis for direct mail promotionals. In fact, the profile of the "ideal" customer can be used as a screening mechanism for identifying potential new customers.

The database marketing approach typically begins with customer demographics. The age, sex, race or ethnicity of current customers is important, as are such traits as marital status and household composition. This is particularly true if the unit to which a product is being marketed is the household or family rather than the individual. The income distribution and educational level of existing customers are important in planning products and promotions, as are such traits as occupational category and the industries in which customers are employed. And, of course, these data are always tied to a unit of geography, such as a county or zip code.

One approach to utilizing a customer database involves the identification of a constellation of goods and services associated with any other purchase. In banking, for example, it was found that customers who purchased certificates of deposit were good candidates for certain other financial services. In fact, there is probably a constellation of services surrounding most purchases that could be exploited if the associated purchases could be identified.

Another approach might be to identify "customer segments" among exiting customers. These segments are categories of customers that require similar services and can be linked to other services across the organization. Some hospitals have found it useful to think in terms of customer segments such as child-bearing age women or senior citizens, for example. Customer segments serve as a basis for marketing programs because they represent internally homogeneous segments with similar consumer behavior patterns. A new mother among your customers is likely to represent a link to another set of products for babies, allowing for the cross-selling of products within the company.

Marketing sequencing is a third approach made possible by database marketing. Many events in individuals lives occur in sequence. Although there is significant variation, in U.S. society the typical individual is thought to complete college, get a job, get married, and start a family, more or less in that sequence. Taking a cue from lifecycle marketing of the past, it is possible to anticipate future needs of existing customers by determining where they are in the current cycle. An individual near retirement age, for example, is a likely candidate for a number of services that probably would not have been considered at an earlier age. The database marketing approach allows marketers to sequence their initiatives in keeping with the specific customer's point in the cycle.

Developing and maintaining a database marketing program is no small undertaking. Many industries are only now developing clear linkages between customers and their purchases and tracking customer behavior is very challenging. However, current computer technology offers the means for developing state-of-the-art databases that not only provide the basis for marketing initiatives but serve as useful management reporting systems.

CATEGORIES OF DEMOGRAPHIC DATA

The variety and amount of demographic data available today are substantial. In fact, when the mass of demographic data is considered by a first time researcher, the volume may appear to be overwhelming. It is helpful to get our arms around this collection of data by identifying some logical categories. Not all students of demography would divide the data sources of the field into the categories below, but this approach is appropriate for a book of this type.

First, data can be categorized as information internal to or external to the organization. *Internally generated data* include the data generated by an organization in the course of normal operations. This encompasses data on a company's existing customer base, sales histories, accounting and financial records, profiles of its "best" customers, and characteristics of clients targeted for cross-selling.

External data focus on the external environment and are usually generated by sources outside the organization. These data are sometimes more difficult to locate and access but are, relative to internal data, more available to the public. This category includes data on the trade area's population or profiles of areas that are targeted for future marketing efforts. The organization's ability to access, manipulate, and interpret these external data is increasingly the difference between success and failure for business planners.

A second distinction can be made between primary and secondary sources of data. *Primary research* involves the direct collection of data for immediate use by those collecting them. Primary data collection involves, for example, surveys, focus groups, and observational studies. While the value of primary research has become well established, as evidenced by the growing number of customer satisfaction surveys and focus groups being conducted, these activities usually generate proprietary data that are not likely to be disseminated outside the institution. Primary research requires a much more detailed treatment than can be afforded here and is better addressed in a research methodology context. Primary data are not emphasized in this chapter since primary research activities are usually focused narrowly on specific issues facing an organization at a particular time under certain conditions.

This chapter focuses on secondary sources of data. *Secondary research* involves the use of data gathered for some other purpose than marketing or planning but that has value in the formulation of strategy and policy. Examples of secondary data include most data obtained through library research either in hard copy or electronically. The data collected by the U.S. Census Bureau are an excellent example. These data are collected primarily for federal statistical purposes but are used secondarily for business planning.

A third way of categorizing demographic data may involve "functional" categories. Each category stands as a substantive area of interest to business demographers. The following are examples of categories in which demographic data may be placed.

Market data refer to the combined demographic data related to a particular market that constitutes a population profile. This process involves identifying basic demographic characteristics of the study area and projecting these characteristics forward to the desired period of time. It also may involve the compilation of demographic data appropriate to the industry under study. A short discussion of the use of demographic data in profiling a market area is presented in Box 3.3.

Customer data constitute the type of demographic data that is closest to home for most corporations. Every organization collects—to a greater or lesser extent—demographic data on its customers. (Note that a "consumer" is a potential customer, while a "customer" is someone that has already established a buyer-seller relationship.) Customer records represent a readily available source of internal data. They typically include demographic profiles of customers, trends in utilization patterns (especially in terms of demographic characteristics), and profiles of different categories of customers. This information is particularly important when repeat sales and cross-selling are pursued.

Box 3.3
Profiling a Market Area

Virtually all business activities focus on a specific geographic area. Consequently, a great deal of effort on the part of business analysts goes into developing profiles of a market area (or trade area or service area or whatever term is utilized). Market data represent perhaps the most straightforward and most frequently utilized category of demographic data. This is typically the first step in assessing business opportunities in a particular area.

Market data refer to the combined demographic data related to a particular market that yields a population profile. This process involves identifying basic demographic characteristics of the study area and projecting these characteristics forward to the desired period of time. It can also involve the compilation of demographic data appropriate to the specific industry under study. A market area profile provides an overview of the targeted area and, depending on the amount of detail, provides the basis for a wide variety of planning studies.

The usual first step in demographically profiling a market involves the delineation of the market area. The analyst must identify the set of zip codes, counties or other geographic units that constitute the market area. In some cases, the boundaries may be obvious and include a manageable geography like a county. In other cases, the boundaries may be irregular and require some creative data collection.

There are two levels of demographic profiling of a market area that can be considered—a basic profile and a more specialized profile focusing on selected characteristics. Virtually all market area profiles involve a basic analysis, which depicts the population in terms of such traits as age, sex and racial/ethnic characteristics. This basic profile is also likely to include socioeconomic characteristics, such as marital status and household structure, educational level, and income characteristics. More detailed data on economic characteristics (e.g., labor force characteristics, housing values) may also be considered. This basic profile includes data that would be useful for virtually any analysis.

For most purposes, the analyst will require population projections for the service area. At the very least, projections of population size at least five years into the future will be necessary. In most cases, projections related to the population's composition are

---

Box 3.3 continued

desirable. After all, it is the market's future age, sex, race, and socioeconomic characteristics that are going to drive demand for products and services in the years to come.

More specialized demographic information is likely to be required for industry-specific analyses. Financial institutions, for example, are likely to require more detailed information on spending behavior, occupational traits and stage in the life cycle. Health care organizations are likely to be interested in the prevalence of health conditions and current hospital utilization patterns.

Developing a basic profile and supplementing it with detailed industry specific data provides the basis for most business decision making. An understanding of demographic data and concepts is obviously needed for these activities. Decision makers now have a variety of data sources to choose from for market intelligence. The type of information that is provided includes information on the demographic, social, political, and economic aspects of the market. The emphasis is on sources of data that support the decision-making functions of organizations.

Consumer data resemble market data in many ways, involving the full gamut of demographic variables and often targeting a segment of the market. Since not everyone is a prospect for your company, consumer data may involve a profile of selected segments of the population. The profiles are to some extent independent of geography in that a list of potential customers (consumers) may contain the names and addresses of persons who are geographically dispersed.

In a way, *competitor data* represent a combination of consumer and customer data. They are often used to demographically profile the customers that are loyal to a competitor and those who are not. (For those with insider information, it would also be worthwhile to determine the demographic profile being targeted by competitors.) Typically, one would desire the same information on competitors' customers that is collected on your own customers. Of critical importance is often the manner in which the two groups of customers differ demographically.

As marketing and business planning have become more sophisticated, demographic data have become not only important in their own right but increasingly important as a basis for deriving other information. For example, knowledge of the demographic composition of a target population is not likely to be the end goal, determining the shopping habits of this population may be. Thus, demographic data help generate utilization or purchasing rates of various types—with packaged goods industries, for example, classifying users as light, moderate or heavy; with health care organizations, dividing the population on the basis of the level of demand for services evidenced by various subgroups.

Business decision makers also utilize information on the demographic processes that contribute to any market profile. The three basic demographic processes of migration, fertility, and mortality are addressed in Chapters 4 through 6. While mortality trends are of limited use for business planning, unless one is in the health care or funeral home industries, an understanding of the fertility and migration processes is critical for most business decision making. Fertility refers to the reproductive activity of a population and, from a business perspective, determines the current size of certain markets and the population structure of current and future consumer groups. Migration involves the movement of members of the population from one place to another and, in many markets, is the major factor in both short- and long-term changes in local market consumer characteristics.

DATA COLLECTION TECHNIQUES FOR DEMOGRAPHIC DATA

Demographic data are collected in a variety of ways. The data collection methods discussed in this chapter are divided into four general categories: censuses, registration systems, surveys, and synthetically produced data. Censuses, registries, and surveys are the more traditional sources of demographic data, although synthetically produced statistics (i.e., population estimates and projections) have become standard tools for most planning activities. Data users have become increasingly aware of the variety of data and services offered by the growing number of data vendors. Because data vendors have become a significant force in most industries, a special section on them is presented below.

Censuses

A *census* is a count of the population in a specific geographic area at a specific time (Shryock, Siegel, and Associates 1973, p. 15). The U.S. Census Bureau has conducted a census every ten years since 1790. A true census, by definition, includes a complete count of the population. While the decennial Census of Population and Housing theoretically counts every resident, a large portion of the data on population characteristics is obtained from a random sample of the nation's households. The use of sampling (about one in six households) significantly reduces the cost of taking the census, but it introduces variability into statistics that are sometimes incorrectly viewed as complete counts. Users of census data should become knowledgeable about their reliability, especially when small geographic units are being studied.

Typical census items elicit data on the number of persons residing in each living unit (e.g., house, duplex or apartment) and the characteristics of those individuals. Information is also gathered on age, race, ethnicity, marital status, income, occupation, education, employment status, and industry of employment. There are also questions about the dwelling unit in which the respondent lives, such as ownership status, value of owned house, monthly rent, and age of dwelling unit. Complete questionnaires for the 1990 Census of Population and Housing can be found in Robey (1989). A summary of items included in the 1990 census appears in Box 3.4.

A key benefit of these data for business analysts is their availability for various units of geography. While national, regional, and state data may be useful to business demographers, it is often data at the county and subcounty levels that are

---

Box 3.4
Short-Form and Long-Form Items
in the 1990 Census of Population and Housing

Short-Form (100%) Items

Population

Household relationship

Sex

Race

Age

Marital status

Hispanic origin

Housing

Number of units in structure

Number of rooms in unit

Tenure (owned or rented)

Value of home or monthly rent paid

Congregate housing

Vacancy characteristics

Long-Form (Sample) Items

Population

Social characteristics:

   Education (enrollment & attainment)

   Place of birth, citizenship, & year of entry to the U.S.

   Ancestry

   Language spoken at home

   Migration (residence in 1985 vs. 1990)

   Disability

   Fertility

   Veteran status

Economic characteristics:

   Labor force

   Occupation, industry, and class of worker

   Place of work and journey to work

   Work experience in 1989

   Income in 1989

   Year last worked

Housing

Condominium status

Plumbing and kitchen facilities

Telephone in unit

House heating fuel

Source of water and method of sewage disposal

Vehicles available

Year structure built

Year moved into residence

Number of bedrooms

Farm residence

Shelter costs, including utilities

Source: Bureau of the Census, 1989. *The 1990 Census of Population and Housing: Tabulation and Publication Program*. U.S. Department of Commerce. U.S. Bureau of the Census. Washington, DC: U.S.

of greatest value. In particular, data for census tracts, block groups, and census blocks can be aggregated in order to approximate a market area. Since business planners often think at the zipcode level, the Census Bureau and private industry have cooperated to convert census data into zipcode categories.

Figure 3.1 presents descriptions of selected Summary Tape Files (STFs) generated by the Census Bureau. The Bureau distributes both the 100 percent data and the sample data in this format on magnetic tape and CD-ROM. For business applications, the STF1A, STF3A, and STF3B datafiles are most often used. These data are easy to access via CD-ROM as discussed in Box 3.5.

Figure 3.1
Selected Summary Tape Files (STF) from the 1990 Census

Summary Tape File (STF)	Description
1A	Short-form data (100% question) for states and their subareas in hierarchical sequence down to the block-group level.
1B	Same as 1A, except down to the census block level.
2A	Short-form data (100% question) for census tracts and block numbering areas (BNAs), and places of 10,000 or more persons.
3A	Long-form data (sample questions) for states and their subareas in hierarchical sequence down to the block group level.
3B	Long-form data (sample questions) for 5-digit zip codes within each state.

Box 3.5
Accessing Demographic Data on CD-ROM

Technological advancements in data storage and retrieval have facilitated the use of data from the census and other sources for a wide variety of business applications. Data from the 1990 Census of Population and Housing and the 1992 Economic/Enterprise Censuses are now available on CD-ROM. The data are available for the following

Box 3.5 continued

geographic units: U.S., states, metropolitan statistical areas, counties, census tracts, block groups and blocks, and zip codes. CDs containing demographic data can be purchased or accessed at no charge in public and university libraries. New public-access mapping software, Landview, is now available on CD at those same libraries, and many private sector mapping packages have become available.

Summary Tape Files (STFs) 1 and 3 contain most of the demographic data needed for market analysis, and there are separate CDs for each category of data. The STF1 CD contains data from the 100 percent questionnaire (population and housing questions) and STF3 contains the more detailed sample data. STF1A includes data with geographic detail down to the block group level, while STF1B contains the data for census blocks. STF3A contains the detailed social and economic characteristics down to the block group, and STF3B includes data for five-digit zip codes. STF2 CD contains more detail for the 100 percent questions and STF4 contains more detail for the sample questions. Data from the STF2 and STF4 files are available only down to the census tract/block numbering area levels, not for census blocks or block groups.

The CDs available from the Census Bureau are very easy to use. Many libraries already have them installed, although installation is no more difficult than placing a music CD in a CD player. The entire process is menu driven. The user selects the category of data needed (e.g., age structure and income distribution) and the geographic units (e.g., counties and census tracts) for which the data are required. The resulting tables can either be printed out or written to diskette for further manipulation.

The analysis in the example below took less than ten minutes, including the time required to print the tables. The project involved a determination of the demographic characteristics for census tract 48 in Omaha, Nebraska, as well as for the five block groups that comprise tract 48. Tract 48 in the Omaha MSA contains the University of Nebraska at Omaha. Using a series of menus, we were able to select Nebraska from among the states on this CD and then Douglas County, which contains census tract 48 as the initial unit of geography. We then selected census tracts, specifying tract 48. Since STF1A provides 100 percent data, we were able to determine that the tract contained 4,506 persons. Other data extracted from the CD included

<u>Census Tract 48</u>

% Population Age 65 & over	10.9
Median Age	31.1
Total Number of Households	2,295
Rental Vacancy Rate	1.5%
Median Value Owner-Occupied Houses	$62,200

By further searching through the block group data we found the populations of BG1 through BG5 to be 499, 740, 687, 1,310, and 1,270, respectively. The same population and housing characteristics available for tracts are also available for block groups.

Next we loaded STF3A in order to access more detailed social and economic characteristics. The same geographic units, tract and block groups, were selected. We found the median household income for the entire tract and its component block groups to be

Box 3.5 continued

<u>Census Tract 48</u>

Entire Tract	$23,315
BG1	$18,125
BG2	$25,956
BG3	$31,042
BG4	$25,529
BG5	$19,118

Additional data on family income, occupation and employment and poverty level were also found.

Users of the CD simply must select the geographic area(s) for which data are desired and use the menu system to select the data needed. Both simple and complex market area analyses are possible with relatively little effort. If the analyst does not know which geographic units are being researched, a census map may be consulted. These maps are available at libraries that serve as repositories for government publications. Mapping is discussed in more detail in Chapter 7.

While the Census Bureau's primary function is the enumeration of population and housing units, it also conducts less well-known economic censuses every five years in years that end in 2 and 7 (e.g., 1992). The industries covered by these economic censuses are retail trade, wholesale trade, service industries, mining, transportation, construction, manufacturing, and agriculture. Government operations are also covered in these federal censuses. This information is presented by Standard Industrial Classification code (SIC), the scheme through which businesses are categorized. The information collected from each establishment typically includes sales, employment, and payroll data, although other more specialized data may be gathered. These data are available for a variety of geographic units, including states, metropolitan areas, counties, larger incorporated places, and zip codes. Formats include magnetic tape, microfiche, CD-ROM, and printed reports. These data releases may be obtained from the same sources and locations that provide population and housing data.

It should be noted that the future availability of census data may be affected by attempts to reduce the federal budget. In fact, at the time of this printing serious consideration was being given to reducing the scope of the census scheduled for the year 2000. Population estimates may have to be used as a substitute for actual counts, particularly in small areas (Rosewicz 1996). Although critics voice concerns about the quality of data and the appropriateness of government meddling into citizen affairs, the cost of the census is probably the major concern regarding Census Bureau activities. In a period of financial retrenchment, the cost of the decennial census is a convenient target for those who are negatively predisposed to federal expenditures.

Although the census will certainly survive in some form (since it is mandated by the Constitution), its scope and detail may well be curtailed. This could result in a decline in the quantity and quality of data available for business planning. The data collected during the census are not only important in their own right, but provide the basis for population estimates and projections for the years between censuses. Unfortunately, the business community has not been very vocal about its data needs, and the cutbacks are being planned without sufficient business input (Hoeffel 1995).

Sample Surveys

Sample surveys differ from censuses in that they collect data from some sample of a target population rather than the entire population. Surveys are useful when it is not practical to canvass everyone (which is most of the time) and when detailed information from a small number of respondents would be better than minimal data from a larger number of respondents.

Sample surveys operate on the assumption that inferences can be drawn for the population based on the responses of a relatively small sample of that population. This assumption only holds, however, if the sample selected is representative of the total population in its characteristics and if everyone in the population has a known chance of being selected. Understandably, statistics generated from a sample of the population may vary from those for the entire population, that is, sampling error will exist. However, if the sample of respondents is properly chosen, the size of the error can be easily determined.

Information collected through sample surveys has several advantages over census data, including opportunities for more frequent data collection and for more in-depth treatment of business issues. The relatively small sample sizes for such surveys allow for easier administration, quicker turnaround time, and more efficient data manipulation compared to larger-scale operations such as a census.

One the other hand, sample surveys have their disadvantages. Since they involve a sample, there may be some slippage in accuracy relative to censuses. The most serious shortcoming related to business decision making, however, is the inability to compile adequate data for small geographic units due to small sample sizes. Also, the special subject areas addressed by some surveys may not be featured on a regular basis, so that the interval between surveys can become lengthy.

Critical to all survey research is the ability to link demographic characteristics to the population attributes or behaviors under study. Most surveys contain lengthy sections that elicit information on the age, sex, race, and socioeconomic status of the respondents and/or their households. These demographic data serve as the basis for segmenting the populations under study and developing subsequent measures of consumer activity.

Registrations

Registrations represent a third source of demographic data. A registration system involves the systematic submission, recording, and reporting of data on a broad range of events, institutions, and/or individuals (Shryock, Siegel, and Associates 1973, p. 27). The best known registration activities in the United States are those related to "vital events"—that is, births, deaths, marriages, divorces, and induced abortions. However, other registry data, such as those compiled by federal agencies like the Health Care Financing Administration (HCFA), the Social Security Administration (SSA), and the Immigration and Naturalization Service (INS) can also prove to be valuable. Registry systems may also exist at the state level, as in the case of drivers license registries.

The collection of vital statistics has a long history in the United States, predating the Declaration of Independence. Standard birth certificate information includes time and date of birth, place of birth occurrence, residence of mother, birth weight, pregnancy complications, a pregnancy history of the mother, parents' age and race (ethnicity in selected states), and mother's education and marital status. Data gathered on the standard death certificate include age, race (ethnicity in selected states), sex, residence, usual occupation, and industry of the decedent, along with the location where the death occurred. In addition, information on the immediate and secondary causes of death, and other significant conditions is collected. A separate certificate is used in the case of a fetal death.

Birth and death statistics are available in government publications, based on both place of occurrence of the event and place of residence of the affected individual. Considerable detail is provided for a wide range of geographies including states, metropolitan statistical areas (MSAs), counties, and urban places. Data for other geographic areas (e.g., census tracts) may be available through state and local government agencies, such as state and county health departments. Yearly summary reports are produced and published by the National Center for Health Statistics, and monthly summaries are also available through its vital statistics reports. Some vital statistics data are available on computer tape and CD-ROM, though not all data elements may be included.

Marriage and divorce registration areas (MRAs and DRAs) cover all but eight states and are made up of component states and structured in the same fashion as birth and death areas. Basic information gathered on the marriage certificate includes age of spouse, type of ceremony (civil or religious), and previous marital status of spouse, as well as the race and educational status of the bride and groom. Data available from divorce certificates are limited to the ages of husband and wife at the time of marriage and divorce, previous marital history, number of children under age 18 involved, and the educational status of husband and wife.

Marriage and divorce statistics are normally disseminated by the National Center for Health Statistics through monthly and yearly reports for states, MSAs, and counties. State agencies and county health departments provide this information at the substate level. Individual-level data (without identifying characteristics such as name and address) are available on magnetic tape.

Data on induced abortions are collected from the 13 states that participate in the reporting program sponsored by the National Center for Health Statistics. Although the coverage is not complete, these data are used as the basis for calculating abortion rates for the entire nation.

Information on immigrants, legalization applications, refugees, asylum applicants, non-immigrant entries, and naturalizations are collected by the

Immigration and Naturalization Service within the U.S. Department of Justice. These data are generated from immigrant visa information that is theoretically available on everyone legally entering the United States. After a person is allowed entry into the United States, visa and adjustment forms are forwarded to the INS data–capture facility for processing. During immigrant processing, data are collected on the port of admission, the country of birth, last residence, nationality, age, sex, occupation, and zip code of the immigrant's intended residence.

Immigration data are made available from the INS through annual statistical summaries, more frequent interim reports, and on magnetic tapes. While the published reports contain data for states and MSAs, tabulations for counties and zip codes can be made from the tapes.

Synthetic Data

Synthetic data are generated by combining existing demographic data with assumptions about population change. The products of this combination are estimates, projections, and forecasts for populations. The large and growing demand for information for noncensus years is being met by government agencies and commercial data vendors that prepare synthetic estimates for various geographic units. These data are particularly valuable since census and survey activities are limited due to budget and time considerations.

Estimates involve the calculation of statistics for a current or past time period. They typically involve the extrapolation or interpolation of actual data (e.g., census data) for one or more known time periods. *Extrapolation* involves an extension of time trends into the future using some established projection method. *Interpolation* refers to the process of estimating population statistics for some point in between two known time periods.

Projections are estimates of population statistics for some future period. As such, projections reflect past trends and carry them forward into the future. Projections may simply extrapolate a trend into the future or may involve adjustments based on known developments in the area for which the projection is being made. *Forecasts* are similar to projections, in that they involve population statistics for some point in the future.

Population estimates for states, MSAs, and counties are prepared each year as a joint effort of the Census Bureau and the agency designated by each state governor to participate in the Federal-State Program for Local Population Estimates (FSCPE). The purpose of the program is to standardize data and procedures so that the highest-quality estimates can be derived. The estimates generated typically provide a population figure for the current year, one for some previous year, and a change figure; some may include data on the components of change (i.e., births, deaths, and net migrants).

Different types of information are available for population projections. One Census Bureau publication focuses on U.S. projections to the year 2080 by age, sex, and race; it also provides data for three sets of fertility, mortality, and migration assumptions (Day 1993). Overall, the Census Bureau produces 30 different series of projections for each year. Most states also generate population estimates and projections that are available through state agencies. However, these figures are often produced at irregular intervals and are often quite dated.

The population estimates and projections generated by government agencies have historically been the only ones available. Today, however, a number of data vendors supplement these figures with proprietary synthetic data. These vendor-generated data have the advantages of being available for subcounty units of geography and are provided in greater detail (e.g., sex and age breakdowns) than government-produced figures. Vendors may also provide data for custom geographic units. Some precision is lost, however, as one develops statistics for lower levels of geography and for population components. However, the ease of accessibility and timeliness of these vendor-generated figures have made them a mainstay of business planners and researchers.

Occupational projections 10 to 15 years into the future for the United States are produced by the Bureau of Labor Statistics within the U.S. Department of Labor (1994). Six models have been created, each containing numerous variables reflecting different scenarios of growth in the total labor force, changes in the aggregate economy, industry demand, and industry employment. Three sets of employment projections are created based on differing sets of assumptions. The occupation projections are available through regularly published reports. The matrix coefficients utilized to generate the percentage distribution for the labor force can also be obtained and these are sometimes used by other organizations to produce subnational projections.

The federal government and, occasionally, other organizations produce compendia of information on specific topics. These publications generally contain extensive demographic data and, in fact, may frame their conclusions in terms of demographically defined segments of the population. Examples of such products are found for the U.S. Departments of Health and Human Services (health statistics), Education (education statistics), and Justice (crime statistics).

These publications are found in most libraries, especially those that serve as repositories for government documents. They are also available for purchase from the U.S. Government Printing Office or through regional centers that sell government publications. These publications are becoming increasingly available in electronic formats. (The list of selected readings at the end of this chapter includes some of these resources.)

SOURCES OF DEMOGRAPHIC DATA

The following sections describe the major sources of demographic data. The data sources discussed are limited to those relating to the United States, although the importance of relevant information from an international perspective is acknowledged.

Government Sources

Governments at all levels are involved in the generation, compilation, manipulation, and/or dissemination of demographic data. The federal government, through the decennial census and related activities, is the world's largest processor of demographic data. Other federal agencies are major managers of data in the related areas of fertility, morbidity, mortality, and migration statistics. State governments generate a certain amount of demographic data, with each state having a state data center for demographic projections and vital statistics. However, states vary widely in the types and quality of data they provide. Local governments may also generate demographic data. City or county governments may produce population projections and county health departments are responsible for the collection and dissemination of vital statistics data. Government-supported university data centers may also be involved in the processing of demographic data.

As noted earlier, census data are available for virtually every geographic unit, including states, counties, zip codes, metropolitan areas, cities, census tracts, block groups, block numbering areas, and blocks. The ability to utilize census geography was dramatically improved for the 1990 census, and the new TIGER (Topologically Integrated Geographic Encoding and Referencing) system allows for the integration of geographic information and data collected as part of the 1990 census. The end result is the significantly enhanced ability to identify the demographic characteristics for virtually any geographic unit.

Most census datafiles are now available on computer tape, diskette, and microfiche, although many users still rely on the large number of published reports. In addition to the computer tape files normally produced, 1990 data are available on CD-ROM.

Census data may be accessed from a variety of other sources. Many libraries are U.S. government repositories and have most or all of the reports in print, microfiche or CD-ROM formats. The U.S. Government Printing Office also makes the reports available to the public at a reasonable cost. Computer tapes, microfiche, and CD-ROM data are sold directly through the U.S. Census Bureau's Data User Services Office. All of these products are relatively inexpensive. After the 1980 census, many private vendors also began to repackage census data and sell it to the public.

Usually, census data are available in aggregated form specific to several geographic units. However, "microdata" from the Census Bureau for individuals and households without personal identification information and most geographic identifiers are available on computer tape and CD-ROM. These data are particularly valuable for conducting customized data analysis.

Most published reports are available for geographic areas no smaller than regions, due to the relatively small sample size. However, manipulation of the data provided on computer tape or CD allows the analyst to generate figures for smaller geographic units such as metropolitan statistical areas, or to conduct individual–level analysis. Users, however, should be aware that smaller area estimates contain a great deal of variability as a result of variation in sample size.

Figure 3.2 lists 18 federal surveys that generate demographic data and these are organized into three categories. This list is not exhaustive but does provide the reader with a sense of the surveys available. Five frequently used demographic/business datasets are featured in Box 3.6.

Figure 3.2
Federal Surveys of Use to Business Demographers

Population/Demographic
Current Population Survey
National Survey of Family
Survey of Income and Program Participation
American Housing Survey

Business
Consumer Expenditure Survey
County Business Patterns
Current Construction Survey
Current Business Survey
Current Industrial Survey
National Medical Expenditure
Foreign Trade Survey

Health
National Health Interview Survey
National Hospital Discharge Survey
National Ambulatory Care Survey
Nation Nursing Home Survey
National Medical Expenditure Survey
National Long-term Care Survey
National Maternal and Infant Health Survey
National Health and Nutrition
Examination Survey

Source: Compiled by authors.

Box 3.6
Demographic Databases Used Frequently by Business

Current Population Survey

The Current Population Survey (CPS) is the Census Bureau's device for gathering detailed demographic information between decennial censuses. The series generates topic-specific reports at regular intervals throughout the year. In addition, a microdata computer tape is available annually that contains information relevant to that specific year. Since 1960, CPS sample size has ranged from 33,500 to 65,500 households. The items collected include many of those gathered in the census of population and housing (e.g., age, race, and education).

These data are available through a variety of published reports as part of the Census Bureau's *Current Population Reports* series. Most published reports include geographic refinements no smaller than regions due to the relatively small sample size. However,

Box 3.6 continued

using microdata the analyst can generate information for smaller geographic units such as MSAs, although users are cautioned that smaller area estimates may contain a great deal of variability. Recently, individual-level data, without identifying information, have become available on CD-ROM.

Consumer Expenditure Survey

The Bureau of Labor Statistics (BLS) has been collecting data on spending behavior and the cost of living for nearly a century. Since 1980, the Consumer Expenditure Survey has gathered data on an ongoing basis; sample households are replaced by others as the cycle of data collection proceeds. The survey consists of two components. The first involves a quarterly interview in which each "consumer unit" is interviewed four times over a 12-month period. The second component requires that a diary of expenses be kept for two consecutive one-week periods. The survey gathers data from 20,000 (5,000 each quarter) consumer units nationally, while the diary sample size is about 5,000 consumer units.

Information gathered includes standard demographic factors (e.g., age, race, and education); income, including sources of income; and expenditures over a broad range of categories. Survey data focus on larger expenditures including housing (e.g., shelter and utilities), apparel, transportation (e.g., automobiles), health care, and entertainment. Diary information is targeted toward smaller purchases such as food and beverages, housekeeping supplies, and personal care products.

The data are available in regularly published reports, and a microdata file may be purchased. Data in the reports are presented by region and for the United States as a whole, although smaller geographic unit data may be produced from the data tapes. However, small sample size and the resulting instability of estimates must be considered. Some of these data are now being repackaged by data vendors and sold in a more user–friendly format.

County Business Patterns

County Business Patterns is an annual series of reports made available annually since 1964 and at irregular intervals since 1946. As the title implies, the data are for counties or county equivalents, although they are also aggregated to the state and national levels, and are available for the District of Columbia, and Puerto Rico. The basic data items are extracted from the Standard Statistical Establishment List, a file of all known single– and multiestablishment companies maintained and updated by the Bureau of the Census.

Statistics are generated on the number of establishments, number of employees, and payroll, along with the total number of establishments categorized by employee size (e.g., 1–4, 5–9). The data are organized by two-, three- and four-digit SIC codes. Because of the extremely small number of establishments in many SIC codes for smaller states and many counties, much of the data is given in ranges and not in absolute figures. The data are available in printed form, or microfiche and diskette, and on CD-ROM.

Box 3.6 continued

National Health Interview Survey

The National Health Interview Survey (NHIS) is an ongoing national survey of the U.S. noninstitutionalized civilian population. Each year, a multistage probability sample of between 36,000 and 46,000 households (92,000 to 135,000 persons) is generated for inclusion and interview. The data gathered are quite detailed and the NHIS contains a number of demographic items. Demographic information collected includes age, race, sex, marital status, occupation, and income. Health questions relate to physician visits, hospital stays, restricted-activity days, long-term activity limitation, and chronic conditions. Recently, questions regarding AIDS knowledge and attitudes have been added to the survey. Food nutrition knowledge, tobacco use, cancer, and polio are also subjects sometimes addressed.

The data are available in published report form (*Current Estimates* reports, Series 10, and the *Advance Data* series) and on computer tape. The data have recently been released on CD-ROM. The data tapes consist of five files, each related to a specific topic: health conditions, physician visits, hospital stays, household characteristics, and person characteristics. Geographic identification is limited to region and MSA if the person lived in one of the larger MSAs. The CD-ROM data are contained on a disk organized into nine files. The data are available for each year from 1969 on.

Annual Survey of Manufacturers

The Annual Survey of Manufacturers (ASM) was initiated in 1949, and is conducted in years in between the Census of Manufacturers. Data are for establishments and cover employment, hours worked, payrolls, value added by manufacture, cost of materials, and inventories, among a longer list of items. The data are organized by SIC code.

The survey is composed of two components. The mail portion of the survey involves a probability sample of about 55,000 manufacturing establishments selected from a total of about 200,000 establishments. These 200,000 establishments represent all manufacturing establishments of multiunit companies and all single-unit manufacturing establishments mailed schedules in the 1987 Census of Manufactures. This mail portion is supplemented annually by a Social Security Administration list of new single-unit manufacturing establishments opened since 1987 and a list of new multiunit manufacturing establishments identified from the Census Bureau's Company Organization Survey.

The data are available for the United States and individual states including the District of Columbia. However, some state data are suppressed to protect confidentiality since some states have small samples. The data are available in published form and CD-ROM.

Data from a variety of federal sources are compiled and presented in Box 3.7. Recently, data have begun to be available on the Internet and through other on-line access options (see Box 3.8).

Box 3.7
Federal Compendia of Demographic Data

Statistic Abstract of the United States: 1,410 tables organized into 30 sections in the 1995 edition. Sections 1–4 focus on population, vital statistics, health and nutrition, and education. Other "demographic" sections include: social insurance and human services, labor force, employmental earnings, income expenditures and wealth, business enterprise, transportation, agriculture, construction and housing, manufacturers, domestic and trade services, and comparative international statistics. Most data are for the entire United States, but some state, MSA, and city data are included. Historical data are included in many tables. Published annually. Available on diskette, CD-ROM and Census Online, as well as hard copy.

County and City Data Book: 220 data items for all states, counties, and cities (incorporated places of 25,000 or more) in the 1994 edition. Data organized into 14 sections, including land area and population, population characteristics, housing and wholesale and retail trade. Little historical data are included. The first three tables provide rankings for counties and cities (e.g., counties with highest number of Hispanic population). Published every five years. Available on diskette, CD-ROM, and Census OnLine, as well as print.

County and City Extra: Similar to *County and City Data Book*, but published annually by Bernan Press. Data for MSAs and Congressional Districts also included. 228 data items, organized into 17 sections (states), 201 data items, 14 sections (states, counties, and cities), 151 data items, 11 sections (cities), and 53 data items, 4 sections (Congressional districts). Published annually since 1992. Available as CD-ROM and hardcopy.

State and Metropolitan Area Data Book: 94 data items organized into six sections in 1991, including many of the same data included in the *Statistical Abstract of the United States* and the *County and City Data Book*. Data are available for states and metropolitan areas. Published every five years. Available in CD-ROM, diskette, and print formats and accessible through Census Online.

Historical Statistics of the United States, Colonial Times to 1970: 615 data items organized into 26 sections ranging from population to agriculture, transportation, and business enterprise. The data are presented for the United States with state breakdowns where appropriate. Historical trends are presented when there are adequate data.

Box 3.8
Accessing Census Data On Line
http://www.census.gov/

New technology has made demographic and business data easier to access and use than ever before. Data from the 1990 Census are now readily accessed via CD-ROMs that are available at little or no cost. Data required for specific market areas can be downloaded from CDs to diskette and analyzed using one of many available spreadsheet software applications. Now, even easier access is possible on the Internet using Census Online.

Box 3.8 continued

Census Online is a site on the Internet which contains a wealth of business-related census data. The information is organized by category, with the main menu containing eight categories: *Population and Housing, Economy, Geography, Data Access Tools, About the Census Bureau, Latest News, Ask the Experts,* and *Market Place.* The ability to manipulate a mouse—that is, simply pointing and clicking—is the main skill needed to view, print, purchase, and/or electronically transfer information. Each of the main menu categories is organized into submenu items. If the latest population estimates for selected states and counties are needed, the starting point would be the main menu, *Population and Housing.* Submenus allow the user to identify the states and counties for which the data are needed. Additional menu-driven commands allow for the data to be printed and/or electronically transferred to a hard drive or diskette. The web site is entered using this Internet address: http://www.census.gov/. By the end of 1995, the Census Bureau web site was being accessed approximately 70,000 times per day.

Census Online is much more than a data archive. National, state, and substate maps are available and these can be printed directly or electronically transferred. Information about the organization and history of the Bureau of the Census is also available. Press releases, organized by topic, can be viewed. For example, the authors of this book have a research interest in health insurance coverage. Examining press releases under the topic *Health* on the menu bar yields several useful press releases on recent publications based on Current Population Survey data. Specific reports are referenced in the press releases and, if more information is needed, these can be purchased or, in some instances, accessed electronically. While not yet fully functional, the Ask the Experts main menu selection allows questions to be posed via e-mail to be subsequently answered by return mail.

CD-ROM products can also be ordered through the Census Bureau's web site. Clicking on *Market Place* calls up descriptions of data available on CD-ROM. Purchases are made by clicking on a "buy" button, using either a credit card or an established census deposit account number.

Finally, Census Online also provides a "bridge" to other web sites which offer demographic data. Web sites at the Universities of Michigan, Missouri and California-Berkeley, for example, provide information on and access to maps and data on CDs that can be printed or electronically transferred.

Private Organizations

A number of private organizations generate, compile, manipulate, and/or disseminate demographic data. Most of these organizations repackage data collected elsewhere (e.g., by the Census Bureau or the National Center for Health Statistics) and present it within a specialized context. The Population Reference Bureau, for example, a private not-for-profit organization, distributes population statistics in various forms. Voluntary health care associations (e.g, the American Cancer Society) disseminate morbidity and mortality data as it relates to their areas of interest. The National Education Association may reanalyze and distribute educational data from the census. Some organizations, like Planned Parenthood, may commission special studies on fertility or related issues and subsequently publish this information. The availability and characteristics of data generated by private organizations varies widely. Each source must be contacted to obtain details on their databases.

Commercial Data Vendors

The increasing demand for demographic data has been partially met by the growing number of businesses (vendors) that offer data services. These services range from the simple provision of population figures for broad market areas to the sophisticated analysis of a variety of market factors for very small units of geography. While the rise in data supply may be viewed as positive, there is a downside to this trend; the increase in suppliers has made quality measurement and comparison more difficult. This issue is made more complex by the proliferation of software packages that are capable of organizing, analyzing, and presenting these data in a visually appealing fashion.

An annual directory is published by *American Demographics* magazine that features companies that specialize in demographic products. The number of companies providing such data has steadily increased, despite some consolidation in the data industry, especially with the rise of resellers of demographic data.

Data vendors offer a wide range of products of use to those involved in business planning, marketing, or research. They range in complexity from basic demographic statistics provided in paper form to sophisticated computer-based analysis systems. The sections below identify the types of resources that are available from vendors, rather than attempting to note specific products, services, or vendors.

The bread-and-butter of data vendors has been basic demographic data. Provided in printed form, on diskette, and/or on-line from a mainframe computer, basic population data have long been utilized for business decision making. Vendors have become progressively more sophisticated in terms of the data that they can generate. The detail in terms of geographic options and population composition is staggering at times. In some environments, data vendors have taken the place of the Census Bureau as the "last word" in demographic data.

Data vendors also have been in the forefront of the integration of demographic and other databases. Vendors have integrated databases from disparate sources in order to provide a comprehensive range of information relative to particular problems. Data vendors have progressed from repackaging existing data to providing various levels of data analysis. Many vendors have developed "canned" models that allow for the analysis of data using relatively rigorous research designs. A typical example would be the vendor that would take a client-identified point (e.g., an intersection or latitude/longitude coordinate) and draw a service area around it to the client's specification. A new "polygon" has now been created that can serve as the geographical unit for analysis. A more complex example would involve the use of modeling, in which the vendor would examine a variety of "what-if" scenarios. A case in point would be the operation of a model that would calculate the number of purchases of a particular product expected to be generated for a particular geography.

Some data vendors have progressed beyond disseminating data to the development of software for analyzing it. Typically designed to work with their databases (which are often proprietary), vendor-developed software packages can be used to manipulate, analyze, and present data from various sources. Box 3.9 provides a general description of desktop marketing systems. For a more thorough treatment of this topic, refer to Thomas and Kirchner (1991).

Box 3.9

Desktop Analysis Systems

Locating prospects for a product or selecting an appropriate site for a retail outlet is a challenging proposition requiring access to extensive amounts of data. Efficiently identifying and targeting markets is difficult even with tried-and-proved research techniques. Until the 1980s, business analysts had few tools at their disposal for the efficient performance of market research.

During the 1980s, data vendors introduced desktop market analysis systems. Advances in microcomputing capabilities and the development of increasing numbers of databases led to the emergence of all-in-one microcomputer-based systems that not only integrated disparate databases but came as close to analyzing and interpreting the data as possible. In short, these desktop systems were designed to turn numbers into information and information into solutions. Able to access multiple databases simultaneously, desktop analysis systems have added a new dimension to business decision making.

Desktop market analysis systems can assist in locating target populations, selecting sites, analyzing competition, planning direct mail campaigns, and determining the appropriate media for reaching a particular population segment. Internal customer data can be interfaced with externally generated market information on demographic, economic, and consumer characteristics.

The systems on the market now are considered either generic or industry specific. Generic systems are those designed to operate in a variety of industrial environments. Industry-specific systems are those designed for a particular industry such as health care. There are a large number of generic systems available but relatively few industry-specific ones. (Financial services and health care provide examples of the latter.)

Desktop market analysis systems have transformed marketing research from a slow, plodding process of questionable accuracy to a highly scientific, accurate, and expeditious activity. Desktop analysis systems have made databases easily accessible and offer software packages that perform a number of sophisticated functions, such as simultaneously using multiple databases and creating "macros" to manipulate variables. Researchers can convert the results into reports, tables, graphics, and maps that depict the characteristics of the market and offer solutions to marketing problems. The availability of affordable geographic information systems has greatly enhanced the capabilities of desktop marketing systems.

Obviously, desktop analysis systems cannot do everything and they certainly cannot "think." The analyst still must possess the requisite background information, market

---

Box 3.9 continued

familiarity, and interpretative skills. The desktop system becomes a formidable tool in the hands of an analyst with these capabilities.

THE FUTURE OF DEMOGRAPHIC DATA

There is both good news and bad news related to the future availability and quality of demographic data. On the positive side, increasing numbers of vendors are generating or reselling demographic data for geographies ranging from the nation down to the household level. This has not only made data more accessible but also more affordable. While demographic data are still available in the traditional forms—in printed reports and on-line from commercial vendors—these data are increasingly available on diskette, CD-ROM, and through the Internet.

Certainly the technology for generating, processing, and disseminating demographic data has improved and, with these improvements, computer processing costs have gone down. It is no longer a challenge to incorporate demographic data into a desktop marketing system--and maintain data for the entire United States on one hard drive. Mapping and graphics technology has made it increasingly easy to convert demographic data into maps and graphics. Public/private partnerships have facilitated the movement of current demographic data from the government sector to the private sector.

The primary concern facing users of demographic data today, however, is the threat of a scaled-back version of the census in the year 2000. Large reductions in the Census Bureau's budget could seriously compromise both the quality and quantity of data on which business users depend. If census activities are significantly altered, the base data from which vendors produce their figures may be seriously flawed. In particular, data for small geographic areas may be limited to just a few statistics. Although there are some ways to work around the data gap that could occur should the census be scaled back, a valuable and at least partially irreplaceable data source could well be lost. Box 3.10 describes the activities of an applied demographer utilizing data from many of the sources discussed.

Box 3.10

Jeff Tayman—Demographer with the San Diego Association of Governments

My title is Senior Regional Planner and I work for the San Diego Association of Governments (SANDAG). I have a Ph.D. in sociology/demography with a minor in applied statistics. I apply a wide range of demographic, statistical, economic, and geographical techniques to issues affecting local and regional governments.

Box 3.10 continued

SANDAG is a quasi-government agency run by a Board of Directors, which consists of an elected official from the 18 incorporated cities in San Diego county and a member of the County Board of Supervisors. It serves as a forum for regional decision making on such issues as transportation, growth management, habitat conservation, housing, and solid waste. SANDAG has 70 full-time employees and I work in the Research and Information Systems Division. My division contains 21 people, most of which are geographers, and I have direct supervision over five people. I am the only demographer at SANDAG and I am the only employee with a doctorate.

My major responsibility is to manage the estimates and forecasts portion of a Regional Information System that supports SANDAG's planning functions. I am responsible for a budget that averages $500,000 each year. A wide variety of demographic and economic estimates and forecasts are maintained in this system. These data are geographically intensive and are generated for areas that are no bigger than a census block—about 26,000 areas within San Diego county. An interdisciplinary approach is used to solve the myriad of technical, data, and modeling issues associated with the implementation of a comprehensive small-area estimation and forecasting system.

Around 35 to 40 percent of my time is spent on the technical aspects and the mechanics of producing and maintaining the estimates and forecast databases. Part of this time involves working with my staff to coordinate their activities and to solve any problems that they or I have noted. Most of my other work in this area focuses on developing, refining, and testing new data, methods, and algorithms to improve our models. It is also very important that each forecasting and estimation system have technical documentation that conforms to a Configuration Management Plan.

Project management activities require about 10 percent of my time. Long- and short-range planning and scheduling are an essential part of my job and are critical to the successful maintenance of the estimate and forecast information. I must also work closely with our data users, both inside and outside of SANDAG, to ensure that we are producing information that meets their needs and demands.

As a government agency, it is important that our information is readily accessible and disseminated to a wide range of users, both inside and outside of government. So, part of my responsibilities involves designing and developing data retrieval systems and writing publications for the nontechnical person that summarize and analyze key trends in the information. I also write position papers that examine the implications of demographic and economic changes on issues affecting the region that are important to elected officials and other decision makers. Part of SANDAG's outreach effort involves face-to-face communication with our constituents. I am the lead spokesman for matters dealing with demography or economics and make 30 to 50 presentations each year to elected officials and a wide variety of organizations and interest groups.

While most of my projects are long term and on-going, occasionally I will be called to work on shorter-term projects that require my particular mix of skills. These projects, usually less than one month in duration, have involved topics such as sampling design, facility location, crime and arrest forecasts, and political redistricting.

REFERENCES

Hoeffel, John (1995). "Shrinking the Census." *American Demographics* (October): 32–42.
Robey, Bryant (1989). "Two Hundred Years and Counting: The 1990 Census." *Population Bulletin*, Vol. 44, No. 1, Washington, DC: U.S. Government Printing Office.
Rosewicz, Barbara (1996). "Census Will Use Estimates to Get a Better Count." *Wall Street Journal* (February 29): B1, B8.
Shryock, Henry S., Jacob Siegel, and Associates (1973). *The Methods and Materials of Demography*. Washington, DC: U.S. Government Printing Office.
Thomas, Richard K., and Russell Kirchner (1991). *Desktop Marketing*. Ithaca, NY: American Demographics Publishing.
U.S. Bureau of Labor Statistics (1994). *The American Work Force: 1992–2005*. Bulletin 2452. Washington, DC: U.S. Government Printing Office.

SUGGESTED READINGS

Ambry, Margaret (1991). *Consumer Power*. Ithaca, NY: New Strategist Publications.
Day, Jennifer (1993). "Population Projections of the United States by Age, Race and Hispanic Origin: 1993–2050." *Current Population Reports*, Series P-25, No. 1104, Washington, DC: U.S. Government Printing Office.
Hughes, Arthur (1994). *Strategic Database Marketing*. Chicago: Probus.
Murdock, Steve H., and David R. Ellis (1991). *Applied Demography*. Boulder, CO: Westview Press, pp. 69–112.
Thomas, Richard K., Louis Pol, and William F. Sehnert (1994). *Health Care Book of Lists*. Orlando, FL: St. Lucie Press.
U.S. Bureau of the Census (Monthly). *Census and You*. Washington, DC: U.S. Government Printing Office.
U.S. Bureau of the Census (Annual). *U.S. Statistical Abstract*. Washington, DC: U.S. Government Printing Office.
U.S. Bureau of the Census (Periodic). *County and City Data Book*. Washington, DC: U.S. Government Printing Office.
U.S. Bureau of the Census (Periodic). *States and Metropolitan Areas Data Book*. Washington, DC: U.S. Government Printing Office.
U.S. Department of Health and Human Services (Annual). *Health, United States*. Washington, DC: U.S. Government Printing Office.

Chapter 4

Migration: Geographic Mobility and Its Implications

INTRODUCTION

Migration, or the permanent movement of individuals or groups from one geographic location to another, has been an intrinsic aspect of American culture. From the first emigrants who fled England for the New World to the pioneer-migrants who ceaselessly pushed the frontier westward to the corporate executive transferred every two years, geographic mobility has played a dominant role in American life. With the exception of certain truly nomadic societies, migration has probably had a greater impact on the American experience than it has on any other country.

The American nation was built by immigrants and much of its population growth, even today, can be attributed to foreigners seeking a new life in the United States. In fact, for much of U.S. history, migration has played as much a part in national population growth as have births. Our culture has the characteristics it does because of the input of millions of immigrants from diverse cultures. Today 100 million Americans can trace their roots to Ellis Island in New York or Angel Island in California—historically, the two major processing centers for immigrants. American culture continues to evolve as different groups of migrants make their contribution to the "melting pot."

America's fascination with mobility does not end at the national border but has served to make migration an integral part of our ethos. Our history has revolved around our westward movement, as immigrants and their descendants peopled the continent. This mass movement has not only served to redistribute the population but has created a cultural experience that even today sets the United States apart from other industrialized countries.

Americans have never outgrown this wanderlust, and the United States is unique in terms of the proportion of the population that changes residence each year.

Whether in search of economic opportunity, a better climate, a new start or simply "a change," Americans are exceptional with regard to their mobility. We accept residential change as a part of our lives, building it into our corporate ethic and making geographic mobility a value in its own right. Indeed, an important maxim in American business has been that would-be executives must "pay their dues" by changing locations several times for the good of the company.

Although the average number of lifetime moves has declined somewhat in recent years, the issue of migration is kept alive by the continued migration flows from one region of the country to another and by the modern-day records being set by immigrants. The U.S. population continues to be redistributed toward the West and the South, while rural areas continue to become depopulated in most parts of the country. Immigrants, now from Asia, Latin American, and Africa rather than Europe, are once again reshaping the American cultural landscape through their presence.

THE IMPACT OF MIGRATION IN THE UNITED STATES

The migration process has had a significant impact on the size and distribution of the American population. As can be seen in Table 4.1, immigration accounted for over 40 percent of total population growth in the United States during the height of European immigration between 1900 and 1920. Its contribution declined with the decrease in immigration in subsequent decades, only to rise again during the 1950s. By the 1970s immigration had increased to account for nearly 20 percent of population growth. This contribution increased to over 25 percent during the 1980s, with immigration's estimated contribution to population growth placed at around one third for the 1991–2000 period.

Immigrants have both direct and indirect implications for population change, and population change affects the business environment. They directly impact population size by virtue of being added to the existing population. They affect growth indirectly by virtue of their fertility and mortality levels once they enter the population. At the subnational level, migration represents the most rapid mode of population growth and decline, especially in the short run. As both birth rates and death rates have fallen, migration has had a proportionally greater impact on growth. Unlike babies, migrants come in all ages, and the effects of migration can be significant for population size and composition at both the point of origin and point of destination.

Equally important is the contribution that migration makes toward the changing composition of the population. Immigration trends are changing the national character of America, and internal migration is steadily reshaping its local markets. Immigrants typically are not representative of the general population in terms of their demographic and socioeconomic characteristics. In particular, immigrants are likely to differ from the receiving country in terms of age and sex characteristics, a situation that influences the population structure of both the sending and receiving countries.

Changing population composition at the local level is primarily a consequence of migration patterns. Migration trends directly affect the demographic composition of an area, with the age structure, racial and ethnic mix, and sex ratio all affected by these trends. Migration patterns also affect the socioeconomic characteristics of an area, modifying the household structure, the income level, the educational characteristics, and the occupational structure. These developments, in turn, affect the social, economic, and political nature of the community and are a major factor in the changing character of local markets.

From a business perspective, migration can have significant implications for local and even regional markets. Business planners have identified a certain constellation of goods and services to serve a particular market and developed marketing plans that respond to the perceived characteristics of that market. The migration process, however, could, and often does, affect the context in which business is conducted. In the face of significant levels of migration, a business may find that its carefully sited outlets are no longer in the right place, that the products that it was marketing no longer appeal to persons who are new to an area, and/or that the existing promotional approach is ineffective with the newcomers.

DEFINING MIGRATION

Migration refers to the physical relocation of persons involving intended permanent change in residence. Permanent change in residence implies that the persons or households in question intend to stay in their new residences for some period of time (although intentions are often difficult to ascertain). A "residence" is defined as the place where a person usually sleeps and eats. Having an established residence implies some type of permanency in "appropriate" housing (e.g., apartments, detached homes), although some segments of society may not have recognized residences (e.g., the homeless).

Formal migration analysis excludes temporary migration, the daily or seasonal patterns of movement to and from jobs or for climatic reasons, although such short-term changes in location clearly have significant business implications. Communities such as Daytona Beach, Florida, experience short-term population increases due to annual migration of "snowbirds" and the even more temporary vacationers. Even a business or professional convention that draws thousands or tens of thousands visitors to a conference center can have a substantial short-term impact on a local market. Daily movement to and from employment, shopping, and other functions is called *commuting* and is addressed separately. (See Chapter 8 for a discussion of day/night population shifts due to commuting.)

In the study of migration, demographers distinguish between international migration and internal migration. Migrants either move between countries (international migration) or within the boundaries of a single country (internal migration). *International migration* refers to the intended permanent movement between one country and another. Of course, there is always the question of the intended permanence of the move and certainly the temporary movement of

Table 4.1
The Contribution of Immigration to Population Growth: 1831–40 to 1991–93

Decade	Population Growth During Period	Percent of Growth Due to Immigration
1991-93	8,487	34.0
1981-90	22,168	28.4
1971-80	23,244	19.3
1961-70	23,979	13.9
1951-60	27,767	9.1
1941-50	19,028	5.4
1931-40	8,894	5.9
1921-30	17,064	24.1
1911-20	13,738	41.8
1901-10	15,978	55.0
1891-1900	13,047	28.3
1881-90	12,792	41.0
1871-80	10,337	27.2
1861-70	8,375	27.6
1851-60	8,251	31.5
1841-50	6,122	28.0
1831-40	4,203	14.3

Source: U.S. Bureau of the Census (1995). *Statistical Abstract of the United States, 1995*. Washington, DC: U.S. Government Printing Office.

populations between countries has to be a consideration for business planning.

The issue of illegal immigration is important in many countries and particularly in the United States. Although illegal immigrants are not citizens and do not enjoy the same rights and privileges that citizens do, they do play a role in both the production and consumption of goods and services.

Persons migrating to a country are referred to as *immigrants*, while individuals moving out of a country are labeled *emigrants*. Every country has laws and policies that govern international migration, especially immigration. In the United States, international migration is regulated by laws that establish the conditions for immigration into the country. Today these laws establish country-specific limits on the number of immigrants who may legally move to the United States in any given year (Martin and Midgley 1994).

Immigration law in the United States has had limited effect on emigration from this country. Most U.S. citizens are free to leave as long as they have a passport and some country will allow them entry. Since there is no systematic method for tracking emigration, the actual level of emigration is difficult to determine.

Internal migration refers to intended permanent movement within a country. Internal migration is less regulated than international migration and, for that reason, is much more difficult to measure. (It is also sometimes referred to as *lateral migration* since one is moving laterally within a country.) Within the United States, internal migration is basically unimpeded, although local laws designed to limit the growth of certain communities have a relatively long history (Barnett and Reed 1985). Demographers refer to internal migrants coming into an area as *in-migrants*, while those leaving an area are termed *out-migrants*.

Internal migrants are divided into subcategories that distinguish between short-distance and long-distance movement. A hierarchy of definitions has been created to reflect variations in distance. Initially, anyone who changes residence (regardless of distance) over a specified time period (usually one year or five years) is classified as a *mover*. However, in order for a mover to be technically a *migrant*, the mover has to change his or her county of residence. The county was chosen for the mover/migrant distinction by federal statistical agencies because it was felt that movement across county lines involved a substantial change in the social and economic milieu. From this perspective, a migrant is a mover but not all movers are migrants. Other useful distinctions also reflect the distance and nature of the movement. For example, *intrastate* migration refers to movement within a state while *interstate* migration involves movement between states.

Demographers utilize a variety of terms related to international migration. *Aliens* are persons living in a country who are not citizens of that country. Some of these aliens may be in the country with the intention of establishing permanent residence. Others may be in the country on a strictly temporary basis and, usually, for a specified period of time. These *nonimmigrant* aliens may be in the country as students, tourists, temporary workers, or in some other capacity. In recent years, nonimmigrant entrants to the United States have outnumbered immigrant entrants by about 20 to 1. The study of the arrival points and eventual destinations of the approximately 20 million annual nonimmigrant arrivees has important business implications.

"Guest worker" programs are common in many countries. Historically, the United States maintained a guest worker agreement with Mexico that allowed "braceros" to enter the country on a temporary basis in response to manual labor shortages in certain industries, although the programs ended in the 1960s. Changes in U.S. immigration laws during the 1980s reestablished these programs.

Refugees comprise a third subcategory of aliens. Refugees are conditional entrants who are allowed to live in the receiving country for an indefinite period of time. The U.S. Immigration and Naturalization Service (INS), a division of the Department of Justice, has strict regulations concerning who is eligible for entry as a refugee. Some refugees eventually return to their home countries, while others remain to become citizens of the receiving country.

Naturalization is the process through which immigrants become legal American citizens. Applicants for naturalization must demonstrate a knowledge of American history and the political system and demonstrate fluency in English. Although naturalization is not required for permanent residence, it is not possible to fully participate in American society without it. Historically, most immigrants became naturalized American citizens. Although large numbers are still naturalized every year, recent immigrants are less likely to become naturalized than their predecessors (Martin and Midgley 1994).

Migration streams involve the flow of relatively large numbers of persons from one area to another. Some of these streams can be massive and have contributed heavily to the redistribution of the American population in past decades. The east-to-west and city-to-suburb movement of the population has changed forever the social, economic, and political structure of the United States. *Rural-to-urban* migration, which began in some areas of the nation as early as 1800, has altered the course of industrial development in this country. In more recent years the migration of persons from what has been labeled the "snowbelt" to the "sunbelt" (*region-to-region* migration) has left both the places of origin and places of destination markedly changed.

Since the 1950s, most, if not all, American cities have been radically altered as a result of *urban-to-suburban* migration. Large numbers of central city residents have abandoned the urban core and settled in surrounding suburbs. This migration pattern has probably done more to change the social, economic, and political character of American cities than any other single factor. More recently, a mild counter trend has developed, in which "urban homesteaders" have reclaimed portions of the inner city and renovated homes in old neighborhoods. This process has been referred to as *gentrification* (Lee, Oropesa, and Kanan 1994).

Migration streams are typically unidirectional. In some cases, however, *return migration* as indicated by a *counterstream* may occur. The flow of African-Americans from the South to the Northeast and the Midwest during the 1930s and 1940s constituted a migration stream. Many of these same migrants returned to the South during the 1970s and 1980s. Thus, they were born in the South, resided outside the South for some period of time, and later migrated back to the South as return migrants. See Box 4.1 for a discussion of migration and rapid population change.

Box 4.1
The Impact of Migration on Local Markets

The various migration processes in operation in contemporary America collectively represent a major force for change for both national and local markets. Local markets in particular are affected, since relatively small numbers of migrants can have a substantial impact within small geographic units. Today, in many market areas migration has a greater impact on population size and composition than either fertility or mortality. In fact, population redistribution patterns reflecting the combined impact of these migration processes are the most important demographic factor affecting local markets today.

A number of different migration processes can potentially affect a local market. Many areas experience a significant amount of international immigration. Some communities

Box 4.1 continued

have recorded substantial changes in the size and composition of their populations as a result of an influx of immigrants. Markets in southern California and south Florida, in fact, have been substantially transformed as a result of immigration. Even markets that do not receive large numbers of immigrants may include subareas substantially affected by a relatively small number of foreign immigrants if ethnic enclaves develop.

While the impact of immigration is relatively selective, virtually all markets are affected by the various processes related to internal migration. Historically, the growth of most American cities has been attributed to the in-migration of individuals and families from the surrounding hinterland. The peopling of America's metropolitan areas during this century can largely be attributed to the influx of migrants from rural areas and small towns. These inmigrants have not only contributed to population growth but brought about change in the area's population composition as well.

By the 1990s this migration process had become less signficant as a force for the shaping of U.S. cities. The number of potential rural-to-urban migrants had diminished and today's in-migrants typically originate in other comparable communities. Movement between metropolitan areas has become the most common process affecting change in a market area's demographic characteristics.

Since the 1960s, the most important demographic process affecting market-level population change has been the internal redistribution process. Within metropolitan areas there has been a persistent trend toward residential decentralization—from the central city to the suburbs. The steady flow of residents to outlying areas has changed the urban landscape and contributed to the depopulation of many inner cities.

In other cases, the outmigrating residents have been replaced by those moving in from other communities both inside and outside the same metropolitan area. Most cities have, in fact, experienced a phenomenon referred to as the "invasion-succession process," whereby successive waves of in-migrants replace their predecessors, only to be succeeded by the next wave of in-migrants. A counter migration process involves the "gentrification" of America's cities, as upscale families "settle" in the inner city and renovate older dwellings.

These migration trends not only affect the size of both the sending and receiving communities, they affect the composition of the populations ultimately residing in both. Changes in population composition are likely to be more important for business planning purposes than are changes in population size. This is more significant the smaller the size of the area being considered. There are cases in which in-migrants more or less resemble the out-migrants, leaving the population composition essentially unchanged. This is often the case for upscale suburbs in which case the newcomers are little different from those leaving the area.

For most areas affected by these internal migration processes, the changes in population composition are significant for business planning purposes. The incoming and outgoing populations are likely to be differentiated on the basis of such characteristics as age and sex composition, as well as in terms of racial and ethnic characteristics. The in-migrants may also differ in terms of marital status and household structure, as when young families replace older residents in established neighborhoods.

Perhaps the most important consideration is the potential for changes in consumer characteristics. To the extent that newcomers differ in their socioeconomic characteristics, they are likely to be characterized by different levels of purchasing power. If they

Box 4.1 continued

differ along other dimensions, they are likely to not only have different consumer preferences but may require a different marketing approach. This is especially the case when the tastes, preferences and attitudes of the two populations differ.

A changing age structure will involve changing purchasing patterns, as in cases where elderly residents are displaced by younger families. Changing household structure will have an important impact on spending patterns. Changing racial and ethnic characteristics will similarly affect the demand for goods and services.

Given that the consumption of most goods and services is linked to the demographic characteristics and consumer attitudes of a particular population, business planners must consider more than the impact of migration on market size. Projections of future demand must also consider the likely future population composition of the market in question.

MEASURING MIGRATION

Of the three components of population change—fertility, mortality, and migration—migration is the most dynamic and complex, as well as the most difficult to measure. While death occurs only once and the average number of births per woman in the United States today is about two, the occurrences of migration are much more frequent and the potential for migration is essentially unlimited. An average U.S. resident will move nearly 12 times in his or her lifetime (Kulkarni and Pol 1994). About 17 percent of the population changes residence each year and, over any five-year period, more than 45 percent of the population moves. Box 4.2 discusses lifetime migration in more detail.

Box 4.2
How Often Do Americans Move?: An Historical Perspective

Recent newspaper, television and radio stories reported that Americans change residences nearly 12 times during their lifetimes. Depending on the perspective of the reader, this number may seem "small," "large," or "just about right." To one of the authors of this book, the number seems "small" because he has lived in over 30 different residences during his lifetime. As with any factoid that appears in the popular media, the question, "so what?" immediately follows. "So what" is a broad question and, at the very least, it is a question that begs for a comparison.

To provide such a comparison Kulkarni and Pol (1994) assembled results from previous studies and calculated migration "expectancy" from the late 1950s through the early 1990s. Using age-specific migration rates from the Current Population Survey (CPS) for several time periods, they calculated expected lifetime residence changes for intracounty and intercounty moves, including those within a state and those between states. The results indicate that migration expectancy dropped by over one lifetime move

> **Box 4.2 continued**
>
> since the late 1950s. However, the decline has not been spread out evenly over all types of moves. State-to-state migration, involving longer-distance residential mobility, has stayed constant over the 30-year period at about 2.2 moves over a lifetime. The decline in intracounty movement is the source of most of the reduction in migration expectancy. In the late 1950s, intracounty migration expectancy was nearly nine moves, but by the early 1990s, this figure had fallen to about seven.
>
> Clearly, a less mobile population has implications for business. Fewer moves means fewer potential home sales, all other factors being equal. On the other hand, fewer moves also imply lower moving costs, leaving additional money to be spent on other goods and services.
>
> *Source*: M. Kulkarni and L. Pol (1994), "Migration Expectancy Revisited: Results for the 1970s, 1980s and 1990s." *Population Research and Policy Review*, 13: 195–202.

An understanding of migration is critical for business planning, since the movement of customers or potential customers may or may not coincide with movement of the population in general. An inflow or outflux of people to or from a particular market area may imply an increase or decrease in potential customers for a particular product or service. However, the nature of the population flows must be understood to determine their impact on the local market. For example, most communities in Florida continue to experience significant population in-migration. Whether or not this means additional customers for a product or service depends on what the product or service is. For many of the communities, most of the inmigrants will be retirees, with needs for specific goods and services.

International migration, specifically immigration, is monitored closely and, therefore, is much easier to measure than internal migration. For purposes of national security and other reasons, most governments maintain relatively careful records on those immigrating across their borders. As stated earlier, the U.S. Immigration and Naturalization Service has the responsibility for monitoring immigration. Nonresident immigrants in the United States are required to periodically report their status INS. The monitoring process is particularly complex in the United States because of the wide variety of visas that are issued to those seeking entry. The INS also has responsibility for controlling illegal immigration.

The measurement of migration is made complex by the fact that a geographic point of origin and a point of destination must be established. Migrants—whether international or internal—appear twice in the standard population change equation, since they count as in-migrants in one place and out-migrants in another. The difficulty in measurement is largely the product of conceptual ambiguity and the lack of clear measurement techniques.

Data on migration within the United States are derived from censuses, surveys, and administrative records. The most consistently utilized method for tracking internal migration is the decennial census, with a survey item related to individual's residence five years prior to the census. The census enumerates the number of persons who moved over the five-year interval in question, and from this, the level of mobility during this period can be calculated. This approach, however, does not consider the number or the nature of the moves that may have occurred between the two dates specified. This makes the tracking of the mobility of frequent movers and certain categories of migrants problematic.

Some federally sponsored surveys also include questionnaire items related to migration patterns. In the Current Population Survey (CPS), administered annually by the U.S. Bureau of the Census (discussed in Chapter 3), the mobility of a nationwide sample of the population is measured from one year to the next (Hansen 1995). In the National Health Interview Survey, respondents are asked low long they have lived at their current address and how many times they have moved in the last three years (Tucker and Urton 1987).

Another indirect source of migration data, administrative records, is being used increasingly to track the internal movement of residents. "Registries" such as Social Security, Medicare, and the Internal Revenue Service files use a two-points-in-time comparison of addresses to identify patterns of internal migration. For some purposes, it may also be possible to use driver's license records to track change of residence.

Both surveys and registries have drawbacks because: (a) they cannot measure moves in between the two reference dates and (b) they cannot assess the intended permanence of the move for either the origin or destination area. Without an actual migration registry, the information on internal migration will always be flawed.

Some commercial data vendors now maintain records (lists) on the population at the household level. Many of them contain detailed data on most or all U.S. households. These data provide the basis for tracking changes in residence over time. They can be used to determine internal migration rates, although these data have seldom been used for this purpose to date.

A number of measures are utilized by demographers in the study of migration. *Net migration* refers to the numerical difference between the number of in-migrants and out-migrants. Net migration represents the difference between the two—that is, the number of out-migrants subtracted from the number of in-migrants. If 20,000 people immigrate to a country during a specific year and 10,000 people emigrate out of the country, gross migration equals 30,000 people and net migration equals a (positive) total of 10,000. *Gross migration* refers to the total volume of in-migration and out-migration characterizing a geographic area. Gross migration is determined by simply adding together the number of in-migrants and out-migrants.

The *net migration rate* can be calculated by dividing the number of net migrants to an area in a given time period (e.g., a specific year) by the population in that area at the beginning of the year. This rate will be an approximation of the actual migration rate at best because the denominator of the equation (i.e., the beginning population) will be modified during the year by births and deaths, and the net migrant numerator may involve multiple moves on the part of some migrants. This first factor may be accounted for by using a midyear population estimate rather than a beginning estimate. Box 4.3 provides the formulas utilized in calculating migration rates.

Box 4.3
The Calculation of Migration Rates

The following are commonly utilized calculations for measuring migration:

$$\text{Net migration rate} = \frac{\text{Number of net migrants to Area X for specified time period}}{\text{Population of Area X at the beginning of the time period}} \times 1,000$$

$$\text{In-migration rate} = \frac{\text{Number of in-migrants to Area X for specified time period}}{\text{Population of Area X at the beginning of the time period}} \times 1,000$$

$$\text{Out-migration rate} = \frac{\text{Number of out-migrants Area X for specified time period}}{\text{Population of Area X at the beginning of the time period}} \times 1,000$$

$$\text{Gross migration rate} = \frac{\text{Total out-migrants and in-migrants to Area X for specified time period}}{\text{Population of Area X at the beginning of the time period}} \times 1,000$$

$$\text{Migration efficiency} = \frac{\text{Number of net migrants to Area X for specified time period}}{\text{Gross migration for Area X for time period}}$$

Examples of the use of these calculations are provided for the Midwest Region of the U.S. for 1975-1980.

$$\text{Net migration rate} = \frac{\text{Number of net migrants } (-1,380,000)}{\text{Population at beginning of the time period } (59,255,000)} = -2.3\% \text{ or } 23.3/1,00$$

$$\text{In-migration rate} = \frac{\text{Number of in-migrants } (2,125,000)}{\text{Midpoint population estimate } (58,285,000)} = 1,000 = 3.6\% \text{ or } 36.5/1,000$$

$$\text{Out-migration rate} = \frac{\text{Number of out-migrants } (3,505,000)}{\text{Midpoint population estimate } (58,285,000)} \times 1,000 \ -6.0\% \text{ or } 60.1/1,000$$

$$\text{Gross migration rate} = \frac{\text{Total out-migrants and in-migrants to Area X for specified time period } (5,630,000)}{\text{Midpoint population estimate } (58,285,000)} \times 1,000 = 96.6/1,000$$

$$\text{Migration efficiency} = \frac{\text{Number of net migrants } (1,380,000)}{\text{Gross migration } (5,630,000)} = .245$$

The identification of an appropriate population-at-risk for determining the migration rate denominator is complicated because each rate has a different at-risk group. Consider, for example, the out-migration rate for a specific city for a one-year period. The numerator of the rate is the number of out-migrants, while the denominator is the population at the beginning or in the middle of a one-year period. However, identifying the population at risk for the in-migration rate is problematic. Anyone who did not live in the city at the beginning of the interval—virtually the entire population of the United States—is at some risk of moving into the city. However, the in-migration rate normally is calculated using the same base as the out-migration rate. Therefore, the base for the rate is no longer a population-at-risk. Instead, the resulting rate should be interpreted as the percentage of population increase that is due to in-migration.

The data required for the calculation of these rates include population counts or estimates as well as figures for the number of in- and out-migrants. These data are specific to the geographic units of interest and a certain time frame. If the time interval is more than one year (e.g., a three-year average), the denominator chosen for the rate is usually the midpoint population of the interval.

Lifetime migration is another relatively crude measure that is sometimes utilized in the absence of better indicators of mobility. The Census Bureau, for example, may compare current state of residence with state of birth, thereby roughly determining "lifetime" migration patterns.

INTERNATIONAL MIGRATION TRENDS

The level of immigration into the United States has fluctuated widely since the nation was legally recognized as a sovereign state. The number of legal immigrants to the United States totaled only one-half million during the 1830s. This number increased significantly during the last half of the nineteenth century and the first quarter of the twentieth century, surpassing 8 million per decade. Between 1930 and 1940, however, immigration levels dropped, with the volume increasing once again after World War II. However, the number of immigrants remained low by historical standards until the 1980s. This decade witnessed an upsurge in immigration equaling the historic records from the turn of the century. In the early 1990s, a record number of legal immigrants were registered and that number is likely to remain large for the foreseeable future because of changes in immigration laws during the 1980s and 1990s. Figure 4.1 presents historical immigration trends for the United States.

As noted earlier, emigration flows are poorly understood. It is estimated, however, that 150,000 to 200,000 permanent residents leave the United States annually for permanent residence in another country. A comparable number of undocumented "permanent" residents also are thought to emigrate each year (Woodrow-Lafield 1995).

Figure 4.1
Immigrants to the United States: 1831-1990

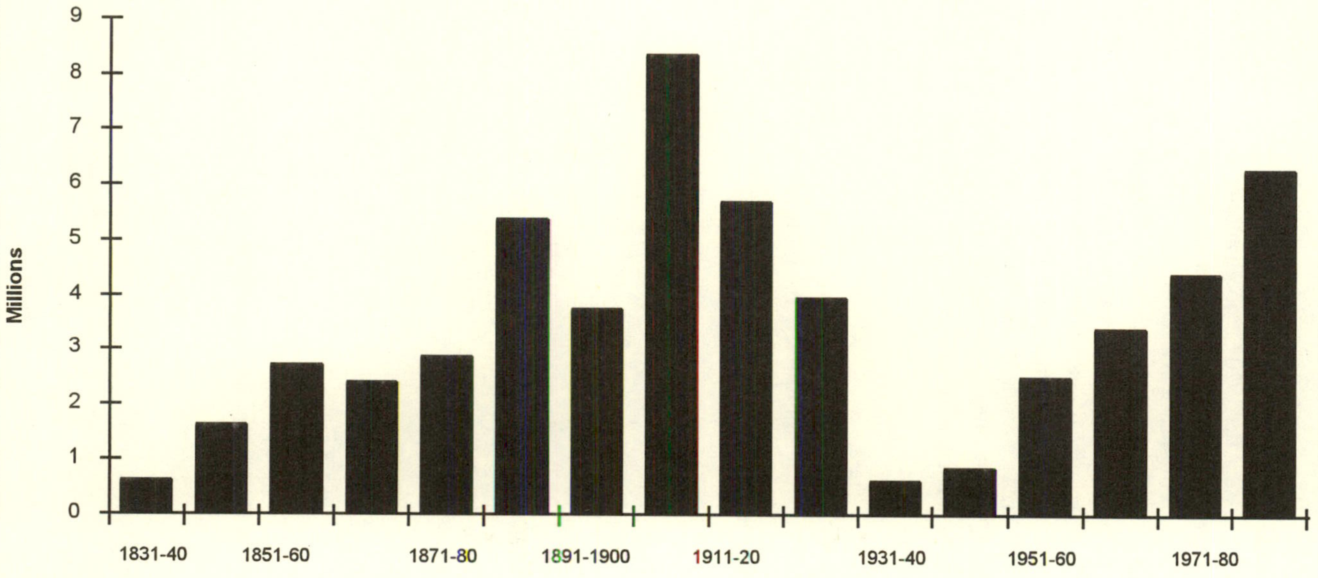

Source: U.S. Immigration and Naturalization Service

Immigrant Origin

The country of origin for immigrants is an important consideration in the study of immigration. Up until 1920, the vast majority of immigrants to the United States came from Europe. After 1920 European immigration declined and most of the share lost by Europe has been gained by Asia. In the decade of the 1980s, nearly one half of all immigrants originated in Asia. All together, 85 percent of all immigrants came from Asia or countries in North and South America in the 1980s and early 1990s. Figure 4.2 illustrates the shift in area of immigrant origin. Table 4.2 indicates that in 1993 the major source of legal immigrants was Mexico with 126,600, followed by China (65,600), the Philippines (63,500), Vietnam (59,600), and the former Soviet Union (58,571). As a result of this shift in country of origin, the current immigrant population differs significantly in culture and language from the majority European-origin population in the United States (U.S. Immigration and Naturalization Service 1994).

Table 4.2
Major Sources of Immigration to the United States: 1993

Origin	Number	Percent
All Countries	904,300	100.0
Mexico	126,600	14.0
China	65,600	7.3
Philippines	63,500	7.0
Vietnam	59,600	6.6
Soviet Union (former)	58,600	6.5
Dominican Republic	45,400	5.0
India	40,100	4.4
Poland	27,800	3.1
El Salvador	26,800	3.0
United Kingdom	18,800	2.1

Source: U.S. Immigration and Naturalization Service (1994). *1993 Statistical Yearbook of the Immigration and Naturalization Service*. Washington, DC: U.S. Government Printing Office.

Immigrant Destination

Immigrants to the United States have generally settled, at least initially, in a few selected areas of the country. Thus, a small number of states serve as the destination

Figure 4.2
Immigrants to the United States by Area of Origin: 1831-1990

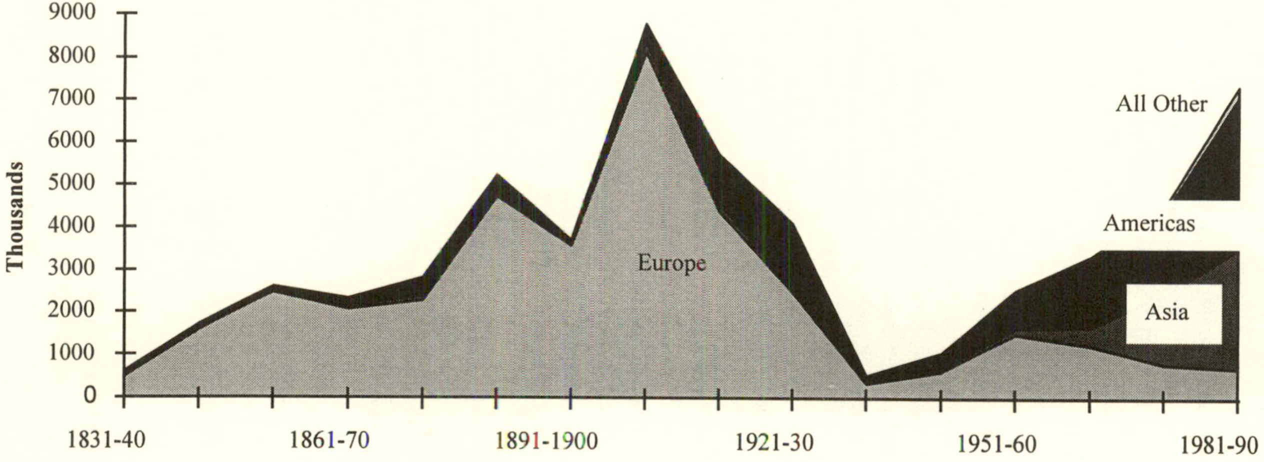

Source: U.S. Immigration and Naturalization Service

for most immigrants. California, New York, and Florida are destinations for nearly 55 percent of all immigrants! The top 10 states receive nearly 80 percent and the bottom 10 less than 6 percent. The East Coast has been the historical settlement area for most immigrants, particularly European immigrants. More recently, the West Coast has become a major destination for immigrants (especially from Asia and Mexico), as have such southern states proximate to countries of origin as Texas (Mexico) and Florida (Cuba and the rest of Latin America). In fact, the volume of immigrants processed at Los Angeles and El Paso combined is equal to that of New York and triple that of San Francisco. The only "inland" state that has historically attracted large numbers of immigrants is Illinois, principally due to the cosmopolitan nature of Chicago.

On the other hand, there are many states that attract virtually no immigrant settlement. Plains states, smaller states in New England, and most southern states have typically not been destinations for immigrants. In 1993, when immigration was at near-record levels (nearly 1 million immigrants), there were several states that were the destination for fewer than 1,000 immigrants.

From the mid-1980s to the early 1990s, some interesting changes occurred in state-of-destination patterns, due primarily to the growing tide of immigrants from Mexico. California became *the* destination for immigrants to the United States, and Texas jumped from fourth to second in the number of immigrants. Maryland and Pennsylvania fell out of the top ten, to be replaced by Arizona and Washington. The latter two were also affected by the increased influx of Mexicans. Even western states like Idaho, historically among the bottom ten in immigrants, recorded a significant influx of Mexican immigrants. Some southern states like Georgia and North Carolina also recorded substantial increases in immigrants, although unrelated to the Mexican influx (see Table 4.3.)

Within the states of destination, immigrants are likely to be concentrated within one or more metropolitan areas. The case of Chicago has already been mentioned; and Los Angeles and New York City account for most of the immigrants in their respective states. Table 4.4 presents a list of ten metropolitan aeas with the greatest number of immigrants in 1993.

Immigrant Characteristics

The immigrant population is typically much younger than the resident population in the receiving country. Nearly two thirds of all immigrants to the United States in 1993 were under age 35, with around 35 percent between the ages of 20 and 34. Only about 4 percent were age 65 or over. For the United States, the comparable figure for the resident population 65 and over is more than 12 percent. The median age of immigrants in 1993 was 27.8 year for males and 28.7 for females versus 32.5 and 34.9 years, respectively, for the nonimmigrant population (U.S. Immigration and Naturalization Services 1994).

Historically, migration streams have been male dominated. In recent years, however, the sex composition of immigrants has shifted. During the late 1970s

Table 4.3
States Receiving the Most and the Least Immigrants: 1993

State	Immigrants in 1993	Percent
High Immigration States:		
California	260,090	28.8
New York	151,209	16.7
Texas	67,380	7.5
Florida	61,423	6.8
Illinois	46,744	5.2
New Jersey	40,285	4.5
Massachusetts	25,011	2.8
Washington	17,147	1.9
Pennsylvania	16,964	1.9
Maryland	16,899	1.9
Low Immigration States:		
Wyoming	263	<0.1
South Dakota	543	<0.1
North Dakota	601	<0.1
Montana	509	<0.1
West Virginia	689	<0.1
Vermont	709	<0.1
Maine	838	<0.1
Mississippi	906	<0.1
New Hampshire	1,263	0.1
Alaska	1,266	0.1

Source: U.S. Immigration and Naturalization Service (1994). *1993 Statistical Yearbook of the Immigration and Naturalization Service*. Washington, DC: U.S. Government Printing Office.

(1977–79), the sex ratio of immigrants to the United States was 111, or 111 male immigrants for every 100 females. However, during the mid-1980s (1985–87), this ratio dropped to 100. By 1993, the sex ratio had dropped to 88 males per 100 females (U.S. Immigration and Naturalization Services 1994).

Because of the past priority given to family reunification in pre-1990 immigration law, nearly 90 percent of all immigrants to the United States were family members of persons who had previously immigrated. Nearly 53 percent of the immigrants in 1993 were married, followed by immigrants who were single (43 percent), widowed (2.5 percent), divorced (1.6 percent), and separated (0.1 percent).

The occupational structure of recent immigrants indicates that over one half (55.5 percent) had a professional specialty or technical occupation in 1993. The leading occupational groups following professionals were executive, administrative, and

Table 4.4
Major Metropolitan Areas for Immigrant Settlement: 1993

Metropolitan Area	Number of Immigrants Settled
New York, NY	128,434
Los Angeles-Long Beach, CA	108,703
Chicago, IL	60,590
Miami-Hialeah, FL	30,484
Washington, DC-MD-VA	27,427
Anaheim-Santa Ana, CA	24,921
Houston, TX	22,634
San Francisco, CA	21,054
Boston, MA	20,414
San Jose, CA	19,473

Source: U.S. Immigration and Naturalization Service (1994). *1993 Statistical Yearbook of the Immigration and Naturalization Service.* Washington, DC: U.S. Government Printing Office.

managerial occupations (21.3 percent); service occupations (11.1 percent); production, crafts, and repair occupations (4.7 percent); and operator, fabricator, or laborer occupations (3.5 percent). Among the professionals immigrating, the leading occupations were engineers, nurses, university professors, and mathematical and computer scientists (U.S. Immigration and Naturalization Services 1994).

Implications of International Migration

The changing characteristics of immigrants to the United States include, in addition to changes in country of origin, the fact that most immigrants today arrive in family groups. The days of the young, single male immigrant are past. This shift has implications for the age structure as well as the business environment. In addition, the typical legal immigrant is no longer an unskilled laborer willing to occupy the lowest rung of the economic structure. With the exceptions of certain countries (e.g., Mexico), nonrefugee immigrants represent a broad spectrum of the sending country's economic structure and are often well established in professions or skilled occupations.

Another factor related to contemporary immigration patterns is the relatively constant contact that is maintained with the sending country. In fact, there is often a high level of travel back and forth between the country of origin and the United States. This continued close relationship with the origin country appears to have had the affect of slowing the assimilation of many of these immigrants into U.S. culture. Unlike the (mostly European) immigrants of the past, these new immigrants are often less eager to become Americanized and more tenacious in maintaining their cultural heritage. Thus, although the proportion of immigrants within the U.S. population is not the largest it has ever been, it is probably safe to say that resistance to the absorption of immigrants into U.S. society is at a record high level. Box 4.4 addresses the issue of important characteristics in more detail.

Box 4.4
The Changing Characteristics of the Immigrant Population

During the 1970s and 1980s the United States experienced a resurgence of immigration. By 1991 new records were being set for annual immigration with 1.8 million legal immigrants recorded that year. This renewed volume of immigration has reestablished immigration as an issue for scholarly research and as a public policy topic in the United States.

These issues have been raised only partially as a result of the high volume of immigration; the nature of the immigrants themselves has become a factor. Historically, most immigrants originated in Europe and, for the most part, came with cultural backgrounds, if not a linguistic background, compatible with that of the dominant culture in the United States. Today, the number of foreign-born residents from these traditional sending countries are declining, with immigrants from Great Britain, Germany and even Canada being replaced by newcomers from quite different cultural backgrounds. Asia and North America (primarily Mexico) are now the major sources of immigrants and, although the numbers are relatively smaller, immigrants from Africa, South America, and the Middle East are growing in importance.

Unlike the well-educated, often professional immigrants that the United States has become accustomed to over the past two decades, these "new" immigrants include large numbers of refugees from the conflicts of Southeast Asia and Latin America. They often arrive with only the clothes on their backs. Those coming from Asia bring very "foreign" ways with them. Similarly, the estimated four to eight million illegal aliens in the United States from Mexico, Central America, and the Caribbean often come from lower socioeconomic backgrounds.

The new immigrants also differ significantly in demographic terms from their turn-of-the-century predecessors. Historically, young males have comprised the largest share of immigrants, making this population very selective in terms of age, sex, and marital status. Today's immigrants are much more likely to enter the United States as family groups. This means that the age, sex and marital status profile of the immigrant population is more likely to resemble that of the native-born population than it has in the past. In addition, current immigration regulations encourage the reunification of families within the United States, meaning that a wide range of ages is likely to characterize immigrants entering the country under the priority provisions for family members. These changes also mean that there is a much higher proportion of women among contemporary immigrant populations. In fact, more women today are emigrating in their own right, rather than simply being companions to immigrating male heads-of-household.

Contemporary immigrant groups also differ in terms of their orientation to American society. Although there remains substantial pressure for integration into the U.S.

Box 4.4 continued

economy, there seems to have been a slowing down in the trend toward complete assimilation into American culture. This is partly due to the fact that the current waves of immigrants come from quite different cultural backgrounds, making assimilation more difficult. They have also entered an environment in which there is less pressure to immediately become "Americanized" than in the past and one that encourages ethnic pride. This resistance to rapid assimilation is probably also a factor of the continued ties that many immigrants maintain with their countries of origin. Many, in fact, freely travel back and forth between the sending country and the United States.

These characteristics of the "new" immigrants present a challenge for the business community. This population is extremely diverse and less likely to accept one-size-fits-all business approaches. The fact that they are increasingly maintaining their ethnic identity means that marketing and other business activities must occur within a context acceptable to these populations. American business must become increasingly culturally sensitive if these emerging markets are to be fully exploited.

One other factor to note is the increase in the number of refugee immigrants. Since the enactment of the 1953 Refugee Relief Act, over 2 million immigrants have entered the United States as refugees. The numbers of refugees entering the country have been increasing decade by decade, with over 1 million refugee immigrants recorded during the 1980s. In 1993 alone, 160,000 refugees were allowed into the country. This represents an influx nearly one and one half times the annual average for the 1980s (U.S. Immigration and Naturalization Service 1994).

The largest numbers of refugees since the 1953 legislation was enacted have been from Asia (primarily southeast Asia) and Iran. The volume of refugees from Europe increased during the 1980s, primarily from Eastern Europe and Russia. The numbers from Africa have increased significantly over the past two decades, while Cubans account for most of the refugees from the Western hemisphere.

In 1993, 21 million nonimmigrants were admitted to the United States. Most of these (78 percent) were tourists. Some 3 million businessmen entered the country along with nearly 300,000 students.

Emigration

Emigration, the outflux of residents from a country, usually receives little attention in the United States. For many countries of the world, however, population redistribution in the form of emigration is a major factor affecting their social, economic, and political systems. Emigration flows may be temporary and limited to certain segments of the population such as displaced agricultural workers. Or they may be sustained and involve a broad cross section of the population. Factors influencing emigration include social conditions (e.g., discrimination), economic conditions (e.g., famine or unemployment), and political conditions (e.g., government repression).

Although America is viewed as a major destination for immigrants, the level of emigration from the United States is significant. Between 1900 and 1979, over 30 million people entered the country as immigrants; during the same time period more than 10 million people left the country as emigrants. The number of emigrants has varied decade by decade, from about 3 million during 1901–1910 to less than 300,000 during the 1940s (Warren and Kraly 1985).

The United States has always recorded a positive net migration flow, admitting more immigrants than there were people leaving the country. The same has been true for most industrialized European countries. However, many countries record a net migration loss and, for those with sustained periods of loss, the social, economic, and political consequences can be considerable. These consequences reflect the fact that emigrants are often self-selected from certain social categories of the sending country. The impact of emigration in the United States is difficult to determine, since many emigrants may return to reside in the United States or may travel back and forth between the United States and their new country of residence.

Illegal Immigration

Illegal immigration refers to the entry of individuals into a country without permission of the immigration authorities. Illegal immigration has always been a consideration in the United States because of its long and largely unguarded borders. Since the 1970s the volume of illegal immigration into the United States is thought to have increased significantly, with most illegals originating in Mexico. Although the statistics are hard to document, some estimates place the number of illegal immigrants entering the country each year equal to the number of legal immigrants, or around 1 million. Some estimates for undocumented aliens entering the United States annually range as high as 2.5 million. The number of illegal immigrants currently residing in the United States is estimated to be between 3.5 million and 4.0 million (U.S. Bureau of the Census 1995).

The issue of illegal immigration had begun attracting increasing attention in the United States by the mid-1990s. Against a backdrop of increasing controversy over immigration, growing frustration with the nation's inability to control the influx of undocumented persons has arisen. Despite stepped up efforts to control this flow—over a million undocumented persons are deported each year—the states most affected by illegal immigration continue to press for more effective solutions. Their contention is that illegal immigration is a national problem, but selected states are having to bear the burden of providing services to these alien populations. Federal legislation passed in May of 1996, which increased the number of border patrol guards and made it legal to deny school entry to children of illegals, is seen by some as effective tools to slow the flow. Critics of the legislation see it as punitive (to children) and unlikely to achieve much success. (See Box 4.5 for a discussion of the impact of immigration on local economies.)

Box 4.5
The Economic Impact of Immigration

The past contribution of immigration to the growth and cultural evolution of American society is well documented. Successive waves of immigrants have not only added numbers to the population but they have melded their characteristics to create a uniquely American culture. The economic contribution of these past immigrants has similarly been documented. These newcomers from foreign lands provided the manpower for an expanding industrial economy. The industriousness and creativity of immigrants from many lands have contributed to the shaping of one of the world's dominant economies.

The implications of immigration for the U.S. economy are being reexamined today in the light of renewed high levels of immigration. In the early 1990s, record numbers of foreigners entered the United States as immigrants. Both the numbers and the characteristics of these new immigrants raise issues concerning their impact on the economy. These newcomers immigrated into a quite different environment than that found by their predecessors, and their relationship with the economy is much more complex. The impact of this immigration is particularly felt by communities experiencing a disproportionate share of immigration.

The analysis of the economic impact of immigration today must involve more than a review of the labor force implications, although that is certainly a key dimension. The extent to which immigrants participate in other programs and consume social services and other benefits in the local market must be factored in. The situation is made more complex by the influx of large numbers of undocumented aliens whose contribution to the economy and consumption of resources are difficult to gauge.

A significant body of research on this topic emerged during the 1980s and 1990s as the demand for information on this issue grew. A number of studies have been conducted that attempt to determine the extent to which immigration affects both the national and local economies. These include case studies of particular industries and markets, econometric studies, and economic mobility studies.

Among the issues that must be addressed in any analysis are the following:

1) The extent to which immigrants participate in the labor force, their level of participation, and the patterns of participation they follow over time;

2) The implications of labor force participation on both the availability of jobs for native-born Americans and on the wage rate in local markets;

3) The extent to which immigrants contribute to the local economy in terms of tax contributions, purchase of goods and services, and other perhaps less tangible contributions;

4) The level of consumption of public services, the costs involved, and the extent to which immigrant contributions offset their use of services; and

5) The manner in which illegal aliens complicate the situation and the extent to which their inclusion in the analysis makes a difference.

Although the findings to date are far from definitive, the available research suggests that recent immigrants are characterized by a high level of participation in the work

Box 4.5 continued

force. In fact, working age individuals constitute a disproportionate share of the immigrant population and, indeed, most immigrants enter the country in search of economic opportunities. Immigrant laborers typically take jobs for which the demand is high but the supply of workers is limited. These often include jobs that the native born consider below an acceptable level of employment.

Although some temporary impact on wage rates has been found, the impact is usually minor and relatively time limited. Reduced employment for native-born workers appears to be offset by increasing opportunities and rising wages for complementary workers, thereby benefiting the economy as a whole (U.S. Council of Economic Advisors 1986).

It appears that recent immigrants and native-born workers at similar socioeconomic levels contribute equally to the local tax base. Immigrants contribute in terms of their consumer practices at perhaps higher levels than a matched group of American-born workers in that they tend to be upwardly mobile and are often in the process of household formation. Some studies have indicated that immigrants contribute to the local economy disproportionately because they earn more than their native-born counterparts (by working more hours and/or having more than one job).

Thus, the consumption of various goods and services may be higher than for a comparable group of native-born workers. Mexican-American immigrants, for example, have been found to be relatively free spenders for various goods, once they have become economically established. However, these findings are being reexamined in view of the characteristics of the current wave of immigrants, a group many consider to be less prepared to participate in the U.S. economy (Borjas 1990).

Although some sensationalized accounts of abuses of social services by immigrants have been published in the popular press, it appears that immigrants utilize services at levels commensurate with their position in the economy. Some may have large families and, thus, use a disproportionate share of public services; others are too self-reliant to use public services, preferring to depend on the resources available informally through the immigrant community. The interaction of the factors above results in an "appropriate" service utilization level given other demographic factors.

Recent research indicates that immigrant workers contribute more to the economy in taxes than they consume in public services (Martin and Midgely 1994). This issue is complicated, however, by the fact that a large share of taxes are paid to the federal government, while services are consumed at the local level. In view of this situation, some analysts have concluded that *all* citizens—whether immigrant or native born—represent a drain on the local economy (Rothman and Espenshade 1992). The most recent studies have found that the rate of participation in welfare is slightly higher for immigrants than for comparable groups of native-born Americans. However, when refugees—who are automatically granted access to welfare services—are factored out, there is essentially no difference in the use of welfare between immigrants and the native born.

Perhaps the most emotional aspect of the issue relates to the role of undocumented immigrants in this equation. It is this group that is most often cited for abusing the system. Although the studies are not definitive, it appears that illegal immigrants do not —and, in fact, cannot—utilize a high level of public services. Except for health care, which cannot be denied in emergency circumstances, undocumented aliens are typically not eligible for public services. On the other hand, they do contribute to the local

Box 4.5 continued

economy to a certain extent by virtue of paying sales taxes and purchasing goods.

Although the debate is far from over, the research to date suggests that the impact of immigration on local economies is more positive than negative. No doubt there are situations when this does not hold true. Additional research will be required that takes into consideration the complexity of the situation.

References

Borjas, George J. (1990). *Friends or Strangers: The Impact of Immigrants on the U.S. Economy*. New York: Basic Books.

Martin, Philip, and Elizabeth Midgley (1994). "Immigration to the United States: Journey to an Uncertain Destination." *Population Bulletin*, Vol. 49, No. 2. (September). Washington, DC: Population Reference Bureau.

Rothman, Erik, and Thomas Espenshade (1992). "Fiscal Impact of Immigration to the United States." *Population Index* 58, No. 3, (Fall): 410.

U.S. Council of Economic Advisors (1986). "The Economic Effects of Immigration," Economic Report to the President. Washington, DC: Council of Economic Advisors.

The future level and type of international migration will depend to a great extent on any changes in immigration law that occur. During the mid-1990s the backlash against immigration that emerged in certain parts of the country spawned attempts to limit access to jobs and community services for immigrants (especially undocumented aliens) and to modify immigration legislation to restrict the flow of immigrants into the United States. States that experienced high levels of immigrant inflows demanded additional support from the federal government for "excess" demand on services.

INTERNAL MIGRATION TRENDS

The level of internal migration in the United States has remained relatively constant for the past half century. An estimated 17 to 21 percent of the population moves each year. The 17 percent mover rate between 1993 and 1994 alone translates into over 43 million persons changing residence. Of that 43 million, 27 million or 64 percent were classified as "movers" (within a county) and nearly 15 million or 36 percent were classified as "migrants" (between counties). Of the nearly 15 million migrants, about 9 million moved within the same state and 7 million moved across a state boundary (Hansen 1995).

When data from the 1990 census are examined, a somewhat different picture of internal migration emerges. In 1990, almost one half of the population five years old and over lived in a different residence than it had five years earlier. Among those who moved, nearly 60 percent did so within the county of previous residence. However, 42 percent of all persons changing residence between 1985 and 1990 (43 million persons) crossed county boundaries. Approximately one half (about 21 million persons) of all inter-county migrants moved to a different state (Hansen 1995).

Short-distance moves, especially those within the same county, are usually made in order to change housing type (i.e., to obtain better or different housing) or in response to lifecycle events such as marriage, birth of children, graduation from college, and workforce entry. Some local moves are involuntary and may include eviction from an apartment or destruction of a housing unit by natural disaster.

Long-distance moves are usually economically motivated. These include involuntary moves such as corporate or military transfers, as well as job-related moves involving a new location. Others may move long distances to be nearer relatives or for access to a different climate or better community amenities (Hansen 1995).

Origin/Destination of Migrants

Past streams of migration have significantly changed the geographic distribution of the population of the United States. Persistent westward movement has pushed the continental United States' population center farther west with each successive decade. This center was in Missouri ten miles southeast of Steelville (Southwest of St. Louis) in 1990.

Since World War II, there has been a substantial net population inflow for the South and the West and a net outflow for the Northeast and Midwest. Declining economic conditions within areas based on traditional manufacturing economies have encouraged out-migration from the portions the Northeast (the "rustbelt"). Expanding economies and a better climate have attracted migrants to the West Coast and the southern states comprising the "sunbelt."

The net migration flows, however, tell only part of the story. While the South had a net loss of 25,000 persons to the West between 1993 and 1994, over 1 million persons moved from the West to the South. The Midwest suffered a net loss of 849,000 people to the South; at the same time over 1 million persons moved from the South to the Midwest.

Although the net migration flows have significant implications for business planning, the demographic characteristics of persons in those flows are also an important consideration. A net gain or loss of 25,000 persons for a region over a five-year period may seem like a small number but, if, for example, the more than 1 million people who left the area was demographically very different from the million that entered it, the impact could be substantial.

Recent patterns of internal migration represent a continuation of past trends. The Northeast and Midwest regions both experienced net out-migration between 1993 and 1994, although the volume was many times greater for the Northeast. Both of these regions benefited from substantial (and approximately equal) immigration during this period. For that year, however, the Northeast still suffered a net loss of 376,000 residents while the Midwest recorded a net gain of 193,000 residents

(Hansen 1995). (Table 4.5 presents information on different migration patterns by region.)

During the same period the South benefited from substantial net in-migration, with a net gain of 576,000. The West, however, experienced essentially the same level of in-migration as out-migration. Both the South and the West benefited from substantial immigration from abroad.

Table 4.5
Mobility Status by Region, United States: 1985–90

Region	Percent Moving 1985-1990
Northeast	11
Midwest	15
South	18
West	20
Total	16

Source: U.S. Bureau of the Census (1993). *Census of Population and Housing*. Washington, DC: U.S. Government Printing Office.

Characteristics of Migrants

Additional insight into internal migration can be gained by examining the respective characteristics of movers and nonmovers. Movers are considerably younger than nonmovers on the average, recording a median age nine years below that of nonmovers. The youth of movers is reflected in the concentration of persons under 35 (75.3 percent) and age 65 and over (3.1 percent). The comparable proportions for nonmovers are 50.7 percent and 13.7 percent, respectively. The group most likely to move is the 20–29 age cohort, although even this group has experienced a decline in mobility since the record highs of the 1960s.

Areas receiving migrants generally gain a younger population while areas losing migrants "age" more rapidly because of the loss of younger persons. Continued gain or loss can have a significant impact on both the size and age structure of the populations sending and receiving migrants. One notable exception to the youth selectivity of migration is the movement of older persons to certain retirement areas of the United States. Even so, the overall proportion of persons above the age of 55 who move is relatively low. Table 4.6 provides mobility status data by age for 1993-94.

The sex composition of migrants has changed during recent years resulting in the "feminization" of internal migration. Women have historically been neglected in the study of internal migration on the assumption that they were primarily dependents of migrating males. Female internal migrants have become increasingly important in their own right and now account for a significant portion of the migration stream.

Table 4.6
Mobility Status of the U.S. Population, by Age: 1992 to 1993

Age Group	Percent Mover 1992-93
Total	16
1-4	22
5-9	17
10-14	13
15-19	17
20-24	35
25-29	30
30-34	17
35-44	9
45-54	6
55-64	5
65 years and older	6

Source: U.S. Bureau of the Census (1995). *Statistical Abstract of the United States, 1995*. Washington, DC: U.S. Government Printing Office.

Differences by race and ethnicity among movers and nonmovers are also apparent. Of the major racial/ethnic groups, Hispanic-Americans are the most mobile in terms of short-term moves, followed by whites and African-Americans. Hispanics are also more mobile with regard to long-distance moves, again followed by whites and African-Americans. However, if one looks merely at persons who moved out of state, a different pattern emerges. Whites are more likely to have moved across state lines than are Hispanics or African-Americans. Thus, not only are there differences in the level of mobility between different racial and ethnic groups, but the type of mobility may also differ.

Overall, movers are better educated than nonmovers. Short-distance movers are less well educated than longer-distance movers, and longer-distance migrants (between states) are more highly educated than shorter-distance migrants. Nearly 50 percent of those moving to a different state have at least some college education, while the comparable figure for nonmovers is 36 percent.

Income levels are also a characteristic of interest to those studying migration. Using married males (with spouses present) as the identifying party, the Census Bureau found that households with upper-middle-class income levels tended to be the most mobile. Overall, mobility increases as income increases, although the highest income groups tend to be relatively less mobile.

Interesting differences in mobility by occupational group can be seen in Table 4.7. The unemployed were much more likely to have moved than the employed. The occupational groupings with the highest level of mobility were sales workers, laborers (except farm), and professional workers. The lowest levels of mobility were among farm workers, craftsmen, and service workers.

Table 4.7
Residential Mobility by Occupational Groups for Employed Persons 16 and Over 1993–1994

Occupational Category	Percent Moving
Total	17.3
Executive/administrative/managerial	14.8
Professional specialty	15.6
Technicians and related	17.4
Sales	18.2
Administrative support/clerical	16.3
Services	20.7
Farming/forestry/fishing	14.8
Production/crafts/repair	17.8
Machine operators and related	17.8
Transport/material movers	17.0
Handlers/equipment cleaners/laborers	22.3

Source: Hansen, Kristin A. (1995). *Geographic Mobility: March 1993 to March 1994*, U.S. Bureau of the Census, Current Population Reports, P20-485. Washington, DC: U.S. Government Printing Office.

Implications of Internal Migration

The impact of internal population redistribution is felt at both the place of origin and the place of destination for the migrant. For the sending regions, states, and communities, the loss of persons is usually symptomatic of economic problems. Since the most economically productive age groups typically migrate, continued population loss only exacerbates the problem at the origin as the tax base shrinks. On the other hand, areas receiving migrants are likely to be characterized by healthy economies. These are typically areas experiencing expanding tax bases and financial health. The major waves of migration in the United States have, in fact, represented a redistribution of labor to locations where jobs have been available.

These same economic forces have influenced the redistribution of population within metropolitan areas. Although urban areas have undergone a decentralization of jobs, the shift of the population from the central city to the surrounding suburbs also reflects the declining condition of America's inner cities. The deterioration of public services and higher central city crime rates have contributed to more than three decades of residential decentralization. The out-migration of residents with higher socioeconomic status has been a major factor in the continued deterioration of the central cities of many metropolitan areas.

Population growth through in-migration does have its downside. Municipalities are sometimes not able to meet the service requirements of rapidly growing areas. The physical environment of the receiving areas may suffer as well, as the rapid increase in residents brings about increased pressure on the environment. The influx of workers may exceed the area's ability to provide jobs, especially if there is a mismatch between job requirements and job skills.

Over the past two decades the U.S. population has become less mobile. There was a maxim in the past that Americans move at least 13 times on the average over a lifetime, with many of these moves driven by transfers within the corporate business sector. As noted earlier, the average number of lifetime moves appears to be declining and the proportion of the population that moves in any given year has declined compared to previous decades. Changes in the economic system, as well as the emergence of a more "sedentary" mind set, have contributed to this trend toward lessened geographic mobility.

For the last half of the 1990s, it appears that population redistribution will follow the same patterns as the past, although the pace will be slower than in previous decades. As a result, by the end of the century nearly 60 percent of the U.S. population is likely to live in the South or the West. Areas with sustained population loss will continue to experience unfavorable economic conditions.

The continued aging of the U.S. population is likely to have implications for the level of mobility within the population. After age 45, the level of mobility has historically declined, even allowing for retirement-related migration. The movement of the large baby boom cohort into the 45 to 65 age group as we enter the twenty-first century may contribute to a further slowing of the level of mobility. However, it is possible that the "cohort effect"—that is, the implications of being a baby boomer—may counter the effect of aging. If baby boomers, for example, have experienced a high level of mobility throughout their lives, it could be argued that they will not change these patterns simply because they are older. It remains to be seen just how much baby boomers will differ from previous generations in this regard.

IMMIGRATION LEGISLATION

National immigration law governs the flow of immigrants into and out of a country. Sovereign countries are particularly concerned about the influx of immigrants across their borders and most immigration legislation tends to be restrictive. There is the occasional exception in which a country encourages an influx of immigrants. Governments are generally less concerned about the outflux of citizens, although in certain cases (e.g., some totalitarian governments) there may be legal restrictions on emigration.

Although America is often perceived by the public as having an "open door" policy with regard to immigration, the country's immigration policies have been relatively restrictive and, at some times in the past, even racist. Selectivity in terms of country of origin has always been a feature of U.S. immigration policy, with immigrants from certain parts of the world favored over those from other parts. Between 1882 and 1917, for example, a series of legislative acts were passed that barred virtually all Asians from immigrating to the United States.

Immigration restrictions have been based on a system of quotas or, stated more positively, by a series of "preferences." Preferences have historically been stated in terms of hemisphere and country of origin. There have also been provisions giving preference to relatives of American citizens or permanent residents and to certain occupational categories. During the 1970s, for example, in response to a perceived physician shortage, an occupational preference provision made it easier for doctors and certain other health personnel to enter the country.

The reasoning behind immigration laws, particularly the more exclusionary ones, tends to be complex. Despite the humanitarian perspective that has often guided this country, practical issues of unemployment and "appropriate" population mix have always been considerations. Although there is evidence to the contrary, there has been a persistent concern that immigrants will take jobs away from American citizens, and organized labor has historically been a factor in the passage of restrictive laws. More recently, much of this economically inspired concern represents a reaction to undocumented immigration. The prospect of immigrants "illegally" taking jobs from Americans typically evokes an emotional reaction. In actuality, it has been difficult to document the negative economic affects of immigration, either legal or illegal. (See Box 4.5 for a discussion of the economic impact of immigration.)

The other issue concerns the *desired* racial and ethnic composition of the U.S. population. Although seldom stated blatantly, there has been an implicit preference in most immigration legislation for immigrants who are the most American-like (i.e., from similar backgrounds as those writing the legislation) or at least for those who are easily Americanized. Both overt and covert attempts have been made to restrict members of populations considered culturally different from native-born Americans, such as the Chinese Exclusion Act that was in place from 1882 to 1943. There have also been composition-oriented preferences that have been politically motivated, such as the preference for immigrants from the Western Hemisphere (i.e., Central America, South America, and the Caribbean).

Interestingly, the volume of immigration into the United States is proportionately smaller than that for a number of other countries. France and Germany, for example, admit a higher volume of immigrants proportional to their population size than does the United States. In fact, many European countries have longer standing conflicts, especially with "guest workers," than have been experienced in the United States. Historically, at least, there has been a greater tendency for immigrants to the United States to become assimilated into the dominant culture than has been the case in many European countries.

While the immigration reform bills of 1986 and 1990 brought about some important changes in immigration law, the impact of that legislation on immigration (legal and illegal) is not precisely known. The 1990 immigration law increased the level of immigration from 513,000 to 700,000 for the fiscal years 1992 to 1994, with a slight decrease in fiscal years 1995 and beyond. The bill also increased the number of visas granted to skilled workers and managers from 54,000 to 140,000. These and other changes are likely to alter both the number and composition of immigrants in the future (U.S. Congress 1990).

As this book goes to press, legislation has been passed by the Congress that modifies existing immigration law. The 1996 bill represents in part a reaction to the perceived threat of uncontrolled immigration and includes provisions that improve controls at U.S. borders, modify deportation procedures, limit immigrant access to public services, and modify the relative preference system for immigrant visas. (See Box 4.6 for a chronological history of immigration legislation in the United States) More restrictive immigration proposals including, for example, a five-year moratorium on all immigration, are also being discussed.

Box 4.6
Selected U.S. Immigration Legislation and Court Actions

1882	Chinese Exclusion Act	Prohibited entry of virtually all Chinese immigrants (not repealed until 1943)
1892	Ellis Island established	The immigrant processing center was moved to Ellis Island, New York
1917	Asiatic Barred Zone	Prohibition of entry by any natives of Burma, India, Siam, the Malay states, East Indies, and Polynesian Islands (not repealed until 1943)
1921	First Quota Act	Limitations on the number of immigrants by nationality according to a quota based on the number of foreign born already in the United States
1924	Second Quota Act	Modified the limitation provisions of the First Quota Act
1929	National Origins Quota Act	Complex procedure for determining the mix of immigrants by country of origin

---

Box 4.6 continued

		within the numerical limitation established
1952	McCarran-Walter Act	Modified existing quota procedures by introducing a preference hierarchy
1965	Immigration Act of 1965	Modified the national quota system and the immigration ceilings for the Eastern and Western hemispheres and reprioritized the preference hierarchy
1976	Immigration Act of 1976	Modified the provisions of the 1965 act in terms of overall ceilings, per country limitations, and the preference hierarchy
1986	Immigration Reform and Control Act (IRCA)	Comprehensive legislation authorizing legalization of currently resident aliens, prohibition of employer use of illegal aliens, increased border enforcement, and reclassification of status of Cubans and Haitians, among other things
1988	U.S./Canada Free Trade Agreement Implementation Act	Specifies reciprocal immigration arrangements between the United States and Canada under the Free Trade Agreement
1990	Immigration Act of 1990	Major overhaul of immigration law, increasing the level of immigration, revising grounds for exclusion, deportation, and nonimmigrant status, naturalization authority and enforcement activities
1996	Immigration Reform	In response to concerns over illegal immigration, includes provisions on border controls, deportation procedures, use of public services and visa preferences

---

Source: U.S. Immigration and Naturalization Service.

BUSINESS IMPLICATIONS OF MIGRATION

The impact of migration on the United States is almost impossible to overstate. From the more than 100 million people who immigrated to the United States between 1831 and 1990 to the extensive redistribution of the population already here, migration has affected virtually every aspect of society. Future immigration as well as internal migration promises to play a significant role in social change at least well into the twenty-first century. (Box 4.7 discusses the implications of

---

Box 4.7
Serving Immigrant Markets

As the number of immigrants has grown in the United States since the mid-1980s, foreign-born residents have become a growing force in the American economy. In 1990 the U.S. population included nearly 20 million foreign-born residents out of a total population of 250 million. This is a significant number of consumers by any standard.

Although some American corporations have aggressively cultivated specific ethnic markets, the potential for serving immigrants and their descendants is only now being tapped. The stereotype of the impoverished immigrant lingers, and it is true that many participants in the recent waves of immigration have originated in undeveloped countries and/or have arrived as refugees. There are challenges to serving this population resulting from its great diversity and the current trend toward slower assimilation into U.S. society.

Not only are the numbers of foreign born large now, but ethnic and racial minority groups in general are expected to grow faster than the non-Hispanic white population for the foreseeable future. In 1990, members of ethnic and racial groups accounted for 26 percent of the U.S. population; this proportion is expected to increase to 48 percent by 2050. Not only are these numbers being boosted by record levels of immigration in the early 1990s, but the fertility rates for most ethnic and racial minority groups are higher than those for the native-born white population.

The largest numbers of foreign-born residents currently in the United States originated from Asia (primarily the Philippines, India, and Korea), Central America (primarily Mexico), and Europe. Since the 1980s the numbers of Asian (boosted by Southeast Asian refugees) and Mexican immigrants have been growing rapidly, essentially doubling between 1980 and 1991. On the other hand, the number of foreign-born residents of European descent declined 15 percent during this same period. Other areas contributing growing numbers of immigrants are the Caribbean and South America.

There are a number of ways in which businesses could approach the immigrant market and some corporations are already using these techniques. These approaches include focusing promotional initiatives on a particular group or in a particular community, repackaging advertising in a manner that appeals to members of an ethnic community (including foreign language versions), restructuring services (e.g., health care) to reflect the cultural perspectives of the consumer, modifying products to appeal to selected ethnic populations, and/or creating new products specifically targeting an ethnic group.

---

immigration for business planning.)

Though the net number of internal migrants and immigrants can greatly affect the population size of a geographic area, the differential in social and economic characteristics for the mover and nonmover subpopulations can exacerbate that impact. Even when the net figure is nearly zero, the differences in characteristics between the in- and out-migrants may be substantial. In some cases, the newcomers will resemble the existing residents and, except for the impact of changes in population size, will not substantially affect the character of the area. In other cases, however, turnover in population results in a modification of the composition of the population at the points of both origin and destination.

Substantial changes in the level and types of services can occur as a result of changing population composition. On the one hand, there is usually rapid growth among the young, working-age population (the 25 to 34 age cohort). At the same time, there may be tremendous growth in two populations that are high utilizers of services—the old and the very young. Florida, of course, is a major retirement area, and in certain areas within the state, the elderly constitute more than 25 percent of the total population. It is difficult for the infrastructure to keep up with the demand for services in such areas. This same situation is true for the high-growth population in the under-five age cohort.

The changes resulting from these patterns of migration are continually modifying the business environment in which organizations must function. At the national level, the population is becoming increasingly heterogeneous, thereby creating new markets for products and services in both the private and public sectors. Internal migration has brought about significant changes in regional and local business conditions. For subnational geographic areas (e.g., states and counties), places experiencing population gain are quite different from those losing persons in terms of the products demanded and in the ability of residents to purchase those products. Organizations providing products in growing or declining regions must either adapt to those new environments or relocate to places where the environment for their businesses is more favorable. In cases where mobility cannot occur (city government, for example), adjustments to the new environment must occur, even if it means a significant change in the way functions are performed.

Box 4.8 describes the role of an applied demographer in an academic setting.

Box 4.8
Demography and Decision Making in an Academic Setting

Stanley K. Smith
University of Florida

I became a demographer quite by accident. I was a first year graduate student in economics at Michigan State University in East Lansing and my wife Rita was working in the University library. She had been an English major in college and had spent a year trying to instill a love of literature in a bunch of rowdy seventh graders, while at the same time teaching them the finer points of grammar, punctuation, and civilized behavior. This experience had convinced her of the potential merit of pursuing another line of work. She enjoyed working in the library and decided to make librarianship her professional career.

Michigan State University did not have a library science program, but the University of Michigan did. Rita was accepted for admission to the University of Michigan and we

---

Box 4.8 continued

decided to move to Ann Arbor. Rather than attempting to commute the 60 miles between Ann Arbor and East Lansing in an unreliable 1965 Mustang, I transferred to the economics program at the University of Michigan. Unfortunately, that program had very little financial aid available for first year graduate students. This created a serious dilemma because we were as poor as the proverbial church mice.

I soon discovered, however, that financial aid was available to students in the economic demography program. After consulting my Webster's to find out what demography was, I decided that this program sounded better than any of our other options, the most likely being starvation. I applied for admission and was accepted. Thus was launched my career as a demographer.

My entry into the field of applied demography was almost as haphazard. I wanted to teach, but there were few teaching positions in economic demography available when I completed my doctorate in 1976. One of the most intriguing was at the University of Florida. It was a joint appointment between the Economics Department and the Bureau of Economic and Business Research (BEBR). The position in the BEBR was to direct the Population Program, which produced annual population estimates for all cities and counties in the state and population projections for all counties. My graduate program had provided little training in the production of population estimates and projections, but I decided to take the plunge. It turned out to be one of the best decisions I ever made.

My job at the University of Florida is a combination of management, teaching, and research. I became the director of the BEBR six years ago, and about 25 percent of my time is now spent managing its five research programs, 20 full-time staff members, and $1.6 million budget. Some parts of the management experience are quite gratifying, such as seeking ways to improve our research programs and seeing our products and services gain widespread acceptance and use. Other parts are less than gratifying, such as refereeing internal disputes, trying to comply with the University's seemingly endless supply of regulations, and dealing with a shrinking budget. Universities have not escaped the down-sizing that characterizes much of the U.S. economy, and cost-cutting and looking for new sources of funds are now a major part of my job. "Doing more with less" has become an inescapable fact of life.

Teaching is much more enjoyable. I have taught several economics courses over the years, but my favorite is population economics. This course covers a wide variety of topics, including the determinants of fertility, mortality, marriage, divorce, and migration; the effects of rapid population growth in less developed countries; the effects of declining population growth in more developed countries; environmental conse-quences of population growth; and public policy issues related to demographic factors. Students are interested in many of these topics because they can see how economic-demographic issues have a direct impact on their lives. Teaching this course also helps me keep up with what is going on in the field.

The most satisfying part of my job, however, is applied demographic research. This has two parts to it. The first is the production of state and local population estimates and projections, which is always challenging and often controversial. It is challenging because it is not a simple task. Methods of estimation and projection may appear to be cut-and-dried when described in a textbook, but they become much less clear-cut when applied in a real-world environment of missing or unreliable data, techniques of

Box 4.8 continued

uncertain reliability, deadlines that are unrealistic but unchangeable, and political pressures of various types. These circumstances cry out for the practice of "creative" demography. Much of what I have learned as an applied demographer has come from dealing with problems that were never mentioned in my graduate training.

The production of population estimates and projections is often controversial because millions of dollars may be riding on the outcome. In Florida, for example, population estimates are used to distribute $1.4 billion of revenue-sharing funds to cities and counties each year. Population projections affect many planning and budgeting decisions. Estimated and projected population trends attract much media attention and can either threaten or enhance civic pride. Population estimates even determine the salaries of some public officials! In these circumstances it is not surprising that the estimates and projects are controversial. Although these controversies are sometimes nerve-wracking, it is gratifying to know that one's work is actually being used for something rather than simply sitting on a shelf collecting dust.

The second part of my applied demographic research deals with analysis rather than production. "Publish or perish" is still a basic tenet of the academic world. I have always tried to merge this requirement with my interest in applied demography. Are some estimation techniques more accurate than others? Under what circumstances? Are complex projection techniques more accurate than simple techniques? How can confidence intervals be established for population projections? Answers to these and similar questions are not only important for the practice of applied demography, but are legitimate topics for academic research. Most of my academic research has thus stemmed directly from my work as an applied demographer.

I believe there are many opportunities for research that is both academically credible and directly useful to applied demographers. Lamentably, many academics view applied research as being less important than other types of research. I hope that this viewpoint will eventually be replaced by a broader, more progressive outlook. I believe that applied demographers working in an academic setting can play a very important role by bridging the gap between academic research and the practice of demography in the real world.

REFERENCES

Barnett, Larry D., and Emily F. Reed (1985). *Law, Society, and Population: Issues in a New Field*. Houston, TX: Cap and Gown.

Borjas (1990)

Hansen, Kirstin A. (1995). Geographic Mobility: March 1993 to March 1994., U.S. Bureau of the Census, Current Population Reports, P20-485. Washington, DC: U.S. Government Printing Office.

Kulkarni, Miland, and Louis G. Pol (1994). "Migration Expectancy Revisited: Results for the 1970s, 1980s and 1990s." *Population Research and Policy Review*, 13: 195–202.

Lee, Barrett A., R. S. Oropesa, and James W. Kanan (1994). "Neighborhood Context and Residential Mobility." *Demography*, 31 (May): 249-270.

Martin, Philip, and Elizabeth Midgley (1994). "Immigration to the United States: Journey to an Uncertain Destination." *Population Bulletin*, Vol. 49, No. 2. (September).

Washington, DC: Population Reference Bureau.

Rothman, Erik, and Thomas Espenshade (1992). "Fiscal Impact of Immigration to the United States." *Population Index* 58, No. 3, (Fall): 410.

Tucker, C. Jack, and William L. Urton (1987). "Frequency of Geographic Mobility: Findings from the National Health Interview Survey." *Demography*, 24 (May): 265–270.

U.S. Bureau of the Census (1995). *Statistical Abstract of the United States, 1995.* Washington, DC: U.S. Government Printing Office.

U.S. Congress (1990). "Legal Immigration Revision." *Congressional Record* (October 27).

U.S. Council of Economic Advisors (1986). "The Economic Effects of Immigration," Economic Report to the President. Washington, DC: Council of Economic Advisors.

U.S. Immigration and Naturalization Service (1994). *1993 Statistical Yearbook of the Immigration and Naturalization Service*. Washington, DC: U.S. Government Printing Office.

Warren, R., and E. P. Kraly (1985). "The Elusive Exodus: Emigration from the United States." *Population Trends and Public Policy* 8 (March). Washington, DC: Population Reference Bureau.

Woodrow-Lafield, Karen (1995). "An Analysis of Net Immigration in Census Coverage Evaluation." *Population Research and Policy Review,* 14: 173–204.

SUGGESTED READINGS

Bean, Frank, George Vernez, and Charles B. Keely (eds.) (1989). *Opening and Closing the Doors: Evaluating Immigration Reform and Control*. Washington, DC: RAND Corporation and the Urban Institute.

Bean, Frank, Jurgen Schmandt, and Sidney Weintraub (eds.) (1989). *Mexican and Central American Population and U.S. Immigration Policy*. Austin: University of Texas at Austin.

Borjas, George J. (1990). *Friends and Strangers: The Impact of Immigrants on the U.S. Economy*. New York: Basic Books.

Castles, Stephen, and Mark J. Miller (1993). *The Age of Migration: International Population Movements in the Modern World*. New York: The Guilford Press.

Edmonson, Barry, and Jeffrey S. Passel (eds.) (1994). *Immigration and Ethnicity: The Integration of America's Newest Arrivals*. Washington, DC: The Urban Institute.

Hollifield, James (1992). *Immigrants, Markets and States: The Political Economy of Immigration in Postwar Europe and the U.S.* Cambridge, MA: Harvard University Press.

Jenson, Leif (1989). *The New Immigration: Implications for Poverty and Public Assistance Utilization*. Westport, CT: Greenwood.

Long, Larry (1988). *Migration and Residential Mobility in the United States*. New York: Russell Sage.

Martin, Philip (1993). *Trade and Migration: NAFTA and Agriculture*. Washington, DC: International Institute of Economics.

Portes, Alejandro (ed.) (1995). *The New Second Generation*. New York: Russell Sage Foundation.

Simon, Julian L. (1989). *The Economic Consequences of Immigration*. Cambridge, MA: Basil Blackwell.

Watkins, Susan Cotts (ed.) (1994). *After Ellis Island*. New York: Russell Sage Foundation.

Chapter 5

Fertility: Reproduction and the Process of Demographic Change

INTRODUCTION

Fertility refers to the total reproductive experience of a population. The reproductive experience of a population involves all factors related to sexual behavior, pregnancy, and birth outcome. The number of births and the characteristics of those births, along with factors describing the mothers and fathers of children born, form the basis for fertility analysis. The primary focus of this chapter is on the population's reproductive patterns and the implications of these patterns for the business environment.

Fertility can be viewed as a social process requiring the biological interaction of two persons within a specific economic, social, and/or political context. The level of fertility is a measure of reproductive performance and is often presented as the average number of children born to women in a specific population. In the United States, births typically occur to women in the age ranges 15 to 44, although it should be noted that in the mid-1990s there were around 14,000 births annually to women under the age of 15 (U.S. Bureau of the Census 1994, Table 92). Fertility is often expressed in geography-specific terms, such as the total number of births occurring in a city, county, or state.

Reported changes in fertility levels in the United States typically refer to a change in the average number of children women are bearing or to a difference in the total number of births reported. While the average number of births per woman and the total number of births are certainly related, knowing the value of one does not guarantee knowledge about the size of the other. For example, although the average number of births per woman in the United States remained fairly stable during the late 1970s, total births rose because more women entered their childbearing years. The effect on fertility of an increase in the number of childbearing-age women can easily offset a decline in average births per woman.

From a business demography perspective, there are at least two important reasons for studying fertility. First, the absolute number of births in any geographic area is a direct indicator of the market potential for a specific set of products and services. For example, the total number of births in a given county indicates the size of the market for diaper services, newborn health care, and baby products such as nursery furniture. Moreover, the customers (i.e., the buyers, not end users) for these products include parents, aunts, uncles, cousins, grandparents, and friends, among others.

Second, fertility is one of the three *demographic processes*. The level of fertility, along with an area's migration and mortality characteristics, determines the size and composition of any market. Knowledge of the size and makeup of a market is crucial for business planning. The ability to project changes in the size and composition of markets provides a business with a strategic advantage. While the material discussed in this chapter may initially appear to be overly "demographic," the presentation is designed to lay the groundwork for a better understanding of how and why markets change in the ways that they do.

A distinction should be made between "fertility" and "fecundity." *Fecundity* refers to the physiological ability of females to reproduce without regard to societal context. A *fecund* woman, in general, has few if any problems conceiving and carrying a child to term. Women who are *infecund,* or more popularly *sterile,* are physically unable to have children. *Subfecund* women have some degree of difficulty conceiving and/or carrying a child to term. Assistance to subfecund women is part of a rapidly expanding collection of fertility-related services that offer significant business opportunities. Another closely related term is *infertile,* which is operationally defined as the inability to conceive after one year of intercourse without contraception.

Estimates of infertility for 1965, 1982, and 1988 indicate that a declining proportion of American women is defined as infertile—11.2, 8.5, and 7.9 percent, respectively (Mosher and Pratt 1990, Table 3). Infertility is affected by age at *menarche*—the onset of menstruation—and by *menopause*—the end of menstruation. There is a strong relationship between age and infertility, and in 1988 the percentage of women classified as infertile ranged from 0.7 at ages 15–24 to 21.4 at ages 35–44 (Mosher and Pratt 1990, Table 1). Furthermore, between the beginning and latter parts of the twentieth century, the average age at menarche in the United States declined by approximately three years, from 15 years of age to 12 years. This fact is important to those in the business of providing education and contraceptive services, particularly to the teenage population.

The *interaction* of social norms, economic and political conditions, environmental factors, biological limitations, and health care standards, influences the level of reproduction in a population. As a result of these various influences, very few populations reproduce at or near their theoretical biological maximum. If, for example, a woman entered a sexual union at age 18, had a child at age 19, and then bore a child every two years until she was 45, 14 births would occur. Today in the United States, women average approximately two births over a lifetime. Even allowing for a certain level of infertility, social factors are clearly operating to limit the reproductive level.

MEASURING FERTILITY

A number of measures have been developed to characterize fertility patterns, and the measurement of fertility at the individual or micro level is relatively easy. The woman in question either did or did not have a live birth during some specified period of time and she had an easily counted number of births over her lifetime. The fact that births are recorded in some systematic manner facilitates these types of calculations. As discussed in Chapter 3, this task is performed by the birth registration system in the United States, managed by the National Center for Health Statistics in cooperation with state and county health officials.

Initially, births are counted in absolute terms and the variation across geographic units (e.g., states and counties) is specified. Since there are situations when simply counting the number of births may not provide all of the needed information, measures have been developed for expressing fertility outcomes in the form of rates. Because some geographic areas have larger populations than others, an increase in the number of births in a geographic area over time may be simply due to the fact that the population increased. Thus, measures of comparison are needed that account for differences in population size.

Rates are usually produced by dividing the reported number of births by a base population figure. There are several types of fertility rates calculated in this manner and, together, they form a logical progression from general rates to more specific rates. Fertility rates are most often expressed in relation to a specific point in time. They are *period* specific and are calculated from figures tabulated for relatively short time periods (one to three years).

Period rates can be misleading, however, in that they do not tell us how a *cohort* of women will behave throughout a lifetime of childbearing. A cohort of women is composed of women with a common set of characteristics—in this case age. Theoretically, an analyst interested in the fertility outcomes of the cohort of women born between 1970 and 1975 must wait until those women complete their childbearing to precisely determine the aggregate number of children born as well as the average number of children the women will bear. Since it is not practical to wait that long to plan for the future, alternative methods of measurement have been devised. Assumptions about consistency or changes in fertility rates are required in order to make judgments about future levels of fertility.

The data required for the calculation of fertility rates are obtained from four of the sources discussed in Chapter 3: (1) population censuses, (2) survey data, (3) synthetic data for population estimates, and (4) vital statistics registration systems. Most rates require birth data and population figures from a census or a population estimate from some other source. A few rates are derived directly from survey data.

Crude Birth Rate

The *crude birth rate* (CBR) is written as the number of births per 1,000 persons for a specified year. Below is the formula:

$$CBR = \frac{\text{Number of births in year X}}{\text{Midyear population in year X}} \times 1,000.$$

The crude birth rate for the United States in 1992 was calculated as follows:

$$CBR = \frac{4,065,014 \text{ (births in 1992)}}{253,667,000 \text{ (midyear population in 1992)}} \times 1,000 = 16.0,$$

or 16 births per 1,000 persons. This compares with a CBR of 16.7 in 1990, 14.6 in 1975, and 24.9 in 1955. A three-year average of births is sometimes used to minimize the affect of year-to-year fluctuations in the number of births, especially in small geographic areas.

While the CBR is adequate for making very general comparisons and has the advantage of requiring only two pieces of information, it has two major shortcomings. First, the denominator includes people who are not *at-risk* of having a birth. Males, very young females and females beyond menopause are not at-risk of giving birth, yet they appear in the denominator of the rate. Second, the CBR masks differences between the age structures of populations. Fertility rates are greatly affected by age structure, particularly for women, and the CBR cannot account for this. Two populations of the same size could easily have dissimilar CBRs simply because females in the childbearing ages accounted for 20 percent of one population but 35 percent of the other. As a result of these shortcomings, more refined measures of fertility have been developed.

General Fertility Rate

The *general fertility rate* (GFR) refines the CBR by adjusting it for age and sex. The denominator in the equation becomes females aged 15–44, more closely approximating the population at-risk of having a child. The GFR is expressed as follows:

$$GFR = \frac{\text{Total number of births in year X}}{\text{Midyear population of women aged 15-44 in year X}} \times 1,000.$$

For 1992 the GFR for the United States is calculated below:

$$GFR = \frac{4,065,014}{59,010,00} \times 1,000 = 68.9,$$

or nearly 69 births per 1,000 women aged 15–44. By comparison, the GFR was 70.9 in 1990 and 88.0 in 1967. In 1955, at the peak of the baby boom, it was much larger

(118.5). While the GFR is clearly a better measure for most purposes than the CBR, its calculation requires an additional piece of information—the number of females 15–44 years of age. This means that the analyst must have access to data on the age-sex structure of the population.

Age-Specific Fertility Rate

The *age-specific fertility rate* (ASFR) is an even more precise measure of fertility. Instead of calculating a single rate, as is the case of the CBR and GFR, multiple rates are calculated, one for each five-year interval for women 15–44. Individual fertility rates are produced for women 15–19, 20–24, and so on, up to the age interval 40–44. Rates for those under 15 or over 44 can also be generated to measure either very early or very late fertility. Five-year intervals are used for convenience and, in cases like adolescent fertility measurement, narrower age intervals may be used.

One additional data requirement must be met for calculating ASFRs: the age of the mother when she gave birth. An ASFR is computed as follows:

$$\text{ASFR} = \frac{\text{Births in year Y to women aged X to X+5}}{\text{Midyear population of women aged X to X+5 in year Y}} \times 1{,}000,$$

where X to X + 5 refers to the age interval for which the rate is being calculated. For 1992 the ASFR for women 20–24 in the United States is calculated as follows:

$$\text{ASFR}_{20-24} = \frac{1{,}070{,}490}{9{,}345{,}000} \times 1{,}000 = 114.6,$$

or 115 births per 1,000 women aged 20–24. The ASFR for women aged 20–24 was 121 in 1973 and twice that, 242, in 1955.

Six separate ASFRs are calculated when five-year age intervals are used (15–19, 20–24, 25–29, 30–34, 35–39, and 40–44). The rates for 1992 can be found in column 2 of Table 5.1. Managing all six rates may become unwieldy because year-to-year comparisons involve multiple relationships. Therefore, demographers have developed three summary measures that incorporate all six ASFRs. These measures are the total fertility rate, the gross reproduction rate, and the net reproduction rate.

Total Fertility Rate

The *total fertility rate* (TFR) is a hypothetical measure of completed fertility. It estimates the number of children born to a cohort of *just* 15-year-old women *if* all age-specific fertility rates remain the same until they are 44. Of course, all ASFRs will not remain constant for this 30-year time interval, but stable fertility rates is a reasonable assumption in the absence of any dramatic change in fertility levels. The only alternative, of course, is to wait until the childbearing years are completed.

Table 5.1
Age-Specific Fertility Rates and Total Fertility Rate Calculations: 1992

Age Interval	ASFR (per 1,000 women in age interval)	ASFR x 5
15–19	60.7	303.5
20–24	114.6	573.0
25–29	117.4	587.0
30–34	80.2	401.0
35–39	32.5	162.5
40–44	5.9	29.5
Total	411.4	2,057.0

Source: Authors calculations. Source data came from *Vital and Health Statistics* and population estimates produced by the U.S. Bureau of the Census.

The TFR is calculated as follows:

$$\text{TFR} = \sum_{i=1}^{n} (\text{ASFR} \times 5),$$

where n is the number of age-specific birth rates. To calculate the TFR, each ASFR is multiplied by five (the width of each age interval) and the products are then summed.

The total fertility rate of 2,057.0 presented in Table 5.1 refers to 2,057 births per 1,000 women aged 15–44. Thus, women in this population average 2.057 births over a lifetime given the underlying TFR assumptions. Comparable data for past years show a great deal of year-to-year variation. TFRs were high during the post–World War II baby boom (1946–1964) and low during the baby bust (1965–1977). During the 1955–1959 time interval, the TFR averaged 3.70. By 1976, the TFR had dropped to 1.7, only to begin rising again in the late 1980s.

Two refinements to the TFR have been developed in order to more adequately reflect a population's reproductive capability. Because females are the only members of the species who are capable of becoming pregnant, an additional measure of fertility reflecting the births of females is required.

Gross Reproduction Rate

The *gross reproduction rate* (GRR) takes the TFR and "corrects" it to account only for female births, resulting in a TFR for female births. The GRR in fact represents a measure of fertility *replacement*. A value of 1,000 means that women are exactly replacing themselves, while values greater than 1,000 or less than 1,000 reflect fertility over or under replacement levels. Much like the TFR, the GRR represents the average number of lifetime female births expected of a cohort of women entering their childbearing years, *if* age-specific fertility rates remain constant. The GRR is calculated by deriving ASFRs for female births, multiplying each ASFR by five (again, the width of the interval), and then summing all ASFRs in the same way used to produce a TFR. The equation is as follows:

$$\text{GRR} = \left(\sum_{i=1}^{n} \text{ASFR}^{F} \cdot 5 \right).$$

ASFR^F is the age-specific fertility rate for female births only. In 1992, the GRR for the United States was approximately 1,004. By comparison, the GRR was 1,212 in 1945, rose to 1,783 in 1960, and declined to 890 in 1982. However, without accounting for deaths to women before they complete childbearing, the concept of replacement-level fertility is somewhat unclear. Since not all female births will survive to the end of their own reproductive years, another fertility measure (the net reproduction rate) has been developed to account for the affects of "premature" mortality among women.

Net Reproduction Rate

The *net reproduction rate* (NRR) adjusts the GRR by accounting for the mortality likely to occur during the time interval in question. For each ASFR^F, a mortality correction factor is introduced to reflect the fact that not all of the female children born will survive to the end of their reproductive years. Those who do die before or during their childbearing years will obviously not be at-risk of having children throughout the entire interval. The calculation follows:

$$\text{NRR} = (\textstyle\sum \text{ASFR}^{F} \times \text{life table mortality correction}).$$

The NRR thus measures the number of female births per 1,000 females of childbearing age that a cohort of women entering their childbearing years would have if age-specific fertility *and* age-specific mortality rages remained constant. (Age-specific mortality rates are discussed in Chapter 6.) In 1992, the NRR was approximately 981, compared with 1,132 in 1945; 1,715 in 1960; and 870 in 1982.

Cohort Measures of Fertility

Cohort measures of fertility reflect the childbearing experiences of women of a given age—enerally the five-year intervals used in calculating period measures of fertility. In censuses and surveys women are typically asked how many children (live births) they have had in their lifetime. Subsequently, these data are categorized by the age of the respondent. This cohort figure, *children ever born (CEB)*, is a measure of completed fertility for women at various ages. So, for example, the CEB for women age 35 to 39 is the number of children born to every 1,000 women age 35 to 39. For women above age 40, CEB may be considered a cohort version of a TFR, except that the assumption about ASFRs remaining constant is no longer required. For women 45–49 years of age, CEB per 1,000 women was 2,492 in 1950; 2,402 in 1960; 2,854 in 1970; 3,096 in 1983; and 2,012 in 1992. It is also possible to examine cohort rates—children ever born—for women who have not completed their fertility. This allows the data user to assess trends in both the overall number of births and the timing (at what ages women have their children) of fertility.

Looking at the cohort age 25–29, the CEB was 1,442 in 1976, 1,171 in 1986 and 1,181 in 1992. Since 1970, the fertility of very young women, as reflected in CEB figures, has increased. Many fertility surveys also include a question regarding how many children a woman expects (birth expectations) to have over a lifetime. For example, the cohort age 15–19 recorded 1,181 children-ever-born in 1992 and is expected to have 2,137 births per 1,000 women over their lifetimes. Box 5.1 provides a summary of rate calculations.

Box 5.1

The Calculation of Birth Rates

Birth rates are relatively easy to calculate and in most instances the data required are readily available. Birth data are available from vital statistics sources, and population figures (rate denominators) are drawn from Census Bureau counts or estimates. The net reproduction rate requires additional vital statistics data on mortality. Information on cohort fertility is gathered via censuses and surveys. Rates for various units of geography can be calculated.

CRUDE BIRTH RATE (CBR)

$$= \frac{\text{Number of births in year Y}}{\text{Population at midpoint (July 1) in year Y}} \times 1,000$$

GENERAL FERTILITY RATE (GFR)

$$= \frac{\text{Number of births in year Y}}{\text{Population of women age 15 to 44 at midpoint in year Y}} \times 1,000$$

AGE-SPECIFIC FERTILITY RATE (ASFR)

$$= \frac{\text{Number of births in year Y to women age x to x+n}}{\text{Number of women age x to x+n at midpoint in Year Y}} \times 1,000$$

Box 5.1 continued

TOTAL FERTILITY RATE (TFR)

$$= \frac{\text{Sum of ASFRs} \cdot 5}{1{,}000}$$

GROSS REPRODUCTION RATE (ASFR ^{F})

$$= \frac{\text{Sum of ASFRs (for female births)} \cdot 5}{1{,}000}$$

NET REPRODUCTION RATE (NRR)

$$= \sum_{i=1}^{n} \frac{B_x}{P_x} \cdot \frac{L_x}{l_0};$$

where B_x/P_x is the female age-specific fertility rate for age x to x + n; L_x/l_0 is the life

table survival rate (see Chapter 6) appropriate for that age interval, and $\sum_{i=1}^{n}$

indicates that all of the products are summed. Given that there are six categories of ASFRs in the previous table, n would be equal to six.

CHILDREN EVER BORN (CEB)

$$= \frac{\text{Number of children ever born to women aged x to x + n in Year Y}}{\text{Population of women aged x to x + n in year Y}} \times 1{,}000$$

TRENDS IN U.S. FERTILITY

Over the twentieth century, U.S. fertility patterns have varied greatly. From 1890 to 1930 the number of births generally increased incrementally due in large part to the increase in population during earlier time periods. During the 1930s, birth rates declined in response to economic hardship although the number of births continued to be buoyed by the growth in population at earlier times. Lower fertility rates and plateauing birth numbers characterized the 1940s, at least until the end of World War II.

From a business perspective, most recent interest in the number of births and birth rates has been focused on the post–World War II era; that is, the period of time which is known for the baby boom, the baby bust, and the baby boom echo. Looking at Figure 5.1, the reader can see the effect of post-World War II baby boom, the period 1946 to 1964. Although arbitrary, the baby boom is considered "over" in

1965 because the annual number of births had fallen below 4.0 million. Starting at a low of 2.9 million births in 1945, this number rose to 4.0 million by 1953 and peaked at 4.3 million for each year from 1957 to 1961. The baby bust is indicated by the decline in the number of births from 4.3 million in 1961 to 3.1 million by 1975. After 1975, the number of births began to increase. The rise in births from 1975 to 1988 is the result of an *echo* effect, that is, the impact of the large number of baby boom women entering their childbearing years. Annual increases in the number of births from 1988 on are the result of slight increases in age specific fertility rates and therefore a rise in the total fertility rate.

Table 5.2 presents data on age-specific fertility rates for 1970, 1980, and 1992. While the rates are low and relatively constant at the youngest and oldest ages, rates for other cohorts have varied considerably over the 20-year period. Between 1970 and 1980 the rates for every age cohort declined, most markedly for the ages 20–24 and 25–29. Between 1980 and 1992, all but one rate increased. In particular, rates for the ages 30–34 and 35–39 rose by 18.3 and 12.7 births per 1,000, respectively.

Trends in the TFR since the end of World War II are presented in Table 5.3. Starting at 2,491 in 1945, the TFR increased by nearly 50 percent to 3,654 by 1960--in only a ten-year period! More dramatically, it declined to less than 50 percent of its peak value over the next twenty years! The net reproduction rate stood at 1,132 in 1945, 1,715 in 1960, and 853 in 1975. The 1975 NRR showed that females were averaging only 0.85 female births over a lifetime, indicating a fertility level considerably below replacement levels. While the TFR had increased to 2,046 by 1993, the NRR of 981 was still below replacement level. The fact that U.S. fertility is presently below replacement level has important implications for long-term U.S. population growth and is discussed in more detail at the end of this chapter.

Table 5.2
Age-Specific Birth Rates for U.S. Women, 1970, 1980, and 1992

Age interval	1970	1980	1992
10–14	1.2	1.1	1.4
15–19	68.3	53.0	60.7
20–24	167.8	115.1	114.6
25–29	145.1	112.9	117.4
30–34	73.3	61.9	80.2
35–39	31.7	19.8	32.5
40–44	8.1	3.9	5.9
45–49	0.5	0.2	0.3

Source: U.S. Bureau of the Census (1994). *Statistical Abstract of the United States, 1995*. Washington, DC: U.S. Government Printing Office, Table 92. Core source data come from the annual reports, *Vital Statistics of the United States*, published by the National Center for Health Statistics.

Figure 5.1
Annual Births to U.S. Women: 1945–1993

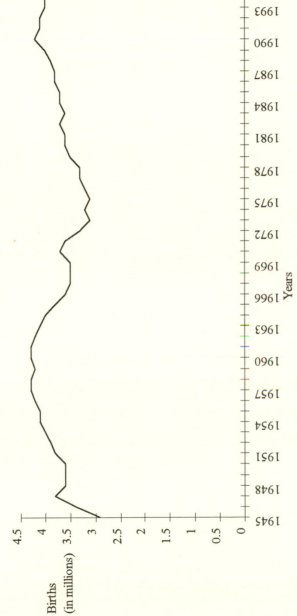

Births
(in millions)

Years

Sources: U.S. Bureau of the Census (1975). *Historical Statistics of the U.S., Colonial Times to 1970*, Part 1, Series B1-4. Washington DC: U. S. Government Printing Office; U.S. Bureau of the Census (1994). *Statistical Abstract of the United States, 1994*, Table 90, Washington DC: U. S. Government Printing Office. Core data from the annual reports, *Vital Statistics of the United States*, published by the National Center for Health Statistics.

Table 5.3
Total Fertility Rate for U.S. Women: 1945–1993

Year	Total Fertility Rate
1945	2,491
1950	3,091
1955	3,580
1960	3,654
1965	2,913
1970	2,480
1975	1,774
1980	1,840
1985	1,844
1990	2,081
1993	2,046

Sources: U.S. Bureau of the Census (1975). *Historical Statistics of the U.S., Colonial Times to 1970*, Part 1, series B11-19. Washington, DC: U.S. Government Printing Office; U.S. Department of Health and Human Services (1995). *Advance Report of Final Natality Statistics, 1993*. Monthly Vital Statistics Report. Vol. 44, No. 3, Table 4.

OTHER FERTILITY-RELATED PHENOMENA

Childlessness

While the decline in the average number of children born per woman has had a profound effect on overall fertility, the impact of *childlessness* is also worthy of note. Childlessness may be divided into two components—*involuntary*, or those women who through no conscious act of their own cannot conceive and/or carry a child to term—and voluntary—those women who through their own volition choose not to bear any children. When data on childlessness are examined, they reflect the contribution of both components. Since the extent of involuntary childlessness is not precisely known, it is difficult to exactly gauge the proportion of women who are choosing not to have children.

The percentages of all women who were childless for two age groups (20–24 and 30–34) for the years 1950–1992 are presented in Table 5.4. It can be observed that over time a relatively large increase in childlessness occurs at both ages. Of particular interest are differences between the percentages exhibited during the post–World War II baby boom period and the most recent years. From 1960 to 1992, the percentage of women in their early twenties who were childless increased from 24.2 to 59.2 percent; between 1965 and 1992 the percentage of women 30–34 years of age who were childless increased from 7.2 to 26.2 percent.

Analysis of survey data has shown that a substantial proportion of women who are childless but say they intend to have children change their minds to a childless preference over a fairly short period of time (Pol and Merwin 1984). Fewer women change their minds in the opposite direction. Therefore, it is quite possible that the relatively high percentage of women who report a childless preference as 20 to 24-year-olds will translate into even higher proportion of childlessness as these women become older. On the other hand, there is evidence that some women are "catching up" on births and are choosing to have their children later in life (Chen and Morgan 1991). This explains the rise in ASFRs for older (over 30) women, but the long-term effect of delayed childbearing on total births needs further study.

Teenage Fertility

Although teenagers accounted for only 12.4 percent of all births in the United States in 1992, teenage pregnancy is an area of growing concern. The age-specific fertility rate for women under 20 in the United States is one of the highest in the developed world—twice as high as the rates for France, Denmark, and Ireland and more than ten times the rate of Japan! The issues related to teenage pregnancy can be categorized into those affecting the welfare of the teenagers who bear children and those related to the health and welfare of the children themselves.

Table 5.4
Percent of All United States Women Aged 20 to 24 and 30 to 34 Who Were Childless: 1950–1992

Year	Aged 20-24	Aged 30-34
1950	33.3	17.3
1954	24.3	13.4
1960	24.2	10.4
1965	28.0	7.2
1970	35.7	8.3
1975	42.3	8.8
1980	40.4	13.7
1984	40.7	15.8
1992	59.2	26.2

Sources: U.S. Bureau of the Census (1986). *Statistical Abstract of the United States, 1986*, Table 92; U.S. Bureau of the Census (1994). *Statistical Abstract of the United States, 1994*, Table 105.

For teenage mothers, there are both health and social considerations related to teenage childbearing. The risk of maternal death is much higher for teenage mothers than for older mothers, and teenage mothers are significantly more likely to suffer from anemia or toxemia than mothers age 20 and above. While the direction of causality is not clear, teenage mothers tend to be poorly educated—eight out of ten mothers aged 17 and under never complete high school—and therefore lack the skills to participate in today's job market. They suffer high rates of unemployment and welfare dependency. Furthermore, if married (48 percent of teenage births are to unmarried women), these marriages tend to be unstable. Early childbearing also contributes to a significantly larger number of births over a lifetime.

With regard to the health of their children, babies born to teenagers are two to three times more likely to die soon after birth than babies born to older mothers. The incidence of low birth weight (less than 2,500 grams, or 5.5 pounds) is twice as high for teenage mothers, and infants born to mothers 15 years old and younger are markedly more likely to suffer from neurological defects than infants born to mothers who are in their twenties. However, there is evidence that the direction of causality, that is, early childbearing causes an adverse effect, is not clear. Some research points to individual and family background factors as being responsible for adverse effects on both teenage mothers and their children (e.g., Geronimus, Korenman, and Hillemeier 1994). Box 5.2 focuses on the health implications of adolescent pregnancy.

Box 5.2
Health Implications of Adolescent Pregnancy

One of the most unsettling trends in the United States today is the increasing proportion of births that occur outside of marriage. While 30 years ago only 5 percent of all births were to unmarried women, today that figure is over 30 percent. This situation is further aggravated by the fact that a large proportion of these births are to adolescents. In the late 1980s, of the roughly 900,000 children born to unmarried women, nearly one third were born to women under age 20. About 140,000 were born to women aged 17 or younger. By comparison, in 1960 there were only 90,000 births to unmarried women under age 20. The fertility rate for unmarried women aged 15 to 19 has more than doubled, from 15.3 births per 1,000 women in 1960 to 32.6 in 1986.

As with other fertility-related phenomena, adolescent pregnancies are not randomly distributed within the population. For example, about 55 percent of all births to white adolescents were born to unmarried women. The comparable figure for African-American women was over 90 percent. These births also are likely to be characterized by attributes that do not facilitate a satisfactory outcome or a long-term healthy existence. Young mothers are much less likely to receive early prenatal care. While less than one half of women giving birth between age 15 and age 17 receive prenatal care in the first trimester, nearly 90 percent of the women aged 25 through 29 receive such care. Furthermore, young mothers are significantly more likely to give birth prematurely.

Regarding the health of the young child, being born to a young mother has its disadvantages. While nearly 14 of 1,000 babies born to women under age 15 are of low birth weight, the comparable figure for women aged 25 to 29 is 6. Though 15 percent of these youngest mothers have babies with low one-minute Apgar scores, only nine percent of the births to older women do. Apgar scores are used to measure the health of a newborn. The combination of low birth weight, prematurity, and the young age of the

Box 5.2 continued

mother contributes to an increased incidence of birth defects, a higher level of mental retardation, and greater levels of infant mortality. About 80 percent of all newborns that die are characterized by low birth weight.

In addition, early childbearing has deleterious effects on mothers. Initially, a greater number of birthing complications occur due to the lack of physical maturity and the shortage of prenatal care. Beyond the immediate physiological dangers are related factors such as lower educational attainment, more lifetime births, and overall lessened earning power. The economic cost of having a child at an early age can be quite high given the opportunity costs involved.

Finally, the indirect health care effects of early childbearing must be considered. A higher incidence of birth defects and mental retardation carries an economic and psychic cost to both mother and society. Many of these children face the long-term prospect of diminished health and the resulting need for long-term health services. There is also some evidence indicating that when early childbearing is combined with poverty and despair, children are more likely to suffer abuse and neglect. Again, this carries an economic and psychic cost.

Induced Abortion

The controversy over abortion in the United States has made the collection and management of abortion data very important. Prior to 1973 abortion data were sketchy, making it difficult to assess the long-term effect of induced abortion on the overall fertility rate. Since 1973, the quality of data has improved and now there are more than 20 years of comparative data available for analysis. The data available for 1992 on induced abortions indicate that there were 379 abortions for every 1,000 live births (or 1.5 million for the year). This represents a reduction in the figure seen a decade earlier (428 per 1,000 live births in 1982) (U.S. Bureau of the Census 1994, Table 111). Since 1980, the number of induced abortions has been relatively constant at between 1.5 and 1.6 million per year. Without induced abortion and assuming that one third of the pregnancies would not have resulted in live births due to spontaneous abortion and other complicating factors, over 1 million additional births would have occurred in 1992. In other words, in the absence of abortion over 5 million births would have occurred in the United States in 1992, rather than the 4,065,014 reported. This represents a 25 percent increase in the number of births in the absence of abortion.

Births to Unmarried Women

The proportion of all births born to unwed mothers has increased steadily in the United States for four decades. In 1955, there were only 183,000 reported births to unmarried women, accounting for less than 5 percent of all births. As late as 1980, births to unmarried women accounted for less than 20 percent of all births. However, since 1980 there has been a marked rise in this percent. In 1992, about 1.2 out of the 4.1 million births registered (or 30.1 percent of the total) were reported as born to unmarried mothers. Figures for 1994 indicate that the number of births to unmarried women has leveled off. This overall rate masks important racial differences in this category of births. In 1992, 22.6 percent of white mothers and 68.1 percent of African-American mothers were not married at the time they gave birth (U.S. Bureau of the Census 1994, Tables 92 and 100).

Labor Force Participation and Fertility

Labor force participation rates for single and married women with children of varying ages for 1950 to 1990 are presented in Figure 5.2. The proportion of single women who were in the labor force decreased by 10 percentage points between 1950 and 1965. These were years in which early marriage followed by childbearing was the norm. Between 1950 and 1990, labor force participation rates for adult single women rose 14 percentage points to nearly 65 percent. For married women with children, however, the pattern of change has been different. Labor force participation rates have risen almost every year for women in this category. The labor force participation rate for women with older children (6–17 years) increased by more than 160 percent over the time interval, and the rate now exceeds that for single women. The increase for women with younger children (under 6) has been truly amazing—a 47 percentage point rise in 43 years—and today it approaches the average participation rate for all women. (Box 5.3 focuses on planning an OB unit.)

Box 5.3

A Case Study in Fertility Services: Planning an OB Unit

The establishment of an obstetrical facility may seem straightforward enough. One need only estimate the likely number of births in an area, arrange for appropriate medical staff and physical facilities, and offer the service. This process, however, masks a great deal of the complexity that surrounds the provision of services for obstetrical needs. In fact, there is virtually no aspect of demography that can be ignored in planning for an OB unit.

From the first step on, the process requires considerable research and the application of a number of demographic concepts. The first problem involves the delineation of the service area for an OB unit. How far is it reasonable to expect pregnant women to travel to deliver a baby (or for prenatal and postnatal services if the obstetrician's office is located near the facility)? Administrators may already have some idea of the facility's service area for general care, but are OB patients different? They are, in fact, and a hospital is likely to attract OB patients from a broader area than patients for many other diagnoses. The delineation of the OB service area will, therefore, depend on the availability of competing services, the location of obstetricians' offices,   and

Figure 5.2
Labor Force Participation Rates for Single and Married Women with Children 1950–1990

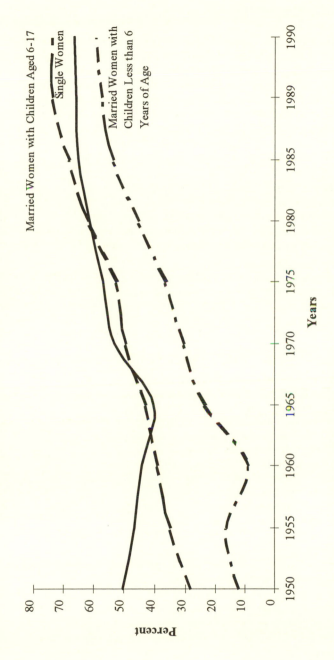

Sources: U. S. Bureau of the Census (1975). *Statistical Abstract of the United States, 1975*, Table 565; U. S. Bureau of the Census (1994). *Statistical Abstract of the United States, 1994*, Washington, DC: U.S. Government Printing Office, Tables 625 and 626.

Box 5.3 continued

transportation access.

Having delineated the appropriate service area, it is then necessary to calculate the demand for obstetrical services.* How many deliveries can be expected annually from the population being served? This, of course, can be forecasted in a number of ways. The simplest—and probably most misleading—of these would be to attach a crude birth rate to the target population. This would be misleading in that it does not take such factors as age, race, and marital status into consideration. Applying the countywide crude birth rate, for example, to your target population at the zip code level may mean that an average is being used that is skewed due to higher African-American birth rates, while in practice you have a predominantly Anglo service area population.

It would be more appropriate to utilize some indicator (e.g., general fertility rate) that takes the age and sex distribution of the area into consideration. It would be best if the actual fertility experience of the target population were known. If it is not, one could apply some standard rate that accounts for age, sex, race, and even income distribution. Any ethnic concentrations within the service area should also be noted, as many such groups (e.g., Hispanics) are likely to display different fertility patterns than the general population.

Incidentally, detailed current population estimates that include age, sex, and racial/ethnic composition may not be readily available. The smaller and more irregularly shaped the service area, the more likely this is to be a problem. The profiling of the service area population may be done by purchasing data from private vendors (usually at the zip code level) or seeking assistance from local planning agencies who often make such estimates. It may be necessary to call on the services of an area demographer if possible, since every service area is likely to have its own peculiar characteristics.

Once the current population has been profiled, it should be possible to apply the appropriate rate and estimate the yield of births from the service area. However, it will be a year or two before the facility is operational, and perhaps five years before it attains financial viability. Some indication of projected births becomes more crucial than current births. How does one forecast births? Here the various projection techniques of the demographer come into play. One might first want to examine overall population trends; that is, is the service area population increasing, decreasing, or stable? A projected decline in the population base does not bode well for a new facility. More importantly, however, is how the composition of the population changing. A growing population will not be beneficial if it is rapidly aging. The planner must project the population in terms of the variables discussed above—age, sex, race, and ethnicity. In addition, some projection of socioeconomic status must be made, unless the patient's ability to pay is not a factor.

Projections can be made using straight-line techniques, cohort analysis, or more reality-based approaches that take factors such as housing stock into consideration. In the short run, the rate of natural increase (difference between births and deaths) or decrease is not likely to be significant, but the migration rate certainly is. The identification of in-migrants and out-migrants becomes essential. What type of people, for example, are moving into the community—retirees, young marrieds, middle-aged empty nesters? Can the identified trends be expected to continue into the future? In addition, will known fertility rates be maintained indefinitely?

Box 5.3 continued

Obviously, a number of assumptions have to be made to develop a profile of the service area population five or ten years into the future, and many of the demographer's tools are necessary for this task. Once a future population has been established, the potential number of births can be projected. The planning does not end here, however, because a number of other factors need to be taken into consideration. The economic status of the target population needs to be evaluated (unless OB services are considered a "loss leader"). Further, the availability of medical manpower needs to be considered, because a new facility with no physician support or an inadequate number of neonatal nurses will not be viable. The risk level of the population must also be considered. Is this a population of high rates of premature and low-birth-weight babies or a population that utilizes little prenatal care? If so, special facilities and services may be necessary.

Two other related factors must also be considered. First, what are the psychographic characteristics of the service area population? Is this a "yuppie" population interested in innovative birthing arrangements, rather than the traditional delivery format this facility is offering? Or is it a traditional population with no interest in the progressive alternative birthing facility being planned? These questions lead directly into the issue of competition. The perception of the organization offering the OB facility will influence utilization levels, so image becomes a key factor. An understanding of how consumers see this facility relative to its competitors is essential.

The subject of competition raises one final point. The projected birth figure for the service area population is only meaningful if there is no competition. In most areas, there will be more than one facility competing for obstetrical cases. The new facility cannot expect to obtain all potential births, but only its "share." The current distribution of births among existing facilities must be determined in order to estimate the share that the new facility will capture. Information on deliveries can often be obtained from state health agencies or purchased from data vendors who calculate market shares. Some realistic estimate of the capturable market share must subsequently be made in order to determine the true potential utilization for the planned facility.

As can be seen, virtually all aspects of demography are utilized in the planning of this type of facility, and the process can even be more complicated than outlined above. This helps explain the booming business in the sale of demographic data and the growing number of individuals with demographic training being utilized by health care organizations.

---

*Obstetrical care is probably the only health service for which the "need" and the "demand" are almost synonymous. Once the process (pregnancy) is set into play, it is essentially irreversible. Many heart patients may back out of bypass surgery, but pregnant women—after a point at least—cannot opt out of the process.

FERTILITY PATTERNS AND THE BUSINESS ENVIRONMENT

Overall, the direction of future American fertility is not clear. Ryder (1990) is correct when he emphasizes the need for short-distance vision and a good deal more study when attempting to forecast future fertility. While the future is unclear, the business implications of what we do know about fertility are easier to identify. The most obvious fertility/business linkage is between the number of births and the need for physicians and hospital services, as well as the baby products linked to pregnancy and birth. Beyond the first days or months of life, infants and young children have a unique set of product and service needs. A fluctuation in the number of births brings with it alterations in the size of these markets. Figure 5.1 showed the 900,000 decline in the number of births between 1962 and 1972, a 21 percent loss in the size of the market for birth-related products and services over a ten-year period! Between 1984 and 1994 the size of this market increased by 300,000, or 8 percent.

In addition, the size of birth cohorts permanently effects the size of that cohort as it ages. For example, the population aged 25 to 34 is projected to decline by nearly 6 million persons between 1990 and 2000. This reduction is in large part the result of the reduction in the annual number of births that took place between 1965 and 1975. To the extent that the demand for certain products and services are directly linked to these ages, the size of the markets made up of persons 25–34 years of age can be projected to be reduced by 13.2 percent during the decade, all other factors being equal.

Fluctuations in the size of markets are clearly linked to population size, and fertility is the major contributor to size. Looking again at Figure 5.1, between 1970 and 1979 there were approximately 33 million births. Over the next decade, 1980–1989, more than 37.4 million births were recorded, for a 12 percent increase in market size. Examination of the data from the early 1990s leads to the conclusion that the number of births for the 1990s will surpass that for the 1980s. In addition, age cohort size differentials begin to account for differences in the number of births 20 or so years later when these individuals begin to have their own children. The post–World War II baby boom ended in 1964, followed by the baby bust (1965–1979). The baby boom *echo* began to be realized around 1980 when annual births rose, not because fertility rates increased, but due to the large number of women entering their childbearing years who had been born during the baby boom.

The baby boom cohorts are now beginning to enter midlife. While it is true that baby boomers do not comprise a homogeneous market, the fact that they are entering middle age is having a considerable impact on the business environment (Bouvier and DeVita 1991). They are contributing to the aging of the U.S. population and the aggregate increase in home ownership. They vote in larger percentages than younger age cohorts and as a result are significantly affecting the nation's political agenda. The next "baby boom"—the 72 million children of baby boomers—are also influencing the market place (Mitchell 1995). They make up the market for *Barney the Dinosaur*, *Power Rangers*, and *Disney World*. As these cohorts age they will reshape the economic and social environment that their parents purportedly changed forever.

The idea that businesses should turn the focus away from younger to older markets is premature. The younger population still comprises a substantial market, albeit a complex one. Because many children are now born into smaller and differently structured households (see Chapter 9), the nature of their consumption and the effect on their parent's purchasing behavior has changed. As a consequence of divorce, remarriage, and cohabitation, about 30 percent of U.S. children are likely to spend time in a step-family (Bumpass, Raley, and Sweet 1995). Some parents provide more leisure products and services for their fewer children because they feel guilty about being away from home. Parental buying behavior is partly driven by the knowledge that different products and services are required by children who spend a great deal of time alone or with other children. Many children find themselves part of two households, and therefore have two sets of parents making purchases for them. Clearly, this information must be linked to demographic shifts in order for businesses to be successful in today's market place.

The reader is reminded that state, county, and subcounty fertility scenarios can be quite different from the national-level trends presented here. Younger populations, and those with larger-than-average percentages of African-Americans and Hispanics, will generate more births, and thus more end users of products produced for babies and infants. While these national trends are important, many business activities are influenced more by subnational trends. It should never be assumed that national-level trends are replicated at the local level, and data for the market area in question should always be consulted before decisions are made. (Box 5.4 contains the short biography of a demographic consultant.)

Box 5.4
A Day in the Life of Thomas G. Exter, Ph.D.

President, TGE Demographics, Inc., Honeoye Falls, New York
Adjunct Professor of Sociology, Rochester Institute of Technology

A day in the life of Tom Exter, if you just consider the professional responsibilities, goes something like this: As the only principal in a demographic consulting firm, I usually get an early start. Up at 6:15 A.M. to take the dog out, I'm in my home office writing by 6:30 A.M. Coffee and computer combine to give me a jump start on the day. Content may include a project report, newsletter text, or a freelance article. I need freelance writing for the income as well as to keep TGE Demographics in the news. Recent articles include: a piece on TIGER 2000 for *Marketing Tools*, how to buy demographic data in the late decade for *Business Geographics*, and data quality issues in Latin America for *Forecast* magazine. Later, I will dedicate up to two hours a day on updating *The Official Guide to American Incomes* (Ithaca, NY: New Strategist, 1996). The home office is essential in order to combine family and work tasks, minimize commuting, and keep productive resources close at hand.

Running TGE Demographics involves several daily responsibilities: Keeping the books up-to-date; answering calls from reporters, editors, vendors, and corporate librarians as well as current and prospective clients; composing e-mail for colleagues, collaborators, and my kids in college; marketing efforts in the form of advertising and networking; and, of course, cranking out tables, charts, maps, and text for project reports. Recent projects include custom household projections for a food marketer and an automobile manufacturer, consumer trend analysis for a cosmetics company,

---

Box 5.4 continued

epidemiological information for a pharmaceutical firm, and site maps for a professional sports franchise. TGE Demographics is a value-added reseller for Environmental Systems Research Institute, Inc. (ESRI) desktop mapping products, especially Arc View. Some clients want the software packaged with data, but most just want color maps right away. For output quality, I do the spatial analysis, compose the maps, then print them out at Kinko's.

In part to get out of the house, but also to expand my networks, I teach on an adjunct basis at The Rochester Institute of Technology. In the past year I have taught sections on Population and Society, Social Change, and Introductory Sociology. On any given day I may be preparing a lecture, correcting exams, or figuring out how to best rig a computer for a presentation. For the Social Change course, I have used Toffler's *Powershift* and Charles Handy's *In the Age of Unreason*. Both suggest that the information worker of the future will be autonomous but connected, noninterchangeable, in a continuous-learning mode, and open to upside-down thinking. If I didn't have to worry about making a living, I might have time to reflect on that.

REFERENCES

Bouvier, Leon, and Carol J. DeVita (1991). "The Baby Boom—Entering Midlife." *Population Bulletin*, Vol. 46, No. 3. Washington, DC: Population Reference Bureau.

Bumpass, Larry L., R. Kelly Raley, and James A. Sweet (1995). "The Changing Character of Step Families: Implications of Cohabitation and Nonmarital Childbearing." *Demography*, 32 (August): 425–436.

Chen, Renbao, and S. Philip Morgan (1991). "Recent Trends in the Timing of First Births in the United States." *Demography*, 28 (November): 513–533.

David, Paul A., and Warren S. Sanderson (1987). "The Emergence of a Two-Child Norm Among American Birth-Controllers." *Population and Development Review*, 13 (March): 1–41.

Geronimus, Arline, T., Sanders Korenman, and Marianne M. Hillemeier (1994). "Does Young Maternal Age Adversely Affect Child Development? Evidence from Cousin Comparisons in the United States," *Population and Development Review*, 20 (September): 585–609.

Mitchell, Susan (1995). "The Next Baby Boom." *American Demographer* (October): 22–31.

Mosher, William D., and William F. Pratt (1990). "Fecundity and Fertility in the United States." *Advance Data*, No. 192. Hyattsville, MD: National Center for Health Statistics.

Pol, Louis, and Mark Merwin (1984). "Childlessness: A Panel Study of Expressed Intentions and Reported Fertility." *Social Biology*, 10: 117–124.

Ryder, Norman B. (1990). "What is Going to Happen to American Fertility?" *Population and Development Review*, 16 (3): 433–454.

U.S. Bureau of the Census (1994). *Statistical Abstract of the United States 1994*. Washington, DC: U.S. Government Printing Office.

SUGGESTED READINGS

Easterlin, Richard (1968). *Population, Labor Force and Long Swings in Economic Growth*. New York: National Bureau of Economic Research.

Easterlin, Richard A. (1987). *Birth and Fortune* (2nd ed.). Chicago: University of Chicago Press.

Easterlin, Richard A., and Eileen M. Crimmins (1985). *The Fertility Revolution*. Chicago: University of Chicago Press.

National Center for Health Statistics (Periodic). *Advance and Final Reports of Natality Statistics*. Hyattsville, MD: U.S. Government Printing Office.

Rindfuss, Ronald, S. Philip Morgan, and Gray Swicegood (1988). *First Births in America: Changes in the Timing of Parenthood*. Berkeley: University of California Press.

Chapter 6

Mortality and Morbidity

INTRODUCTION

Death, like taxes, is certain, and mortality is a topic that most would prefer not to discuss. However, from a business perspective, the occurrence of death presents significant opportunities even if some may find them distasteful. At the most basic level, deaths are responsible for the existence of the funeral business. Even in a small state like Nebraska (1.6 million population), the funeral business is significant. In 1992, Nebraska had 182 funeral and crematory service enterprises employing 730 persons. The payroll for these enterprises was $14.2 million. These businesses reported $55.9 million in annual sales (U.S. Bureau of the Census 1994a, Table 1a).

If one focuses on the broader picture and includes morbidity (or sickness) as a consideration, the number of business concerns increases astronomically. There were over 2,300 health services providers in Nebraska in 1992, employing nearly 27,000 persons. These enterprises accounted for over $1.5 billion in sales and about $700 million in payroll (U.S. Bureau of the Census 1994a, Table 1a). Nationwide, there were 15,647 funeral service and crematory enterprises employing 88,328 persons in 1992. At the same time, there were about 441,000 health services establishments employing over 4.4 million persons (U.S. Bureau of the Census 1994b, table 1a).

The death experience of a population is important from both a demographic and business perspective. Along with fertility and migration it is one of the three components of population change. Between 1991 and 1992, the estimated population of the United States grew from 250.7 to 253.7 million. The components of change were 4.1 million births, 2.2 million deaths, and 1.0 million net immigrants (U.S. Bureau of the Census 1994c, Table 4). At both the national level and the local level, the number of deaths is a critical concern in business decision making. For this reason, an understanding of both mortality and morbidity is necessary.

MEASURING MORTALITY

Mortality refers to the death experience of a population. It is normally measured by a count of the number of deaths, the calculation of death rates, and the determination of life expectancy. *Death* is defined as the permanent cessation of life after birth has taken place. (Deaths prior to a live birth, fetal deaths, are recorded as a separate category.) While the definition of death may seem simple and straightforward, recent medical and legal developments have added a great deal of complexity to death-related issues. Some of these issues affect business decisions, particularly those made by hospitals and health personnel.

Death Rates

Deaths, like births, are often discussed in terms of rates. While the absolute number of deaths is required for some planning purposes, rates are most often used to assess intermarket differences. Although the rates shown in the next several pages are for the United States as a whole, rates can also be calculated for metropolitan statistical areas (MSAs), regions, states, counties, and subcounty markets.

The *crude death rate* (CDR) is simple to calculate and measures the mortality level per 1,000 population. The CDR is calculated as:

$$CDR = \frac{\text{Number of deaths in year X}}{\text{Midyear popluation in year X}} \times 1,000.$$

The CDR for the United States is 1992 can be derived as follows:

$$\frac{2,175,613}{255,082,000} \times 1,000 = 8.5$$

This equation yields a CBR of 8.5 deaths per 1,000 persons.

The numerator data are obtained from the death registration system described in Chapter 3 and the denominator represents either an actual count of a population or an estimate for the year in question. If there are known or suspected year-to-year fluctuations in the number of deaths (e.g., in smaller market areas), a three-year average of deaths should be produced, with the middle year being the year for which the rate is calculated. For example, the CDR for Douglas County, Nebraska, for 1994 could be calculated by averaging the number deaths for 1993, 1994 and 1995 and dividing that number by the estimated 1994 population. This is the same denominator used for calculating the crude birth rate in Chapter 5.

The CDR is considered "crude" because it does not take into account age, sex, or any other factors that explain death rate differences. To refine the measurement of mortality, demographers have developed more specific death rates. For example, in modern societies, the probability of dying varies greatly by age. The proportion of infants that die in their first year of life in the United States is 0.8 percent. The proportion of 10 to 15-year-olds who die during a five-year interval is about one tenth of 1 percent. At the ages 80–85, the proportion dying during a five-year period increases to over 30 percent. Because of this variation, it is important to consider the *population-at-risk* concept introduced in Chapter 5. While everyone in a population is at risk of death, the wide variation in the likelihood of death at different ages calls for measures of mortality specific to age. *Age-specific death rates* (ASDRs) are arrived at through the following formula:

$$\text{ASDR} = \frac{\text{Deaths to persons age X to X+5 in year Y}}{\text{Number of persons age X to X+5 in year Y}} \times 1{,}000,$$

where X to X + 5 is a five-year age interval. In 1992, the ASDR for 20 to 24-year-olds in the United States was as follows:

$$\text{ASDR}_{20-24} = \frac{20{,}137}{19{,}050{,}000} \times 1{,}000 = 1.06 \text{ deaths per 1,000 persons aged 20-24.}$$

A five-year age range is typically used in the calculation of ASDRs. However, ASDRs for wider or narrower age ranges can also be calculated. In fact, at ages where mortality levels tend to be unusual, such as the very young or very old ages, it is not unusual to calculate one-year rates.

The *infant mortality rate* (IMR) has been developed to measure the occurrence of death during the first year of life. By definition, the IMR involves only the population under one year. Infant mortality is calculated separately because, as noted above, the probability of death during the first year of life is relatively high, while probabilities beyond the first year are much lower. The formula for the IMR is as follows:

$$\text{IMR} = \frac{\text{Deaths to persons under 1 year of age in year X}}{\text{Births to persons in year X}} \times 1{,}000.$$

Note that the denominator is the number of live births in year X and *not* the population younger than one year of age. The IMR for 1992 in the United States is calculated as follows:

$$\text{IMR} = \frac{34{,}628}{4{,}065{,}014} \times 1{,}000 = 8.5 \text{ deaths per 1,000 live births.}$$

The IMR is often divided into the following two components: *neonatal* and *postneonatal* mortality rates, with the former measuring mortality in the first 28 days of life and the latter reflecting mortality between 29 days and one year. This distinction is made due to variation in the causes of death during the first year. In general, deaths within the first 28 days are related to congenital abnormalities and problems arising during pregnancy. Deaths beyond 28 days are more likely to reflect environmental factors such as nutrition and postnatal care that, for the most part, are unrelated to the birth experience.

In 1991, there were 30,160 infant deaths in the United States, of which 22,978 (or 76 percent) were classified as neonatal. The infant, neonatal, and postneonatal mortality rates for that year were 8.9, 6.8, and 2.1, respectively (National Center for Health Statistics 1995a, Table 8-1). By comparison, in 1970 there were 74,667 infant deaths, and 56,279 (75 percent) were classified as neonatal. The infant, neonatal, and postneonatal mortality rates were 20.0, 15.1, and 4.9, respectively (National Center for Health Statistics 1974, Table 7-1).

Other measures of early mortality include the *fetal death ratio* applied to stillbirths; the *perinatal mortality rate*, which measures late fetal deaths and early infant mortality; and the *maternal mortality rate*, which is a measure of mortality for women who die during childbirth.

Fetal deaths include fetuses who are dead at birth and who have a stated or assumed gestation period of 20 or more weeks. The fetal death ratio divides the number of fetal deaths in a given year by the number of live births in that same year. In 1991, there were 30,160 fetal deaths in the United States, resulting in a fetal death ratio of 7.3 per 1,000 live births, about one half the ratio for 1970 (National Center for Health Statistics 1995a, Table 8-2; National Center for Health Statistics 1974, Table 7-2). In 1970 there were 52,961 fetal deaths for a ratio of 14.2 per 1,000 live births. Maternal mortality rates are expressed in terms of maternal deaths per 100,000 live births. In 1992, there were 318 deaths to mothers due to complications of pregnancy, childbirth, and the puerperium for a rate of 7.8 per 100,000 live births (National Center for Health Statistics 1995b, Table 29).

Cause-specific mortality rates can also be calculated. For example, the 1992 crude death rate of 8.5 deaths per 1,000 persons includes 2.81 deaths per 1,000 persons due to diseases of the heart, 2.04 deaths per 1,000 persons attributable to malignant neoplasms (cancer), and 0.56 deaths per 1,000 persons caused by cerebrovascular diseases. It is possible to determine the percentage of overall mortality attributable to a specific cause by dividing the number of deaths attributable to a given cause by the total number of deaths. In 1992, diseases of the heart accounted for 33 percent of all deaths, with malignant neoplasms and cerebrovascular diseases accounting for 24 percent and 7 percent, respectively.

Rates that consider both cause of death *and* age can be easily produced, since death records include both pieces of information. An examination of cause-of-death data for infant deaths, for example, indicates that the leading causes of death are congenital abnormalities (21.5 percent of all infant deaths), sudden infant death syndrome (14.1 percent), and disorders relating to short gestation and low birth weight (11.6 percent).

Box 6.1 focuses on rate comparisons between two markets (areas) when the age structure of those markets are different.

Box 6.1
Standardization—A Technique for Adjusting Rates

Demographers frequently use a technique called *standardization* to make comparisons of rates for different populations (Das Gupta 1993; Smith 1992, pp. 49–72). Standardization represents an "adjustment" of the populations in question to make them comparable for statistical purposes. This technique is frequently used to compare crude death rates for two countries, two regions, two markets, or two points in time, although more than two comparisons can be made.

The crude death rate is a function of the number of deaths occurring in an area, as well as that area's age structure. Given the very different probabilities of dying evident for various ages, a younger population produces fewer deaths than an older one, even if the size of both populations is the same. For example, Mexico has a lower crude death rate (5 per 1,000) than the United States (9 per 1,000). The lower CDR for Mexico reflects the fact that Mexico has a much younger age structure than the United States and, therefore, a higher concentration of persons in the least-likely-to-die age categories. A standardization method that accounts for age differences is required to make comparisons between the two populations meaningful.

Age-specific death rates, which combine to make up the crude death rate, can be applied to a common age structure. The crude death rate is then recalculated. When standardization is performed on the two populations in question, the *age-adjusted crude death rate* is higher for Mexico than for the United States. The same principle would hold in comparing death rates for two or more states or substate areas with different age structures. The crude birth rate as well as other demographic and nondemographic rates can be adjusted for differences in population characteristics such as age, education and income.

The basic principles of standardization are illustrated in the following simplified table. Starting with five age intervals and the corresponding age-specific mortality rates, Death Rates (1), we have constructed part of the table needed for standardized comparisons.

Age	Death Rate (1)	Death Rate (2)	Population	Expected Deaths (1)	Expected Deaths (2)
< 1	8.1	7.6	3,900	31,590	24,008
1–4	0.4	0.3	15,528	6,211	4,658
5–14	0.2	0.1	36,449	7,290	3,645
15–24	1.0	0.8	36,124	36,124	28,899
			92,001	81,251	61,210

Death Rate (2) is the ASDRs for the population to which the comparison is to be made. The population column is the 1992 U.S. age structure in 1,000s. Expected Deaths (1) and (2) are produced by multiplying the ASDRs by the age-specific population figures.

Box 6.1 continued

As can be easily observed, the lower ASDRs in the comparison population reduces the number of expected deaths markedly. The CDR for the United States for the ages 0–24 in 1992 was 81,251/92,001,000 or 0.883 per 1,000 population. The CDR for the comparison population, *assuming that they have the same age structure*, is 61,121/92,001,000, or 0.665 per 1,000 population.

For a standardized comparison, we need the CDR_{0-24} for the comparison population, irrespective of population age structure. That figure is 0.765 (data not shown in the table). Therefore, the nonstandardized comparison is 0.883 to 0.765, a 0.115 difference. The standardized comparison is 0.883 to 0.665, a 0.215 difference, meaning that the different age structure of the comparison population was masking the extent of the rate difference. Additional discussion of the use of standardization in a business context can be found in Chapter 11.

Life Tables

A relatively complex but extremely useful technique for analyzing mortality patterns is the *life table*. Life table construction begins with age-specific death rates and produces a number of functions, including life expectancy for each age interval in the table (Schoen 1988). Life tables are generated by actuaries for use by insurance companies in the determination of premiums and by epidemiologists to analyze patterns of mortality. Edmund Halley, of comet fame, was an early pioneer in the construction of life tables. He calculated the premium a purchaser should pay for an annuity, given that the purchaser has at each age some estimated probability of dying. Life tables provide a great deal of information about the patterns of mortality within a population, including the probability of dying and the life expectancy at any age.

Multiple decrement life tables allow for the joint, or multiple, probabilities of events that result in a person's exiting from a population. For example, a life table can be constructed that takes into account both the probability of dying and the probability of retiring. This type of life table is quite useful to a business attempting to assess its health benefits liabilities for both current workers and future retirees. Another application would combine the probabilities of dying with the probabilities of becoming disabled.

An abridged life table for the United States in 1992 is presented in Table 6.1. Based on age-specific mortality rates, death probabilities can be calculated for each age. The other functions of the life table subsequently are derived from this information. All life table functions taken together are based on one assumption: age-specific death probabilities remain constant over the period of the life table. That is, if life expectancy at birth is 75.8 years, then age-specific death probabilities at all ages must remain constant as an age cohort progresses from birth until the point where all have died. A change in any of the probabilities results in shorter or longer

Table 6.1

Abridged Life Table for the Total Population, United States: 1992

Age interval	Proportion dying	Of 100,000 born alive		Stationary population		Average remaining lifetime
Period of life between two exact ages stated in years	Proportion of persons alive at beginning of age interval dying during interval	Number living at beginning of age interval	Number dying during age interval	In the age interval	In this and all subsequent age intervals	Average number of years of life remaining at beginning of age interval
(1)	(2)	(3)	(4)	(5)	(6)	(7)
x to x+n	$n^q x$	l_x	$n^d x$	$n^L x$	T_x	e_x
0-1	0.00851	100,000	851	99,275	7,577,757	75.8
1-5	0.00172	99,149	171	396,195	7,478,482	75.4
5-10	0.00102	98,978	101	494,615	7,082,287	71.6
10-15	0.00121	98,877	120	494,152	6,587,672	66.6
15-20	0.00418	98,757	413	492,848	6,093,520	61.7
20-25	0.00528	98,344	519	490,448	5,600,672	56.9
25-30	0.00601	97,825	588	487,654	5,110,224	52.2
30-35	0.00765	97,237	744	484,369	4,622,570	47.5
35-40	0.01001	96,493	966	480,187	4,138,201	42.9
40-45	0.01305	95,527	1,247	474,740	3,658,014	38.3
45-50	0.01822	94,280	1,718	467,420	3,183,274	33.8
50-55	0.02799	92,562	2,591	456,739	2,715,854	29.3
55-60	0.04421	89,971	3,978	440,481	2,259,115	25.1
60-65	0.06800	85,993	5,848	416,137	1,818,634	21.1
65-70	0.10084	80,145	8,082	381,393	1,402,497	17.5
70-75	0.14673	72,063	10,574	334,799	1,021,104	14.2
75-80	0.21189	61,489	13,029	275,667	686,305	11.2
80-85	0.31480	48,460	15,255	204,369	410,638	8.5
85 and over	1.00000	33,205	33,205	206,269	206,269	6.2

Source: U.S. Department of Health and Human Services (1995). *Advance Report of Final Mortality Statistics, 1992, Monthly Vital Statistics Report,* Vol.43, No.6, Washington, DC: Public Health Service, Table 3.

life expectancy, depending on whether the probabilities increase or decrease over time. Therefore, life expectancies derived from any life table must be interpreted with caution, especially in view of prospective changes in medical and health technology that might affect life expectancy.

While life expectancy at birth in 1996 in the United States is about 76 years, overall age-specific death probabilities are likely to decrease over time. Any cohort of children born now should have a life expectancy somewhat greater than 76 years. One unknown in this equation is the impact of acquired immunodeficiency syndrome (AIDS) on life expectancy. Life expectancy could actually decline in the future for some groups (e.g., white males) due to increased mortality as a result of AIDS.

The x to x + n column of the life table refers to the age intervals, such as 5–9 years for the population. Single-year intervals could have been chosen along with other age, sex, and race combinations. Other life table functions are defined in Box 6.2

Box 6.2
Life Table Functions

$n^q x$ the proportion of persons alive at the beginning of the interval who died during the interval. For example, 0.85 percent of the population born died during their first year of life.

l_x known as the radix; an arbitrary 100,000 persons are chosen as the starting point. As deaths occur during each interval they are subtracted and l_x becomes smaller; 100,000 minus 851 ($n^d x$, which is the number of deaths in the interval 0–1 year) equals 99,149, the number of persons alive at age 1.

$n^d x$ the number of deaths occurring during the age interval given the number of persons alive at the beginning of the interval, l_x, and the proportion of persons dying during the interval. Deaths in the age interval $n^d x$ are derived by multiplying $n^l x$ by $n^q x$.

$n^L x$ the number of person-years lived during the interval. This involves multiplying the number of persons alive at the end of the interval by the span (number of years) of the interval and adding that product to the assumed number of years lived by those dying during the interval. To calculate $n^L x$ for the ages 1–4 in the life table, the following factors were considered: Persons in the l_x column for the ages 5–10 years have all lived four years. Multiplying 98,978 by 4 years equals 395,912 person-years. In addition, the 171 persons dying lived an average of 1.66 years based on official death records. Multiplying 171 by 1.66 equals 283 person-years. The sum of 395,912 and 283 equals 396,195, the number appearing as $n^L x$ in column 5, row 2.

T_x the reverse sum of $n^L x$ values. For example, T_{80-85} is equal to the sum of T_{85} and over and T_{80-85}, or 206,269 + 204,369 = 410,638.

e_x the life expectancy at any age. For example, life expectancy at age 5 is 71.6 years. This column is derived by dividing T_x by l_x. Life expectancy at birth, for example, divides 7,577,757 by 100,000 and yields 75.8 years.

Life tables provide extensive information about the impact of mortality on life expectancy, and it is possible to trace trends in mortality by assembling life table data for more than one time period. Comparative life table analysis can yield information on life expectancy differentials by sex and race for any age. For example, life expectancy at birth is more than seven years longer for females than it is for males, the difference narrows to six years at age 40, three years at age 60, and two years at age 80. If race and sex differences are simultaneously examined, larger variations emerge. African-American females outlive African-American males by nearly nine years from birth. White females outlive African-American males by 14 years from birth.

These data have serious social, economic, and political implications, as well as business implications. At the market level, the identified life expectancy differentials indicate that two very different populations exist when race and sex are considered. When race- and sex-based segmentation and targeting are important, differential life expectancies must be incorporated in order to develop the most effective business plans. Using the African-American male versus white female example, the life table indicates that out of 100,000 white females born (l_0), over 85,000 are alive at age 65 (l_{65-70}). For African-American males, the figure (l_{65-70}) is approximately 57,000, or only about two thirds of the white female population. This differential has serious implications for the segmentation of the mature market.

Based on the above data, it can be concluded that the African-American male population is considerably younger than the other three sex/race groupings, and that the older population is "whiter" than might be expected. Coupled with additional psychographic and behavioral information, specific strategies regarding products, advertising appeals, and distribution channels can be developed for each distinct market segment.

Survival ratios use the life table to calculate the proportion of persons surviving from one age interval to the next. These ratios can be used to determine the percentage of persons alive at a particular point in time who can be expected to be alive at some point in the future. Survival ratios are derived by dividing one L_x (person years lived) figure by another L_x, depending on how far forward or backward the user wishes to look. For example, the survival ratio from Table 6.1 for the age interval 75–80 living to the interval 80–84 is shown below:

$$\text{Survival ratio} = \frac{L_{80-84}}{L_{75-80}} = \frac{204,369}{275,667} = 0.741, \text{ or } 74.1 \text{ percent.}$$

Thus, approximately 74 percent of the persons who were alive at age 75 will also be alive at age 80. This market clearly undergoes significant attrition as it transitions from 75–80 to 80–84.

Cause-specific life tables measure the effect of the hypothetical removal of certain causes of death on overall life expectancy. For example, demographers can produce life tables with the hypothetical removal of cancer to determine the increase in life expectancy that would result if it were possible to eliminate that cause of death.

The same basic life table principles could be used to learn more about the hypothetical effect of changing business conditions on business failures. Studies that identify the reasons for business failure could also assign individual or joint probabilities of failure (e.g., poor management skills or poor management skills *and* undercapitalization). Then the impact of correcting for these factors (removing the probability of failure due to these reasons) on business survival could be measured.

TRENDS IN MORTALITY

Over the past several decades, the United States has experienced a steady increase in the annual number of deaths. This trend is presented in Table 6.2 for the United States between 1935 and 1994. As can be seen, the number of deaths occurring each year has increased by nearly 900,000 over the 60-year period. Further increases in total deaths are inevitable as the age structure of the United States becomes older.

Table 6.2
Total Number of Deaths in the United States: 1935–1994

Year	Deaths[a]
1994	2,286
1990	2,148
1985	2,086
1980	1,990
1975	1,893
1970	1,921
1965	1,828
1960	1,712
1955	1,529
1950	1,452
1945	1,402
1940	1,417
1935	1,393

[a]Deaths in 1,000s.

Sources: U.S. Bureau of the Census (1975). *Historical Statistics of the United States, Colonial Times to 1970*. Bicentennial Edition Part I, Washington DC, U.S. Government Printing Office, Series B 1-4; U.S. Bureau of the Census (1986). *Statistical Abstract of the United States 1986*. Washington, DC, U.S. Government Printing Office, Table 109; U.S. Bureau of the Census (1994), *Statistical Abstract of the United States 1994*. Washington, DC, U.S. Government Printing Office, Table 117; National Center for Health Statistics (1995). *Annual Summary of Births, Marriages, Divorces and Deaths: United States, 1994. Monthly Vital Statistics Report*, Vol. 43, No. 13 (October 23). Washington, DC: Public Health Service.

The increase in the number of deaths has resulted from an increase in the size of the U.S. population and the aging that characterizes it. Death *rates*, on the other hand, have declined, as health services and the standard of living have both improved. Conditions that accounted for a significant proportion of all deaths at an earlier date are now minor contributors. Age-specific mortality rates for eleven age categories for three time periods between 1935 and 1994 are presented in Figure 6.1. Significant reductions in mortality rates can be identified for several ages groups. The most significant reductions include 87 percent for age younger than 1, over 90 percent for ages 1–4, 87 percent for ages 5–14, and 78 percent for ages 25–34! Even at the older ages, mortality rates have declined by 48 percent for ages 75–84

Figure 6.1
Death Rates by Age for the United States: 1935–1994

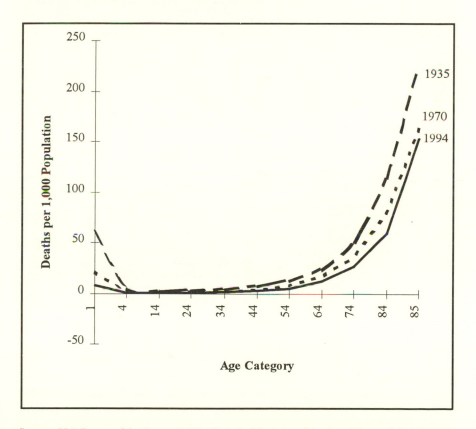

Sources: U.S. Bureau of the Census (1975). *Historical Statistics of the United States, Colonial Times to 1970.* Series B 181-192; National Center for Health Statistics (1995). *Annual Summary of Births, Marriages, Divorces and Deaths: United States (1994).* Monthly Vital Statistics Report, Vol. 43, No. 13. Washington, DC: Public Health Service, Table 5.

and 32 percent for ages 85 and over. While mortality has decreased at all ages, the greatest improvements have come at the younger ages, particularly in the age group characterized by relatively higher mortality.

The infant mortality rate in the United States has declined dramatically during this century. However, the rate of decline has slowed in recent years, leaving the United States with a higher infant mortality rate than most other industrial countries. Table 6.3 presents infant mortality rates from the years 1920–1992 along with maternal mortality rates. In 1992 the infant mortality rate was only 10 percent of what it had been in 1920. The maternal mortality rate had declined to only about 1 percent of its former figure.

Table 6.3
Infant and Maternal Mortality Rates in the United States: 1920–1992

Year	Infant Mortality[a]	Maternal Mortality[b]
1992	8.9	0.8
1990	9.2	0.8
1985	10.6	0.8
1980	12.6	0.9
1970	20.0	2.2
1960	26.0	3.7
1950	29.2	8.3
1940	47.0	37.3
1930	64.6	67.3
1920	85.8	79.9

[a]Deaths per 1,000 live births.

[b]Deaths per 10,000 live births.

Sources: U.S. Bureau of the Census (1975). *Historical Statistics of the United States, Colonial Times to 1970*, Series B 136-147; U.S. Bureau of the Census (1986). Statistical Abstract of the United States, 1986, table 112; U.S. Department of Health and Human Services National Center for Health Statistics (1986). *Advanced Report of Final Mortality Statistics, 1984*. Monthly Vital Statistics Report, vol. 35, No. 6, Table F; U.S. Bureau of the Census (1994), *Statistical Abstract of the United States, 1994*, Table 120.

Evidence of increased longevity for the U.S. population is provided in Figure 6.2, which presents life expectancies at birth for males and females for 13 time periods starting in 1900 and ending in 1994. Over that time span, life expectancy increased by nearly 31 years (or 64 percent) for females and by 26 years (or 56 percent) for males.

The changing differential in life expectancy between males and females reflects the reduction in maternal mortality. In 1900 the sex differential in mortality was only two years (females living longer). As maternal mortality rates declined, life

Figure 6.2
Life Expectancy at Birth by Sex in the United States: 1900–1994

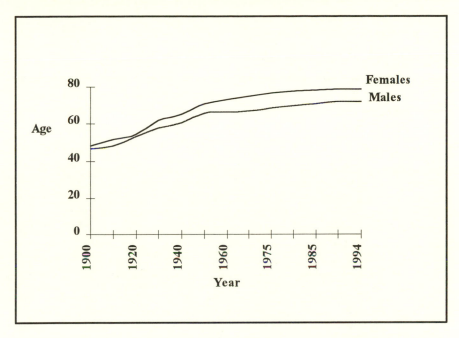

Source: U.S. Bureau of the Census (1975). Historical Statistics of the U.S., Colonial Times to 1970. Series B 107-115; National Center for Health Statistics (1995). *Annual Summary of Births, Marriages, Divorces, and Deaths: United States, 1994.* Monthly Vital Statistics Report, Vol. 43, No. 13. Washington, DC: Public Health Service, Table 7.

expectancy differentials increased. By 1960, when maternal mortality rates had fallen to extremely low levels, the male-female difference in life expectancy had increased to 6.5 years. However, after 1970 the male-female difference narrowed, from 7.7 years in 1970 to 6.7 years in 1994. While the explanation for the narrowing of sex differences includes many variables, increased female labor force participation and subsequent stress-induced mortality and morbidity are critical factors. The increase in the percentage of females who smoke also suggests that women are adopting lifestyles that contribute to earlier death.

Life expectancy data focusing only on two ages, 65 and 85, are shown in Table 6.4. These ages were selected for presentation because they represent ages characterized by recent large increases in absolute numbers (age 65 and over) as well as substantial percentage increases (age 85 and over). Overall, life expectancy at the older ages is surprisingly high. While life expectancy at birth is 75.8 years for both sexes, it rises to 76.6 years if a person survives to age 5. At the older ages, life expectancy far exceeds 75.8 years. Examining the data from row 2 of column 1 of Table 6.4, it can be concluded that life expectancy at age 65 in 1990 was 82.2 years

(17.2 years plus the 65 years that already have been lived). Recent research suggests that life expectancy for healthy older persons is 83 for males and 93 for females (Rogers 1995).

Table 6.4
Life Expectancy at Age 65 and 85 in the United States: 1950–1992

Year	Age 65	Age 85
1992	17.5	6.2
1990	17.2	6.1
1985	16.8	6.1
1980	16.4	5.9
1975	16.0	6.2
1965	14.6	4.7
1955	14.2	5.1
1950	14.1	4.9

Sources: U.S. Department of Health, Education and Welfare (1954). *Vital Statistics of the United States 1950.* Volume 1 Washington DC, U.S. Government Printing Office, Table 8.06; U.S. Department of Health, Education and Welfare (1957). *Vital Statistics of the United States, 1955.* Volume 1, table Az; U.S. Department of Health, Education and Welfare (1967). *Vital Statistics of the United States, 1965.* Volume II— Mortality, Part A, Table 5-4; U.S. Bureau of the Census (1977). Statistical Abstract of the United States, 1977, Table 96; U.S. Bureau of the Census (1984). *Statistical Abstract of the United States, 1984,* Table 103; U.S. Department of Health and Human Services, National Center for Health Statistics (1986). *Mortality Statistics, Monthly Vital Statistics Report,* Vol. 35, No. 6, Table 3; U.S. Bureau of the Census (1994), *Statistical Abstract of the United States, 1994,* Table 116.

By looking at trends over the last 30 years, a more precise measurement of the contribution to overall life expectancy due to increases in life expectancy at ages 65 and 85 is possible. Between 1950 and 1992, life expectancy increased by 10 percent for both males and females (data not shown). The increases in life expectancy at ages 65 and 85 (both sexes combined—data from Table 6.4) were 22 and 20 percent, respectively. Thus, while life expectancy at birth increased substantially over the thirty-two year period, increases at the older ages were even greater.

Closely related to increases in life expectancy are the changes in mortality structure evidenced in Table 6.5. These cause-specific rates were selected from a much longer list of rates. The causes selected reflect the major causes of death in 1900 and 1992. As can be seen, the major causes of death have changed radically since the turn of the century. While cardiovascular disease is the single leading group cause of death for both years, the rate per 100,000 increased by only 4 percent over the 92 year period. On the other hand, the rate for malignant neoplasms rose more than 219 percent, from 64 to 204 deaths per 100,000 population. More remarkable, however, was the decline in rates for the two remaining diseases, influenza and pneumonia, and tuberculosis, 85 and 99 percent, respectively.

Table 6.5
Selected Causes of Death in the United States: 1900–1992

Year	Major Cardiovascular Diseases	Pneumonia & Influenza	Tuberculosis	Malignant Neoplasms
1992	358.8[a]	29.7	0.7	204.1
1990	368.3	32.0	0.7	203.2
1980	436.4	24.1	0.9	183.9
1970	496.0	30.9	2.6	162.8
1940	485.7	70.3	45.9	120.3
1920	364.7	207.3	113.1	83.4
1900	345.2	202.2	194.4	64.0

[a]Deaths per 100,000 population.

Sources: U. S. Bureau of the Census (1975). *Historical Statistics of the United States, Colonial Times to 1970*; Series B 167-180; U.S. Bureau of the Census (1986). *Statistical Abstract of the United States, 1986*. Table 114; U.S. Bureau of the Census (1994), *Statistical Abstract of the United States, 1994*, Table 125.

Ultimately, the key to using any of the measures in a business context is knowing which information is needed. If the business analyst is interested in the growth or decline of the children's market, for example, then fertility and migration data provide the initial information concerning changes in that market. However, mortality, particularly infant mortality, must be accounted for in adjusting market size estimates. On the other hand, the analyst with a need for data on the mature market will be more interested in life expectancies and survival ratios at the older ages, as well as the relative social, economic, and health status of the persons surviving to those ages.

Life table functions are used to determine premiums for various types of insurance. Actuaries must make factor in such phenomena as the ability of ships to survive in convoys during wartime, the probability of plant shutdowns, or the likelihood of a fire. There is even the threat of "failure-to-predict" malpractice suits against actuaries for their failure to adequately assess the risk of a certain phenomenon. There are also a variety of non-insurance-related uses of life table principles that are useful to business executives. The same principles are applied to the life expectancies of products such as automobiles. Those with the most favorable expectancies could use that information in promotional efforts. These same techniques are used to help direct production of spare parts, as well. The requisite probabilities of survival and life expectancies might be calculated by prospective lenders to help determine the creditworthiness of businesses that wish to borrow money. Life table calculations also could help retailers more effectively measure the turnover of goods sold, including the proportion that could be expected to still be on the shelf after one week, two weeks, three weeks, and so on.

MORBIDITY

Morbidity refers to the level and type of sickness and disability within a population. While death certificates are required by law for persons who expire, no such registration exists for sickness. Sickness is recorded by physicians and other health care personnel, but only when it is observed and correctly diagnosed. For example, many persons with influenza never see a health care professional and these cases go unreported. More serious illnesses, however, are generally correctly diagnosed and recorded. Unless they involve certain contagious diseases, however, incidents of sickness are not systematically recorded.

For demographers, morbidity analysis involves identifying both the static and dynamic aspects of sickness, as well as the ways in which those patterns affect mortality. Static dimensions include not only a profile of diseases within a population, but information on the geographic distribution of these conditions. The dynamic dimension focuses on the connection between population change (size, composition, and distribution) and the morbidity profile. As national and subnational population change occurs, the morbidity profile of the affected populations is altered. Today, for example, the aging of the American population has transformed the morbidity profile for the United States from one dominated by acute conditions to one dominated by chronic conditions and disorders of the elderly such as cancer and heart disease.

MEASURING MORBIDITY

Several measures have been developed for morbidity analysis. The first involves the simple counting of officially recognizable conditions. "Reportable" conditions are those for which information is systematically collected, tabulated, and published by the Centers for Disease Control and Prevention (CDCP) and by state and local health offices. Public health officials are particularly interested in these conditions since they have the potential to spread to epidemic proportions. From a business perspective, the providers of prevention and treatment services need to know the size of the potential market.

There are some other conditions that are monitored through reports from health facilities, sample surveys, and ongoing panel studies. Panel studies involve the periodic interview and/or examination of a sample of persons over time. Most surveys, on the other hand, occur only once for a given sample of persons or households. Federal health agencies conduct periodic surveys of hospital inpatients and ambulatory patients utilizing clinics and other outpatient services. In addition, databases have been established for the systematic compilation of data on inpatient utilization and, to a lesser extent, outpatient utilization. These data collection efforts allow for the identification of cases for a wide variety of conditions and the monitoring of the level of these conditions over time. While this information is invaluable, coverage is far from complete. It also should be noted that these compilations include only reported cases. If individuals afflicted by various disorders are not diagnosed and treated, they will not show up in these studies.

Another approach to the development of morbidity indicators is the use of symptom checklists in sample surveys. A list of symptoms that has been statistically validated is utilized to collect data for the calculation of a morbidity index. These symptom checklists are utilized to derive health status measures for both physical and mental illness. Usually there are 15 or 20 symptoms, since it is hard to retain respondents' attention much longer. In the calculation of an index, the number of symptoms is simply summed and this figure becomes the index score for that individual. In some cases, the symptoms may be weighted on the assumption that some may be more important than others in the determination of morbidity levels. For example, chest pains may be given more weight than an occasional cough.

Another group of health status measures might be generally referred to as disability measures. Like other aspects of morbidity, disability is extremely difficult to operationalize. While it would appear simple to enumerate the sight, hearing, or mobility impaired, the situation is actually quite complex. A wide variety of other conditions that are not so clear-cut cloud the picture. Does lower back pain that interferes with work constitute a disability? When does an arthritic condition become disabling? How is mental retardation classified, and at what point? Even those disabilities that appear obvious defy easy categorization due to the subjective dimension of disability. There are many hearing impaired individuals and amputees, for example, that would take exception to being classified as disabled. The extent of this definitional problem has been recognized by the U.S. Census Bureau, which (after an unsuccessful data collection attempt in 1970) decided to discontinue a question on disability. No one could agree on what constituted a disability. Another attempt at calculating the level of "work disability" within the population was made with the 1990 census. Future efforts at measuring disability could be based upon the definitions of disability provided in the Americans with Disabilities Act passed by the U.S. Congress in 1990.

This definitional problem is partly resolved by the utilization of more objective and easily measured indicators as proxies for disability. These might be referred to as "restriction" indicators, since they reflect the extent to which affected individuals are restricted in terms of work or school activities. Measures in this category include: work-loss days, school-loss days, bed-restricted days, and limitation of activity indicators. The number of days missed from work or school, the number of days individuals are restricted to bed, and the extent to which individuals cannot carry out routine daily activities can all be calculated and used as proxy measures of morbidity. While such measures increasingly are being used, it should be remembered that much of this information is available only from sample surveys. It is possible that many "cases" go undiscovered and uncounted. Nevertheless, significant variations have been identified in terms of the demographic correlates of disability as measured in this manner.

Assuming that high-quality morbidity data are available, several other measures can be utilized. Two of the most useful measures are incidence and prevalence rates. An *incidence rate* refers to the number of new cases of a disease or condition over a certain time period expressed as a number per 1,000; 10,000; or 100,000 population-at-risk. A *prevalence rate* divides the total number of persons with the disease or condition in question by the population-at-risk with respect to a specific point in time. Again, the population-at-risk is the number of persons who have some nonzero probability of contracting the condition in question.

Incidence and prevalence rates both serve a useful planning purpose. If the analyst knows, for example, that the incidence rate for a certain medical procedure is 17 per 1,000 population aged 65 years and over, then the demand for that procedure five years in the future can be projected if the size of the population of persons aged 65 and over for the market area in question is known. Of course, this assumes that the rate is constant over the five-year period, although additional assumptions about rate changes can be used as a basis for adjustment. If demographers can provide the population projections, the task of projecting demand may be a relatively simple one—multiply the incidence rate by the population projection. The prevalence rate can be used in much the same way when the condition is a chronic one. This is the precise approach many hospitals and other health care providers use to forecast demand for their services. A more useful set of figures can be generated by creating a set of projections based on different assumptions (likely scenarios), given that incidence and prevalence rates may change over time and that population projections may vary.

The incidence rate is also a valuable measure in epidemiological investigations. If a new or mysterious condition afflicts a population, epidemiologists can trace the spread of the condition through the population by backtracking using incidence data. Such was the case in the 1995 outbreak of the Ebola virus in Africa. The cause or population of origin of a new disease can often only be determined by identifying the characteristics of the victims and the conditions under which the disease was contracted. The exact date of occurrence becomes crucial if the epidemiological detective is to link the onset to a particular set of circumstances. Quite often the key is the demographic characteristics of the victims. AIDS is also a case in point, wherein the means of transmission is identified based on the characteristics of the victims. While a general rate for AIDS shows a steady increase, the rates specific to those subpopulations experiencing the vast majority of cases show the sharpest rises. Geographical information systems are increasingly being utilized in epidemiological analyses and these are discussed in Chapter 7.

Two additional rates utilized by demographers and epidemiologists are case rates and case fatality rates. A *case rate* is merely an expression of the reported incidence of a disease per 1,000; 10,000; or 100,000 persons and is not as finely tuned as a rate that is adjusted for the population at risk. The *case fatality rate* is a measure of mortality from a specific disease. It is generated by dividing the number of persons who die from a certain disease by the number of persons who contracted that disease. The quotient is expressed as a percentage. For example, the 1987 case fatality rate for children who were diagnosed as having AIDS in 1983 was about 67 percent; that is, about two thirds of the children diagnosed as having AIDS in 1983 had died by 1987 (Monmany 1987). It is possible to refine the above rates to include more narrowly defined populations at risk. However, measurement techniques are in need of further development, especially now that there is access to the detailed data required for such expansion and improvement.

TRENDS IN MORBIDITY

The major development in morbidity in this century has been the shift from the dominance of acute conditions to the emergence of chronic conditions as the main cause of ill health. The trend away from acute conditions can be seen in part in the reduction of the incidence rates for many infectious and parasitic diseases. While there were approximately 47,400 reported cases of measles in 1970, there were only 876 in 1994. This same downward trend can be seen over the same time period in the data for tuberculosis (37,100 to 18,452), mumps (105,000 to 1,225 cases), and malaria (3,100 to 929 cases) (U.S. Bureau of the Census 1994c, Table 204; U.S. Department of Health and Human Services, 1995b, Table 11).

On the other hand, cardiovascular diseases and cancer, the two leading causes of death in the United States today, typically do not immediately result in death and, therefore, require a different health care delivery system from one dominated by acute conditions. In fact, an estimated 80 percent of contemporary health conditions are neither immediately fatal nor curable (Strauss 1986). Thus, a large proportion of our population is under lifelong management for such conditions as hypertension, arthritis, or diabetes. For example, in 1992, 22 million, 28 million, and 33 million Americans had heart disease, high blood pressure, or an arthritic condition, respectively (U.S. Bureau of the Census 1994c, Table 208).

Diseases and health conditions have been linked to the demographic characteristics of those more likely or less likely to be afflicted. Even among the elderly who have higher rates of morbidity, wide differences exist in chronic disease prevalence. While about 45 percent of the population aged 65 and over has high blood pressure (a chronic condition), about 15 percent report cancer, diabetes, and/or a previous heart attack. Women are more likely than men to report high blood pressure, cancer, hip fractures, and diabetes (Brown 1989). Women are also more likely to report having anemia, nervous disorders, and respiratory conditions. Similar sex differences in chronic conditions have been reported at all ages (Verbrugge 1988).

The infectious but chronic disease receiving the greater amount of current attention is AIDS. The number of diagnosed cases has increased from 199 in 1981 to over 500,000 as of November 1995 (U.S. Department of Health and Human Services 1995a, Table 1). The spread of this disease has become a major concern, since it is fatal in virtually every case and is spread by means of social interaction. In 1994 alone, nearly 42,000 persons died from complications of the AIDS virus. Moreover, there is evidence that AIDS deaths are under reported by 5 to 8 percent (Lindan and Associates 1990). In addition, pediatric AIDS cases are on the rise. In 1987, 753 children age 0–12 were diagnosed as having AIDS. Between 1987 and 1995 the number of cases diagnosed annually increased to 6,064 (U.S. Department of Health and Human Services 1995a, Table 1).

Lifestyles and environmental factors have been increasingly linked to morbidity. Heart disease has been linked to health-related behavior in the early years of life. New research shows a strong association between high cholesterol levels in the blood of teenagers and the early stages of atherosclerosis. A combination of smoking and high levels of low-density lipid (LDL) cholesterol has a deleterious effect on artery walls. Tobacco and alcohol consumption have both been directly linked to a host of diseases and ultimately to increased levels of mortality. Public pressure from sources ranging from the Surgeon General's statements with regard to the relationship between smoking and lung cancer to congressional actions limiting the advertising of tobacco products have contributed to a reduction in cigarette consumption in the United States.

BUSINESS IMPLICATIONS OF MORTALITY AND MORBIDITY

There are both direct and indirect implications of mortality and morbidity for the business environment. As discussed earlier, the funeral business is relatively large in the United States. Moreover, additional death-related services such as hospice and bereavement counseling are important as well. The health services industry, more closely associated with morbidity, is a major source of business growth and employment. The United States currently spends approximately 14 percent of its gross domestic product (or $884.2 billion in 1993) on health services. Between 1990 and 1993 alone, annual health care expenditures increased nearly $185 billion.

Indirect effects include the impact of the decline in death rates on the aging of the U.S. population. While age composition is a major focus of Chapter 9, it should be noted that the older, and, in general, healthier population of today constitutes a very different market for products and services from that seen just a few decades ago. At the same time, improvements in mortality have resulted in an older population that will spend more years dependent on others because of increased prevalence of disability (Crimmins, Hayward, and Saito 1994). In addition, the importance of mortality on the rate of growth and absolute number of persons for markets of all sizes must be considered. Lower death rates result in fewer deaths, all other factors being the same, and thus higher rates of growth.

Business activities associated with the prevention and treatment of the major causes of death in the United States have increased dramatically since World War II. While the cancer and cardiovascular disease "industries" have received a great deal of media attention, other less well known potential medical breakthroughs could affect mortality rates and the physical and mental health of the entire population. A drug designed to block some of the ills of aging, for example, was initially tested in humans in 1986. Antiaging total skin supplements, that is said to minimize the signs of aging by reducing facial wrinkles are now being produced. Drugs for the treatment of debilitating diseases such as arthritis are continually being developed and tested. As drug treatment advances are made and breakthroughs occur, the quality of life for the entire population will improve and the business opportunities related to the development and distribution of these drugs will grow.

Several other significant developments have already occurred. Diagnostic test kits for HIV, although surrounded by controversy, are already big sellers. A recently developed AIDS vaccine, for example, would have to be administered every two weeks for life, although most recent reports are not optimistic about a "cure" for AIDS being available in the near future. Given the large number of vaccine users, the projected profits would be enormous. Obviously, the business opportunities related to AIDS detection and prevention are significant. While the social and moral motivations for entering such a market are important, the profit motive should not be overlooked.

Declining mortality, increased life expectancy, and changing patterns of mortality and morbidity are all helping to reshape the business environment. New business opportunities are appearing and the characteristics of customers are changing. Future breakthroughs in medical technology as well as progress in combating disease and death will continue to affect the size and composition of markets.

REFERENCES

Brown, Scott C. (1989). "Chronic Conditions in Older Americans: What Roles Do Age, Sex, and Location Play." Paper presented at the Annual Meeting of the Southern Demographic Association, Durham, North Carolina.

Crimmins, Eileen M., Mark D. Hayward, and Yasuhiko Saito (1994). "Changing Mortality and Morbidity Rates and the Health Status and Life Expectancy of the Older Population." *Demography*, 31 (1): 159–175.

Das Gupta, Prithwis (1993). *Standardization and Decomposition of Rates: A User's Manual*. U.S. Bureau of the Census, Current Population Reports, Series P-23-186. Washington, DC: U.S. Government Printing Office.

Halli, Shiva S., and K. Vaninadha Rao (1992). *Advanced Techniques of Population Analysis*. New York: Plenum.

Linden, Christian P., and Associates (1990). "Underreporting of Minority AIDS Deaths in San Francisco Bay Area, 1985–86." *Public Health Reports*, 105 (July–August): 400–404.

Manton, Kenneth, L. S. Corder, and Eric Stallard (1993). "Estimates of Change in Chronic Disability and Institutional Incidence and Prevalence Rates in the U.S. Elderly Population from the 1982, 1984 and 1989 National Long Term Care Survey." *Journal of Gerontology*, 48 (5): 170–182.

Monmany, Terence (1987). "Kids with AIDS." *Newsweek* (September 7): 51–59.

National Center for Health Statistics (1974). *Vital Statistics of the United States, 1970*, Vol. 11, Mortality, part B. Washington, DC: U.S. Public Health Service.

National Center for Health Statistics (1995a). *Vital Statistics of the United States, 1991*. Vol. 11, Mortality, part B. Washington, DC: U.S. Public Health Service.

National Center for Health Statistics (1995b). *Advance Report of Final Mortality Statistics, 1992*. Monthly Vital Statistics Report, Vol. 43, No. 6 Washington, DC: U.S. Public Health Service.

Pol, Louis G., and Richard K. Thomas (1992). *The Demography of Health and Health Care*. New York: Plenum.

Rogers, Richard (1995). "Sociodemographic Characteristics of Long-Lived and Healthy Individuals." *Population and Development Review*, 21 (March): 33–58.

Schoen, Robert (1988). *Modeling Multigroup Populations*. New York: Plenum.
Smith, David P. (1992). *Formal Demography*. New York: Plenum.
Strauss, Anselm (1986). "Chronic Illness" in Conrad, Peter and Rochelle Kern (eds.), The Sociology of Health and Health Care. New York: St. Martin's.
U.S. Bureau of the Census (1994a). *1992 Census of Service Industries*, Geographic Area Series, Nebraska. Washington, DC: U.S. Government Printing Office.
U.S. Bureau of the Census (1994b). *1992 Census of Service Industries*. Washington, DC: U.S. Government Printing Office.
U.S. Bureau of the Census (1994c). *Statistical Abstract of the United States, 1994*. Washington, DC: U.S. Government Printing Office.
U.S. Department of Health and Human Services (1995a). *Morbidity and Mortality Weekly Report*. Vol. 44, No. 46 (November 24) Washington, DC: U.S. Government Printing Office.
U.S. Department of Health and Human Services (1995b). *Morbidity and Mortality Weekly Report*. Vol. 44, No. 44 (November 24) Washington, DC: U.S. Government Printing Office.
Verbrugge, Lois (1988). "Life and Death Paradox." *American Demographics* (July): 34–37.

SUGGESTED READINGS

Farley, Reynolds, and Walter R. Allen (1987). *The Color Line and the Quality of Life in America*. New York: Russell Sage Foundation.
Manton, Kenneth G., and Eric Stallard (1984). *Recent Trends in Mortality Analysis*. Orlando, FL: Academic Press.
Rosenwaike, Ira (1985). *The Extreme Aged in America*. Westport, CT: Greenwood Press.
Rowe, John W., and Robert L. Kahn (1987). "Human Aging: Usual and Successful." *Science*, 237: 143–149.
Smith, David W. E. (1993). *Human Longevity*. New York: Oxford University.
Suzman, Richard M., David P. Willis, and Kenneth G. Manton (eds.) (1992). *The Oldest Old*. New York: Oxford University Press.
Vallin, Jacques, Stan D'Souza, and Alberto Palloni (eds.) (1990). *Measurement and Analysis of Mortality: New Approaches*. Oxford: Clarendon Press.

Chapter 7

Geographic Concepts and Measures

INTRODUCTION

Business demographers need a command of geography for one basic reason: virtually every business application is linked in one way or another to some specific geographic unit. Business decisions are made in the context of these geographic units. Even when a market is delineated as some combination of demographic and psychographic factors (e.g., Asian males 25–34 years of age who live an "average" lifestyle), a more precise identification of where that market is physically located must eventually be established in order to develop appropriate business responses.

In the preparation for site location studies, analysts compile data for various geographic units and make comparisons of the relevant characteristics. If the site is intended for a business where customers are very time and/or distance sensitive, the location of the store must be in proximity to the target audience. If the store is a new entrant in the market, data will be gathered by zip code, census tract, block group, or some other unit that offers the business planner the ability to define the market at a low level of geography.

Assuming that the market area is thought to be the population within a two-mile radius of three prospective sites, for example, the researcher would first draw circles with a two-mile radius around the three sites and collect demographic and other data that describe those potential markets. Comparisons along relevant dimensions would lead to the identification of the "best" of the three potential sites. Box 7.1 provides a brief discussion of the importance of geography to business decision making on the part of a health maintenance organization (HMO).

Relatively recent developments in data accessibility for a variety of geographic units have resulted in more refined and better quality business demographic studies. Demographic data now are available for a myriad of geographic units in formats that are easy to use (e.g., CD-ROM, internet, and diskette). Data for a collection of block

Box 7.1
Geography Does Make a Difference

Does geography make a difference? Most often when people talk of the difference in living in rural versus urban areas or metropolitan versus nonmetropolitan areas they think in terms of amenities and lifestyle. From a business perspective, owners and managers think in terms of market size, product distribution, and location with respect to competitors, among a host of factors that vary by the size and the nature of markets. However, there are other factors worthy of consideration.

The spread of health maintenance organizations (HMOs) and other managed health care programs has been swift. Today, about 16 percent of all Americans receive health care coverage through an HMO, up from 4 percent in 1980. Not all managed care markets are the same, however. HMOs are reimbursed at different rates in different areas for patients who are covered by Medicare, for example. The federal government uses what is called average adjusted per capita cost (AAPCC) to determine the level at which to reimburse service providers. The national average is $400 per month, which means that for each Medicare-eligible person who is covered by an HMO plan, $400 is paid monthly to the HMO. Nevertheless, there is a great deal of geographic variation in payments. For example, in Los Angeles an HMO is paid $558 per member per month. The highest amount is $646 in New York City and the lowest $176 in many rural counties.

Some health care experts contend that because of low AAPCC-based payments, managed care companies have not been able to offer comprehensive plans in sparsely populated areas. When HMO services are offered in rural areas, copayments are often required for office visits, prescriptions, and eye glasses. On the other hand, large-market HMOs can provide these services without copayments. They may also offer "free" services such as dental coverage.

This profit margin differential clearly serves to discourage potential providers of rural health services. Per capita cost reimbursement differences have not gone unnoticed by the business community. Rural areas have fewer HMO options, if they have any at all. Potential providers of health services find investments in urban markets much more attractive.

groups can be aggregated to approximate the boundaries of a uniquely shaped market area.

A second recent development relates to the *geocoding* of nondemographic data. Individual customer records, transaction reports, competitor locations, and other valuable data are being assigned geographic identifiers (e.g., latitude and longitude), which enable the information to be aggregated by virtually any unit of geography. This availability of demographic and nondemographic data specific to targeted geographic units enables the business planner to know more about a market area than was ever before possible. A longer discussion of the most recent developments in this arena is provided at the end of this chapter.

TYPES OF GEOGRAPHIC UNITS

Business planners organize geographic units into logical categories to facilitate their use. Figure 7.1 presents a simple typology of geographic units designed to assist the reader in distinguishing these categories. Geographic units may result from a legal designation or be produced for statistical purposes or some other use. National, state, county, and city boundaries are set by law and, with the exception of city boundaries, changes are infrequent. In the cases of cities, annexation and other legal changes in boundaries are frequent occurrences. In some areas of the United States, however, annexation activity is quite limited or has totally ceased because most, if not all, contiguous land has already been annexed. Users of city data, in particular, must take boundary changes into consideration if data for two or more time periods are being used. Often the apparent change over time is due to the addition of population through annexation and *not* because the population within the original boundaries has changed.

Figure 7.1
Categories of Geographic Units

Political	Statistical	Other
National	Region	Zip Codes
State	Division	Markets
County	Metropolitan Statistical Area	Target Audience
City	Urbanized area	Area of Dominant
Congressional Districts	Census Tract	Influence
State Legislative Districts	Census Block Numbering Area	
School Districts	Census Block Group	
	Census Block	

Congressional district, state legislative, and school district boundaries are reconfigured periodically. Congressional boundaries are redrawn after each census, and there is a long history of "unusual" boundaries being drawn to serve the political, social, or economic needs of certain constituencies (Terrie 1996). Recent court decisions may place greater restrictions on how these boundaries are drawn. School district boundaries can change more frequently, such as when districts are combined and/or annexation takes place. School-specific boundary changes within districts also can occur frequently in areas experiencing rapid population growth or decline.

Statistical boundaries have been created for a variety of purposes, but primarily to allow federal and state agencies to aggregate data in a consistent and useful fashion. Standards for metropolitan areas and other statistical units are set by the Office of Management and Budget and almost always adhered to. Metropolitan boundaries do change, as urban influence expands. Because the entire United States was divided into census blocks for the 1990 census, small area boundaries will be much more stable in the future. Users of data who wish to focus on change are cautioned to check for boundary changes in the places of study before analyses are performed.

Types of boundaries other than those discussed above are central to many business applications. These "other" boundaries may represent the combination of units identified in the political and statistical categories, although this is not always the case. Given the technological capabilities now available, it is now much easier to use customized boundaries.

Two commonly used areas, zip codes, and areas of dominant influence (ADIs), were created for purposes other than data collection and should be recognized for this limitation. It is rare, for example, for a zip code to approximate a market area; thus the use of zip code areas for business analysis must be carefully considered. Zip code usage, even with zip + 4, may result in suboptimal information and, ultimately, poor business decisions. The boundaries for many geographic units frequently utilized in business analysis are subject to change, but in the cases of markets, target audiences and other business-related boundaries, this is an accepted fact of life.

Figure 7.2 presents the hierarchy of statistical data collection at the federal level. It begins with the highest level of geography and ends with the lowest level recognized in government statistical analysis. The geographic units shown in Figure 7.2 are the end product of a statistical system designed to aggregate individual-level data for persons, households, or businesses. The criteria for aggregation at a statistical level are likely to be different from those used for business decision making. Figure 7.3 presents a map of the United States with state, divisional, and regional boundaries.

The geographic units discussed over the next several pages are assigned Federal Information Processing Standards (FIPS) numerical codes. States, metropolitan areas, counties, and cities all have a set of codes. Census tracts, block numbering areas, block groups, and blocks are coded as well. For example, the state/county code 101 refers to Montgomery County in Alabama. Codes 1180 and 5240 refer to the city and MSA designation, respectively, for Montgomery.

States, Regions, and Divisions

States are the major political units of the United States. This includes the 50 states, with the District of Columbia treated as a state equivalent. Census *regions* have been created by grouping states for data presentation and analysis purposes. There are four regions designated by the federal government, and their boundaries are based on geographic proximity and economic/social homogeneity. These four regions are divided into nine *divisions*, each composed of several states.

As can be seen in Figure 7.3, the Midwest Region is divided into the East North Central and the West North Central divisions. The East North Central division is composed of Wisconsin, Illinois, Michigan, Indiana, and Ohio. Again, geographic proximity and economic/social homogeneity are the criteria for grouping, and these boundaries have remained unchanged since they were originally established.

Figure 7.2
Hierarchy of Federal Statistical Data Aggregation

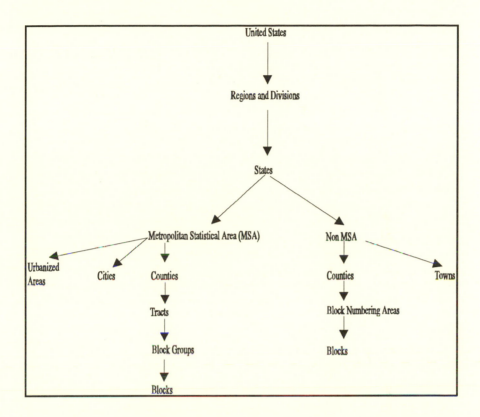

Metropolitan Statistical Areas

The *metropolitan statistical area* represents an attempt to standardize the definition of heterogeneous urban areas. Metropolitan refers to a large urban agglomeration of people. An MSA is a geographic area consisting of a large population nucleus together with adjacent communities having a high degree of economic and social integration with that nucleus. The major purpose of designating MSAs is to enable all federal agencies to use the same geographic definitions in tabulating and publishing data for large urban agglomerations. The use of standard metropolitan boundaries also gets around the problem of comparing cities that are defined in varying ways. While metropolitan definitions have been developed for statistical use by federal agencies, state and local governments, as well as private business firms, have often found the definitions helpful in understanding and presenting data for market areas.

Figure 7.3
Census Regions and Geographic Divisions of the United States

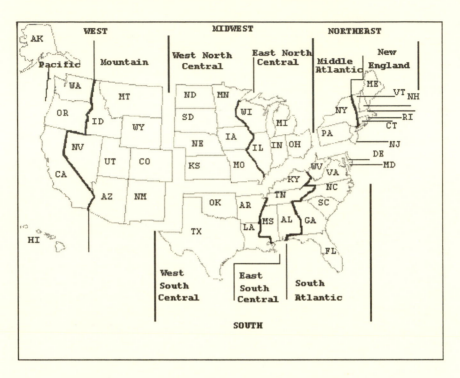

The basic geographic unit of an MSA is the county. In certain states, however, an MSA may be defined in terms of townships, boroughs, or parishes because these geographic units are utilized as county equivalents. An area qualifies for designation as an MSA in one of two ways: (1) it includes a city of at least 50,000 or more inhabitants or (2) it includes a Census Bureau–defined "urbanized area" of at least 50,000 inhabitants with a total MSA population of at least 100,000 (75,000 in New England).[1] In addition to the county or county equivalent containing the main city or urbanized area, a MSA may include additional outlying counties that have certain metropolitan characteristics. A metropolitan area may contain more than one city of 50,000 population and may cross state lines.

Within metropolitan complexes of 1 million or more persons, separate component areas may be defined if specified criteria are met. Such areas are designated *primary metropolitan statistical areas* (PMSAs). Local opinion must support separate recognition of PMSAs, with local area leaders surveyed to ascertain

---

[1]An urbanized area is made up of a large city, usually 50,000 or more persons, and the densely inhabited areas adjacent to the city (e.g., suburbs)

agreement for the distinction. When PMSAs are established, the MSA of which they are a component part is redesignated as a *consolidated metropolitan statistical areas* (CMSA). Besides the 21 CMSAs, there were 19 MSAs of 1 million or more persons in 1990 within which no component PMSAs were established. For example, the Akron (Ohio) PMSA is part of the Cleveland-Akron-Lorain (Ohio) CMSA.

All MSAs are titled using the names of their largest cities; up to three city names may appear. Each area title also includes the names or abbreviations of the states into which the area extends. The New York-Northern New Jersey-Long Island CMSA, for example, includes areas from New York, New Jersey, and Connecticut. One or more central cities are specified in each CMSA and MSA; all cities included in MSA names are central cities, but some areas also have additional central cities not included in the area title.

Counties

The primary political divisions of the states are termed *counties*. In Louisiana, these divisions are known as *parishes*. In Alaska, which has no counties, the county equivalents are the organized *boroughs* and *census areas* that are delineated for statistical purposes by the State of Alaska and the Census Bureau. In four States (Maryland, Missouri, Nevada, and Virginia), there are one or more cities that are independent of any county organization and thus constitute a primary division. These are known as *independent cities* and are treated as equivalent to counties for statistical purposes. The District of Columbia has no primary divisions and the entire area is considered equivalent to a county for statistical purposes.

Cities

The designation *city* generally refers to a political subdivision of a state within a defined area over which a municipal corporation has been established to provide local government functions, facilities, and services. The city category includes any area incorporated as a city, village, borough (except in Alaska and New York), or town (except in the six New England states, New York, and Wisconsin).

Urbanized Areas

Urbanized areas are defined by the Bureau of the Census to include the entire densely settled area in and around each large city. An urbanized area must have a population of at least 50,000 and a population density of at least 1,000 persons per square mile, although the boundary may include some less densely settled areas within the corporate limits. Nonresidential areas such as industrial parks, railroad yards, and golf courses may also fall within the urbanized areas.

Box 7.2 offers a detailed series of definitions for MSAs and their component parts. Because MSAs are often used to delineate market areas, it is important that persons who utilize MSA-specific data know a great deal about this unit of analysis.

Box 7.2
Official Standards for Establishing MSAs

Basic Standards

    Basic standards apply to all states except the six New England states listed in Figure 7.3.

1.   Population size requirements for qualification:
    A.   Each MSA must include a city that, with contiguous, densely settled territory, constitutes a Census Bureau–defined urbanized area with at least 50,000 population.
    B.   If the MSA's largest city has less than 50,000 population, the urbanized area must have a total population of at least 100,000.

2.   Central counties:
    A county is designated as a central county of the MSA if:
    A.   At least 50 percent of its population lives in the urbanized area that resulted in qualification under section 1A, or
    B.   At least 25 percent of its population lives in a central city of the MSA.

3.   Outlying counties:
    A.   An outlying county is included in an MSA if any of the four following conditions is met:
        (1)   At least 50 percent of the employed workers residing in the county commute to the central county or counties, and the population density of the county is at least 25 persons per square mile.
        (2)   From 40 to 50 percent of the employed workers commute to the central county or counties, and the population density is at least 35 persons per square mile.
        (3)   From 25 to 40 percent of the employed workers commute to the central county or counties, the population density is at least 35 persons per square mile, and any one of the following conditions also exists:
            (a)   Population density is at least 50 persons per square mile.
            (b)   At least 35 percent of the population is urban.
            (c)   At least 10 percent, or a minimum of 5,000, of the population lives in the urbanized area that resulted in qualification under 1A.
        (4)   From 15 to 25 percent of the employed workers commute to the central county or counties, the population density is at least 50 persons per square mile, and any two of the following conditions also exist:

Box 7.2 continued

        (a)   Population density is at least 60 persons per square mile.

        (b)   At least 35 percent of the population is urban.

        (c)   Population growth between the last two decennial censuses is at least 20 percent.

        (d)   At least 10 percent, or a minimum of 5,000, of the population lives in the urbanized area that resulted in qualification under section 1A.

   B.   If a county qualifies on the basis of commuting to the central county or counties of two different MSAs, it is assigned to the area to which commuting is greater, unless the relevant commuting percentages are within five points of each other, in which case local opinion about the most appropriate assignment is considered.

4.   Central cities

Recognized as the central city or cities of the MSA are:

   A.   The city with the largest population in the MSA.

   B.   Each additional city with a population of at least 250,000 or with at least 100,000 persons working within its limits.

   C.   Each additional city with a population of at least 25,000, an employment/residence ratio of at least 0.75, and outcommuting (lives in city, works elsewhere) of less than 60 percent of its resident employed workers.

   D.   Each additional city of 15,000 to 25,000 population that is at least one third as large as the largest central city, has an employment/residence ratio of at least 0.75, and has outcommuting of less than 60 percent of its resident employed workers.

Standards for New England

In the six New England states, the cities and towns are administratively more important than the counties, and a wide range of data are compiled locally for these entities. Therefore, the cities and towns are the units used to define MSAs in these states. The New England standards are based primarily on population density and commuting. The basic standards for New England MSAs are discussed in 5 and 6. As a basis for measuring commuting, a central core is first defined for each New England urbanized area, corresponding to the central counties that are identified in the states outside New England.

5.   New England central cores

A central core is determined in each New England urbanized area through the definition of two zones.

Box 7.2 continued

  A. Zone A comprises:

      (1) The largest city in the urbanized area.

      (2) Each other place in the urbanized area or in a contiguous urbanized area that qualifies as a central city under section 4, provided at least 15 percent of its resident employed workers work in the largest city in the urbanized area.

      (3) Each other city or town with at least 50 percent of whose population lives in the urbanized or a contiguous urbanized area, provided at least 15 percent of its resident employed workers work in the largest city in the urbanized area plus any additional central cities qualified by 12A(2).

  B. Zone B comprises each city or town that:

      (1) Has at least 50 percent of its population living in the urbanized area or in a contiguous urbanized area, and

      (2) Has at least 15 percent of its resident employed workers working in zone A.

  C. The central core comprises zone A, zone B, and any city or town that is physically surrounded by zone A or B, except those cities or towns that are not contiguous with the main portion of the central core are not included.

  D. If a city or two qualifies under 12A through C for more than one central core, it is assigned to the core to which commuting is greatest unless the relevant commuting percentages are within five points of each other, in which case local opinion as to the most appropriate assignment is also considered.

6.   Outlying cities and towns

  A. A city or town contiguous to a central core as defined by 12 is included in its MSA if:

      (1) It has a population density of at least 60 persons per square mile and at least 30 percent of its resident employed workers work in the central core, or

      (2) It has a population density of at least 100 persons per square mile and at least 15 percent of the employed workers living in the city or town work in the central core.

  B. If a city or town has the qualifying amount of commuting to two different central cores, it is assigned to the MSA to which commuting is greater unless the relevant commuting percentages are within five points of each other, in which case local opinion as to the most appropriate assignment will also be considered.

  C. If a city or town has the qualifying level of commuting to a central core but has greater commuting to a nonmetropolitan city or town, it will not be assigned to any MSA unless the relevant commuting percentages are within five points of each other, in which case local opinion as to the most appropriate assignment will also be considered.

Box 7.2 continued

7.   Applicability of basic standards to New England MSAs

    A.   An area defined by 5 and 6 qualifies as an MSA provided it contains a city
        of at least 50,000 population or has a total population of at least 75,000.
    B.   The area's central cities are determined according to the standards of 4.

Source: U.S. Bureau of the Census.

Census Tracts, Block Numbering Areas, Block Groups, and Blocks

Census tracts are small statistical subdivisions of a county established by the
Census Bureau for statistical purposes. In theory, census tracts contain relatively
homogeneous populations, but population transitions within MSAs over time often
alter the original homogeneity. Besides their statistical value, tracts also serve as
planning areas for state and local governments, and, more recently, they have proven
useful for business planning. Census tracts are established for all metropolitan areas
and other densely populated counties by local census statistical area committees
following Census Bureau guidelines. Six states (California, Connecticut, Delaware,
Hawaii, New Jersey, and Rhode Island) and the District of Columbia are covered
entirely by census tracts.

Census tracts do not cross county boundaries. The spatial size of census tracts
varies widely depending on the density of settlement, and although the average size
is about 4,000 persons, it is not unusual to find tracts with fewer than 1,000 and
more than 7,000 persons. Census tract boundaries are established with the intention
of being more or less permanent so that statistical comparisons can be made from
census to census. However, physical changes in street patterns caused by highway
construction and other new developments may require occasional revisions. Census
tracts often are subdivided in response to substantial population growth or combined
as a result of substantial population decline. Census tracts are referred to as "tracts"
in all 1990 census data products. In counties without census tracts, for the most part
nonmetropolitan counties, *block numbering areas* (BNAs) have been established.
They also average about 4,000 persons, but are made up of larger areas of land.

Census tracts are further subdivided into *block groups*, smaller geographic areas
averaging around 1,000 persons. The term block group is used for both census tracts
and BNAs, although the land area for block groups within BNAs is larger. The
populations of block groups contain are typically more homogenous than those of
the larger census tracts.

Block groups are further subdivided into census blocks. Census blocks are small
areas bounded on all sides by visible features such as streets, roads, streams, and
railroad tracks, and by invisible boundaries such as city, town, township, and county

limits, property lines, and short, imaginary extensions of streets and roads. The greatest level of homogeneity is found in *blocks*. Average block size for tracted areas is 30 persons. Blocks within BNAs average about 35 persons, and the land area is somewhat larger. As noted earlier, the entire United States was divided into blocks in conjunction with the 1990 census.

It is relatively easy to incorporate census data for tracts, block groups and blocks into business analysis. Printed data and CD-ROM data files afford the analyst two inexpensive and simple ways to access the data. The data are available in tabular form and the tracts, blocks and block groups are numbered in a logical manner. This format facilitates the downloading of the data to spreadsheet and other formats suitable for continued analysis. It should be noted that not all census data are available for all levels of geography. In particular, block level tables contain only 100 percent census questions (see Chapter 3) and are not available in printed form. Printed reports on the 7 million census blocks would be prohibitively expensive and the data are available in other formats (i.e., diskette, magnetic tape, and CD-ROM). At the block group and higher levels of geography, both 100 percent and sample data are available.

As noted earlier, each tract within an MSA has a unique number assigned to it, and within census tracts, block groups, and block numbers are nonoverlapping. The analyst merely needs to obtain a map of the tract/block group/block boundaries (the maps may be purchased or found in a public library in printed form or on CD-ROM) and select those areas appropriate for analysis. Data can be aggregated for a combination of units (e.g., block groups from more than one census tract). When the data are on CD, they can be downloaded easily to diskette and spreadsheet software used to aggregate and manipulate data for multiple tracts or other geographic units.

The value of census data at the tract, block group, and block level is maximized by combining them with other data (e.g., location of competitors and sales data). The ability to geocode business data facilitates the interfacing of demographic data with other information While combinations like these are at the heart of business demography, the use of tracts, block groups, and blocks without the accompanying demographic data is valuable in certain situations. For example, an analyst might simply wish to measure the change in sales volume across relatively small geographic units. Geocoded sales data for multiple points in time could be plotted on a tract map, for example, and the pattern of redistribution determined. Differences in sales by number, dollar amount, frequency, and other factors specific to the geographic units in question could be used to calculate absolute and percentage change over time. Box 7.3 addresses the issue of whether or not to use zip codes in business analysis. Box 7.4 discusses the geocoding of customer lists. Box 7.5 focuses on using federal statistical units to approximate market-based boundaries.

Box 7.3
To Zip or Not to Zip

Address lists for both customers and prospects usually contain a full address field, including zip code. Increasingly, these fields include zip + four codes, or the nine-digit zip code designating carrier route. Since this geographic identifier is already a part of the customer record, business owners and managers often use the zip code as a way to geographically categorize these lists and potential customers. The availability of demographic data and other types of data at the zip code level—much of it produced by commercial data vendors—encourages owners and managers to use zip code-based data for their business analyses. Unfortunately, business owners and managers often do not clearly understand the advantages and disadvantages of using zip code geography.

But, what is a zip code? A zip code is a numerical identifier established by the U.S. Postal Service for the efficient delivery of mail. Zip code boundaries delimit an area that can be efficiently served by a postal delivery center. Most zip codes are relatively large geographically, including several square miles and usually encompassing several census tracts. They also contain large numbers of residents, exceeding 30,000 in population in some cases. The standard five-digit zip codes have been supplemented by nine-digit zip codes that indicate the carrier route within the delivery area. The nine-digit zip code represents a relatively small area in terms of both geography and population.

Since zip codes have been established for postal service administrative purposes and for the efficient delivery of mail, the boundaries can change frequently in response to postal service needs. This is true of carrier routes as well. This means that there are potential problems in attempting to compare data at the zip code level for two or more points in time.

Out of convenience, business analysts often used zip codes as a basis for defining market areas. After all, there is a large amount of data available at the zip code level. However, market areas seldom correspond to zip code boundaries, so the market area may be underbounded or overbounded as a result of trying to delineate it in terms of zip codes. When demographic and other data are compiled at the zip code level, a misleading picture of the market area may be produced, if there is not a clear match between the market area boundaries and the zip codes being utilized.

There are alternatives to using zip codes to specify market area boundaries. In almost every case, a combination of statistical geographic units (e.g., census tracts, census block groups) can be used to provide a better approximation of the market area. With this approach, detailed data from the census can be used to profile the designated market area. Although census data are only collected every ten years, commercial data vendors are constantly improving the data available at the census tract level. Many data vendors can perform special tabulations based on a specified combination of census tracts or even smaller levels of geography.

Box 7.4
Geocoding a Customer List

Businesses of all sizes are geocoding their customer records by attaching geographic identifiers such as latitude and longitude, census tract, block group, and block number. For businesses with larger geographic coverage, state and county identifiers may be added, although in most instances state identifiers already can be found in existing records. Businesses usually begin with the full address of a customer, including nine-digit zip code.

A few basic principles should be understood by businesses using geocoding. First, there are data requirements: (1) a *complete* list of customer addresses and (2) a *master* list of street addresses, continuously updated to include newly developed residential and commercial areas. The master list also contains the geographic identifiers that will eventually be "written" to the customer records. Second, geocoding software is required to perform the match. If we have a customer address of 14520 Burdette Street, Omaha, Nebraska, 68116-4110, software is needed to search the master list (which is organized into street address ranges) to find a match. Once the match is made, the geographic identifiers (e.g., census tract and block number area) are appended to the customer record. Once the identifiers are added, it is possible to link a host of census and other data to these records. Not all records can be matched, of course. Owners and managers need to determine from the vendor performing the service the "hit rate" of the address matching process.

And now you ask, "Well, while it's true that my market area does not correspond neatly into one or more zip codes, how can the use of tracts, block groups and blocks help?" The response is simple. While business owners and managers do not think in terms of census statistical geography, they do think in terms of market or service areas. Combinations of tracts, block groups, and blocks can be assembled to yield very close approximations of market or service areas. Then the demographic and other data available can be aggregated to the boundaries specified by a given business.

So, the "new" customer record contains the old address, the new geographic identifiers, and the potential to be linked to a myriad of other datasets which can provide even more information about the business environment.

Box 7.5
Using Federal Statistical Units to Determine Market Area Boundaries

While business owners and managers want to identify the boundaries of their market areas, few engage in a process that accurately provides the needed information. Market areas are often defined in general terms, by one or more zip codes, for example, which results in a poorly defined set of market boundaries (see Box 7.3). However, simple procedures are available to more accurately identify the area in question.

First, customer addresses should be plotted on a map. If a full address list is not available a sample of customers can be asked to provide the closest street intersection to their residence (yes, customers *will* answer this question). Second, the addresses, or

---

Box 7.5 continued

street intersections, can be plotted on a map that contains small-area census geography, in particular, census tracts and block groups. Census CD-ROM-based software called Landview II, can provide the maps. Third, since some customers will undoubtedly come from a distance, perhaps even from another state, a decision must be made regarding where to draw the boundaries. Often, business owners decide to include the market area that comprises 80–90 percent of the total number of customers. Fourth, once the boundaries are established the market area can be defined in terms of tract and block group combinations, which generally provide a very close approximation of the actual market area.

This methodology removes most of the ties to preconceived market area boundaries and allows for customization based on more precise customer location information. Periodic surveys or frequent customer list evaluation allows business owners to measure changes in the market area, especially if the business strategy involves expanding the customer base by marketing to other areas. If place-of-work information is important in establishing market area data, the focus of the surveys can be changed to gather the needed data. Moreover, by defining the market area in statistical terms, other data become available, which can be used to better understand the market area.

AN APPLICATION

The best way to demonstrate the utility of the geographic units discussed in this chapter is to offer an illustration. Let's assume that the focus of a particular analysis is on several demographic variables for a specific census tract and its subdivisions. This tract is assumed to be a market area for a particular enterprise that has been identified using the distribution of sales data.

Figure 7.4 depicts census tract 50 in the Omaha, Nebraska, MSA in 1990. The map was generated by the Census Bureau's *Landview II* software available on CD-ROM. The CD is easy to install and operations are menu driven. The map seen in the figure was loaded on to *Windows* where *Paint Brush* was used to customize the map. The maps can be produced in color to enhance detail and contrast.

Census tract 50 is approximately two miles from downtown Omaha. The boundary for the tract is identified by the darkest borders (e.g., Dodge Street on the south). The areas within the tract are block groups and blocks and can be easily identified by the streets appearing on the map. The darker of the two remaining boundaries (e.g., N. 40th Street to the west) identify the block group. The lightest boundaries are for blocks. The six number labels appearing on the map are the population centroids of the six block groups making up tract 50. The numbers serve as block group identifiers for the tables that follow.

Assuming that the market area of interest is tract 50, all that remains is to "look up" the tract-specific data for the Omaha MSA. Table 7.1 presents selected characteristics for Tract 50. As can be seen, in 1990 the tract contained about 4,100 persons, 766 families, and 2,268 housing units, of which 473 (20.8 percent) were owner-occupied. There were 465 African-Americans and 326 persons age 65 and

Figure 7.4
Census Tract 50: Omaha MSA, 1990

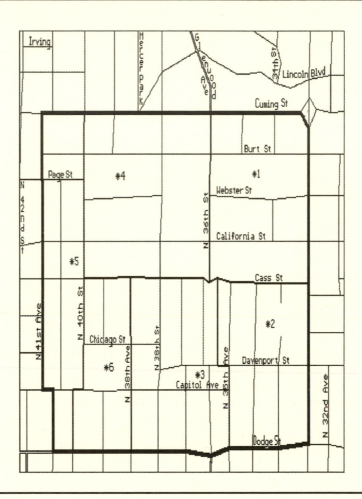

over. The median family income was $25,346. Now, let us also assume that we are interested in intercensal changes in the market area. Census tract 50 has changed considerably since 1980. The second column of the table provides data for the same variables for 1980. Although population size remained fairly constant, there were substantially fewer persons age 65 and over in 1990. The number of employed persons and housing units increased over the decade, and there was a considerable rise in median housing value. The data presented provide a wide range of information about the market area and represent only a fraction of the total data available.

Table 7.1
Social and Economic Characteristics for Omaha MSA Census Tract 50: 1990 and 1980

Characteristic	1990	1980
Total Population	4,109	4,097
African-American Population	465	194
Number of Persons 65 and over	326	547
Number of Families	769	736
Total Number of Employed Persons	2,469	2,149
Number of Housing Units	2,268	2,069
Owner-Occupied Housing Units	473	510
Median Value of Owner-Occupied Housing Units	$49,900	$29,700
Median Contract Rent	$276	$164
Median Family Income	$25,346	$17,500

Source: U.S. Bureau of the Census (1983). *Census Tract Data for the Omaha, Nebraska, Iowa MSA*, 1970 and 1980. Washington, DC: U.S. Government Printing Office; U.S. Bureau of the Census (1993). *Population and Housing Characteristics for Census Tracts and Block Numbering Areas, Omaha, NE-IA MSA*, Washington, DC: U.S. Government Printing Office.

Suppose that the analyst is interested in intramarket variation, in particular the demographic characteristics of block groups 1 and 6 within census tract 50. Table 7.2 provides 1990 data for block groups 1 and 6. The data were retrieved in a matter of seconds from the CD-ROM containing the information for block groups, tracts, and larger geographic areas such as counties and metropolitan areas. Once again, these data are but a sample of the total amount of information available. As can be

Table 7.2
Demographic Profile for Omaha MSA Census Tract 50, Block Groups (BG) 1 and 6: 1990

Characteristic	BG1	BG6
Population	913	640
Percent African-American	13.0%	9.7%
Number of Persons 65 and over	46	33
Number of Households	396	298
Percent Using Public Transportation to Travel to Work	13.5%	7.2%
Median Family Income	$26,442	$27,273

Source: CD-ROM for 1990 Census Data—STF1A, STF3A.

seen in the table, BG1 is larger than BG6 and a higher percentage of its population is African-American. Moreover, a higher percentage of the workers in BG1 use public transportation to travel to and from work. Median family incomes are similar with less than a $1,000 difference, although it should be noted that the range in income for all block groups in census tract 50 is from about $18,000 in BG 2 and BG 3 to over $35,000 in BG4. Clearly there is heterogeneity among the subdivisions of tract 50, and, to the extent that this type of information is considered important, it can be easily gathered and analyzed.

DEMOGRAPHY AND GEOGRAPHIC INFORMATION SYSTEMS

Recent developments in spatial mapping are proving to be very useful in business analysis. Because so much demographic data are linked to geographic units, Geographic information systems (GIS) are finding increasing acceptance by business analysts. Business demographers have learned that GIS offers new and exciting ways to conduct market analyses, site selection, and competitor evaluations.

GIS applications in business demography are driven by three main forces. First, and foremost is the desire to examine data in new and better ways. GIS offers a way to "view" data in a manner that tables and charts do not offer. More complex maps with overlays, colors, shading, and icons allow the analyst to supplement tabular and statistical analyses. The second driving force is the increased interest in the geocoding of business information. Now that business analysts understand the value of geocoded data, particularly for database marketing efforts, they are investing in data systems that allow customer records, sales locations and competitor locations to be mapped. As noted in Box 7.4, data users are matching collections of customer records with master lists of addresses in order to append geocodes to those customer records. The geocodes then can be linked to counties, tracts, block groups, and blocks for areal identification or to latitude and longitude for specific locations. Once geocoding is accomplished, the records can be mapped along with demographic, competitor and other data. The third driving force is the technological developments (hardware and software) that facilitate the production of high-quality maps. In today's business environment, a variety of software packages are available that fit the needs and ability to pay for almost any business.

There is also a wide range of support materials and services—conferences, books, CD-ROMs, and diskettes—available to new and experienced GIS researchers and those who simply want to know more about GIS applications. Introductions to GIS from both a general and managerial perspective are found in Star and Estes (1989) and Aronoff (1991). The advantages of and shortcomings in map usage are clearly specified by Monmonier (1991). More specialized applications with respect to consumer spending, financial institutions, retail trade, real estate and health care can be found in Castle (1993) and Hallsworth (1992). Statistical analysis of spatial data is presented by Cressie (1993). New magazines such as *GIS World* and *Business Geographics* focus on GIS applications. Conferences under the title *GIS in Business* are held annually in the United States and Europe. A database of companies, products, services, data sets, and articles related to the GIS industry is published annually under the name *GIS WorldSource*. This database is organized into 12 sections including those that focus on GIS technology, companies (over 520 GIS-related businesses), software (over 450 GIS software packages), and data sources. The *GIS WorldSource* database is also available on CD-ROM. The CD version has keyword search engines that allow the user to look for companies with specific characteristics as well as articles that have specific applications.

Given the rapid developments in technology, greater ease of use, falling software prices, and improved data availability, the temptation is to map everything. However, mapping without a clear sense of the questions/issues that need to be addressed is likely to result in less-than-optimal and often useless information. The construction of data tables and the production of graphics in business applications require a great deal of planning before a map is drawn. Moreover, maps are limited in the sense that too many mapped variables generally result in a picture that may be confusing and even misleading.

Software Availability

Currently there are hundreds of firms offering mapping software. Fortunately, there are publications that evaluate these competitors. In particular, the *Business Geographics Buyers Guide*, published annually, offers in-depth analysis of software systems, including evaluations of technical support, information on linkages among GIS software companies and providers of demographic data such as *D&B Marketplace* (a product of Dun and Bradstreet) and *Business America* (a product of American Business Information). It lists nearly 200 different companies that produce GIS-related products. The company listings include telephone, fax numbers and e-mail addresses, as well as a brief description of the products sold by each company. In addition, the buyers guide evaluates each company with respect to georeferenced data (e.g., do they have census geodemographic data?), software features, and services (e.g., do they provide support and training?).

While some GIS systems cost over $30,000 and are a challenge to implement, other software is available for less than $1,000 and is relatively easy to use. Although decisions regarding which software to purchase must be driven by price, users should first ascertain the anticipated uses, hardware requirements, and capabilities of competing software before a decision is made. Many software applications can be examined via demonstration disk, although many of these "demos" are light on application, installation and use detail and heavy on the marketing of the product.

The most recent versions of much of the software can be loaded into *Windows* and are menu-driven, making use much easier. Map options are selected and data menus appear. Selected data provide the "overlays" or colors for the maps, although histograms and other tabular and graphical presentations can be requested for one or more of the geographic units selected. For example, one can select an MSA map by aggregated census tracts (market area) and overlay varying concentrations of high-income households (by tract or block group with the area). Then, a histogram or other graphic presentation of the income distribution for one or more of these subareas can be chosen.

Most GIS software enables the user to import data from a variety of sources for mapping purposes. This capability enables the user to merge customer records with census data, competitor locations, and other worthwhile information. For example, health care analysts using *Sachs Market Planner* software and data management system can map the residences of discharged patients (both their own patients as well as estimates for subareas of the total market) with an overlay of the location of competitor service providers. By clicking a mouse on the icon of a service provider, data on that provider (e.g., types of services offered and number of affiliated physicians) immediately appear on the screen. This type of analysis can be used to assist a service provider in making site location decisions. More detail on this type of application is provided in Box 7.6.

Box 7.6
Locating New Physician Clinics

Public Care Hospital, a health care provider in a mid-sized metropolitan area in the Midwest, was developing a strategy to extend and strengthen its network of physician clinics in what it considered to be underserved areas of the MSA. The *Sachs Market Planner* GIS software and data management system had been recently purchased and was used for the analysis. The general thrust of the analysis was to identify locations for clinics based on an evaluation of existing services and to follow that with financial forecasts.

Three distinct data sets were required for the analysis. The first involved data internal to the hospital and included the location of clinics affiliated with the hospital and the residential location of the hospital's patients. The second data set was a list of competitor clinics, specifically focusing on location, services offered, number of affiliated physicians, and staff size. The third data set involved demographic and nondemographic data internal to the Sachs GIS system—1990 Census of Population and Housing information and updates for subcounty units of geography, physician and hospital visit rates from the *National Ambulatory Medical Care Survey*, physician productivity rates from the *AMA Socioeconomic Survey*, and physician supply data from the American Medical Association Physician master files.

Estimates of the expected number of patient procedures were produced for over 300 procedure categories using rates from the demographic and health care data. Using data from existing clinics and "expected" ratios of physicians to clinics, underserved areas were identified. Using overlays of the location of affiliated clinics, Public Care Hospital was able to *view* areas for potential expansion. However, data on competitors were needed before decisions could be made. At this point, data on affiliated and competitor physicians (by specialization) were combined for each geographic unit in order to ascertain the level of service "coverage." Using various assumptions regarding appropriate patient-to-physician ratios, geographic areas were classified as overserved,

---

Box 7.6 continued

underserved, or adequately served. Underserved tracts were targeted for further consideration.

Of particular value in this process was the fact that the mapped icons (e.g., hospitals and physician clinics) could be "clicked" and a summary of service provider information (e.g., number of physicians and services offered) would appear on the screen. While the quantitative analysis proceeded with the application of rates to produce service needs estimates, a qualitative component was added through the visualization of competition.

By mapping Public Care Hospital discharges, analysts were able to study the market area and visually understand the relationship between the residence of patients and the location of affiliated clinics. Once this relationship was better understood, the extent to which clinic expansion would positively affect hospital discharge figures became clearer. During the presentation of this information to hospital board members, it was possible to alter the analysis and assumptions in "real time" and produce new maps and graphics based on questions that were raised. The ability to alter the analysis and see the results during the presentation was of substantial value in the decision making process.

The key to maximizing the value of demographic data and analysis in business decision making lies in linking demographic and nondemographic data. The availability of 1990 Population and Housing and 1992 Economic Census data on CD-ROM facilitates the importing of such data into mapping software. Some companies package a variety of datasets by linking various sources of data and mapping capabilities in one system. For example, *Claritas, Inc.*, incorporates census data, including estimates and projections, with county business patterns, physician, hospital, restaurant and other business data from *MapInfo, Intergraph, SAS Tactician*, and *ESRI* for use in GIS software. *Decisionmark Corporation's Proximity* interfaces data from the 1990 Census of Population and Housing with data from *Market Statistics, Equifax/National Decision Systems*, and *American Business Information*, among others, for use in a mapping system that utilizes company-specific and competitor data as well. Other companies simply provide mapping software that makes it relatively easy to import needed data. Still other full-service consultants, like *CACI Marketing Systems*, provide custom map development services. The case vignette in Box 7.7 focuses more specifically on a GIS application.

Box 7.7
Retail Market Boundary Changes

A local clothing retailer in a midwestern city wished to better comprehend the boundaries of her market. More specifically, she wished to understand the nature of suspected market area boundary shifts and whether or not some of the shifts were related to marketing efforts. Instead of relying on wall maps and stick-pins, she decided to

---

Box 7.7 continued

invest in some GIS software. The GIS software she chose to purchase was compatible with the PC she already owned. Also, she had a relatively complete customer list for the past three years that could be mapped. Her business was relatively small and for the most part limited to the county in which the business was located. She began by plotting current customer addresses on the county map and identified not only her market area boundary but the geographic concentration of customers within the boundary as well. Next, she decided to overlay the current boundary on the boundary from three years earlier. Over the three-year period she had expended a considerable amount of money in an attempt to expand her market westward toward more affluent suburban neighborhoods. Of course, she performed a microanalysis to identify the exact location of new customers, but she thought that "seeing" the boundary overlay would provide additional understanding. She chose two different colors for the overlay and observed that in fact there was considerable growth in her customer base to the west.

However, she also observed "shrinkage" in her existing market. That is, instead of expanding her market area, it had simply been shifted to the west. In fact, the geographic size of her market area had changed little in the three-year period. She then wanted to learn more about the population size and characteristics of areas that had been "lost" over the three-year period. At this point, the analysis became more demographic. Using census tract and block group boundaries as another overlay, she was able to more clearly identify areas gained and lost over the three-year period. Using 1990 Census of Population and Housing data, she "profiled," or examined, the composition of the tract and block groups gained and lost and learned that, while her strategy of attracting customers who lived in the more affluent suburbs had been successful, some of the customers lost also came from reasonably well-to-do areas. Because a major competitor had located near her business more than a year earlier, she suspected that her lost customers had been "stolen" by the competitor. The analysis provided significant input into a new strategy designed to recapture some of the old customers and provided feedback on the previous strategy designed to attract new customers.

THE FUTURE OF GIS AND BUSINESS DEMOGRAPHY

The impact of GIS business/demographic analyses is only beginning to be felt in the corporate boardroom. Advances in database marketing are providing a significant expansion in the internal data sets required to perform detailed analyses. Increased competition is improving GIS technology, increasing user friendliness of available software, and driving down prices. GIS as a presentation tool in the corporate boardroom is no longer an anomaly. Even in smaller businesses, the reduction in cost and increased ease of use has made GIS an accessible analysis tool.

The industry trend is to offer "packages" of data and software and this trend is likely to continue. For example, Decisionmark Corporation's *Proximity,* mentioned earlier in this chapter, offers data on agriculture, consumers and businesses for all 3,141 U.S. counties and all 226,000 block groups; the accompanying mapping software costs less than $2,000. The software is menu-driven, and its icon-based interface runs with *Windows*. Similar packages are offered by *ESRI*, *MapInfo*, and *Strategic Mapping Inc.*, among a host of other companies.

The industry appears to be moving toward marketing "add-ons" (e.g., data sets and enhanced graphics) to existing software systems. Prices should continue to fall, making GIS analysis available to even a broader range of businesses. Current and potential users of GIS have every reason to be optimistic about the anticipated developments in GIS capabilities.

REFERENCES

Aronoff, Stan (1991). *Geographic Information Systems: A Management Perspective*. Ft. Collins, CO: World Publications.

Castle, Gilbert H. (ed.) (1993). *Profiting from a Geographic Information System*. Ft. Collins, CO: GIS World.

Cressie, Noel A. C. (1993). *Statistics for Spatial Analysis*. New York: John Wiley and Sons.

Hallsworth, Alan G. (1992). *The New Geography of Consumer Spending: A Political Economy Approach*. New York: John Wiley and Sons.

Monmonier, Mark (1991). *How to Lie with Maps*. Chicago: University of Chicago Press.

Star, Jeffrey and John Estes (1989). *Geographic Information Systems: An Introduction*. New York: Prentice Hall.

Terrie, Walter (1996). "Several Recent Supreme Court Decisions and Their Implications for Political Redistricting in Voting Rights Act Context," *Population Research and Policy Review* (forthcoming).

SUGGESTED READINGS

Business Geographics. Monthly magazine published by GIS World, Ft. Collins, Colorado.

Myers, Dowell (1992). *Analysis with Local Census Data*. New York: Academic Press.

Plane, David A., and Peter A. Rogerson (1994). *The Geographical Analysis of Population*. New York: John Wiley and Sons.

Chapter 8

Population Size, Concentration, and Distribution

INTRODUCTION

The size of the population in a geographic area is typically the simplest and most straightforward of demographic attributes. At the same time it is often the most important. While population composition and other factors are important in determining the market area characteristics of a specific geographic unit, the size of that population is arguably the most significant factor in assessing market potential. After size, the pattern of concentration of persons across geographic areas and their distribution within the area(s) of interest are probably next in importance for business planners.

Demographers generally begin by providing information on the size of a population in very basic terms. In fact, many of the measures used in these presentations are familiar to the general public. Statistics that describe the size and distribution of various populations—along with information on growth—are common in the popular press. For example, the national and regional press wrote extensively on the lack of population growth for several Midwestern states during the 1980s, while concomitant population increases in California, Florida, and Texas were duly noted. The subsequent slowing of growth in some of those same high growth areas has received significant attention in the 1990s.

In census years, population losses and gains are discussed in the context of lost and gained seats in the U.S. House of Representatives and when state legislative redistricting takes place. Between the 100th Congress (1987) and the 103rd Congress (1994), for example, California gained seven House seats (from 45 to 52) and New York lost three (from 34 to 31). These gains and losses reflect the population growth differentials experienced by California and New York.

Data on the size and distribution of the population also provide the basis for descriptive statistics such as rates and ratios. Population counts are used to calculate fertility and mortality rates and the extent of market penetration for products and services. As noted in Chapters 5 and 6, the calculation of rates facilitates comparisons between areas of different size.

CONCEPTUAL AND MEASUREMENT ISSUES

Size

The first demographic "fact" usually desired about a population is its *size*. Size simply refers to a count of the population for "a specified area at a specified date" (Bogue 1985, p. 13). A "count" implies that some organized and systematic effort such as a census is made to identify and record individuals, households, and/or families linked to some specific geographic unit. The areal component of the definition concerns the assignment of persons counted to geographic units or places based on their addresses. Beginning with a basic street address, virtually any type of geographic aggregation is possible. Moreover, the concept of counting and therefore determining size can be expanded to include enterprises. Box 8.1 discusses accessing size and distribution data on CD-ROM.

Box 8.1

Accessing Population and Housing Data from CD-ROM

Technological advancements in data storage and retrieval have facilitated the use of census and other data for a number of business applications. Data from the 1990 Census of Population and Housing and the 1992 Economic/Enterprise Censuses are available on CD-ROM. These CDs can be either purchased or accessed at no charge in public and university libraries. The data are subdivided into the geographic units discussed in Chapter 7—U.S., states, metropolitan statistical areas, counties, census tracts, block groups, and blocks, as well as zip codes. In addition, new public-access mapping software, LandView II, is now available on CD at those same libraries. Many private sector mapping packages are also available, as discussed in Chapter 7.

Summary Tape Files (STF) 1 and 3 from the 1990 census contain most of the data needed for analysis, and there are separate CDs for each data category. As noted in Figure 3.1, STF1 CDs contain data from the 100 percent questionnaire (population and housing questions) and STF3 contain the more detailed sample data. The STF1A data file includes data with geographic detail down to the block group level, and the STF1B files contains the data for census blocks. The STF3A file contains the detailed social and economic characteristics down to the block group, while the STF3B file includes data for five-digit zip codes. STF2 CDs contain more detail for the 100 percent questions but only down to the census tract/block numbering area (BNA) level of geography. STF4 CDs contain more detailed data for the sample questions, again down to the census

---

Box 8.1 continued

tract/BNA.

The CDs are very easy to use. Many libraries already have them installed, although installation is no more difficult than inserting a music CD in a home CD player. The entire operating process is menu driven. The user selects the data elements of interest (e.g., size, age structure, and income distribution) and the geographic units (e.g., counties and census tracts) for which the data are required. The tables produced can either be printed out or written to diskette for further manipulation. (As noted in Chapter 7, a census map must be consulted if the user is not familiar with the geographic units under study.)

The analysis that follows took less than ten minutes, including the time required to print the tables. Census Tract 48 in the Omaha MSA contains the University of Nebraska at Omaha. We wished to ascertain the demographic characteristics for this area, as well as those for the five block groups that comprise tract 48. Using a short series of menus, we were able to select Nebraska from the list of states on the CD and Douglas County which contains the census tract of interest as the initial units of geography. We then selected census tract 48 from the list of census tracts presented. As stated earlier, the STF1A file provides 100 percent data and we were able to determine that the tract contained 4,506 persons. Among other factors, we found:

Tract 48

Total Population	4,506
% Population Age 65 & over	10.9
Median Age	31.1
Total Number of Households	2,295
Rental Vacancy rate	1.5%
Median Value Owner-Occupied House	$62,200

Accessing the block group (BG) data using another menu we found the populations of BG1 through BG5 to be: 499; 740; 687; 1,310; and 1,270, respectively. The same population and housing characteristics provided for tracts are also available for block groups.

Next we selected the STF3A file for more detailed social and economic characteristics. The same geographic units were accessed. We found the median household income for the entire tract and its component block groups to be:

Tract 48

Entire Tract	$23,315
BG1	$18,125
BG2	$25,956
BG3	$31,042
BG4	$25,529
BG5	$19,118

Additional data on family income, occupation and employment and poverty, among other information, were also found.

Box 8.1 continued

Users of the CD can simply select the geographic area(s) for which data are desired and use the menu system to select the data needed. Both simple and complex market area analyses are possible with relatively little data access effort.

Concentration

Once a population count has been completed, it is possible to calculate measures of population concentration. The concentration of the population is usually measured in terms of density. Density measures the concentration of persons within a standard unit of geography. Density is typically presented in terms of persons per square mile or square kilometer. More broadly viewed, concentration measures can be generalized to include any phenomenon of interest, such as the concentration of sales or potential customers. In relation to business, density measures facilitate the efficient expenditure of marketing resources and assist in identifying areas with high market potential.

Distribution

In addition to size and concentration, the *distribution* of persons within and among geographical areas is determined. Distribution refers to the proportion of the total population living in specified geographic areas and subareas. Populations are not evenly distributed across regions, states, counties, and cities. Thus, the consideration of population size without knowledge of population distribution does not yield particularly valuable information.

In the United States, population count and distribution data are derived primarily from the decennial census. In the process of gathering data on the number of persons in a household or other living units, information on the location of that unit (a street address) is also collected. Aggregation of individual living-unit data to a geographic area (e.g., a zip code) generates size data for that area.

METHODOLOGICAL CONCERNS

Concentration and Distribution

When population concentration and distribution are considered, two types of measurement are of interest. Each of these measures yields a different but related piece of use-specific information. Density measured in terms of persons per square mile provides information regarding a population's concentration within a given geographic area. On the other hand, proportional measures of concentration relate a population count for a certain area to a larger total, such as that of the United

States. For example, the percentage of the U.S. population living in each of the various states can be derived. Both measures assume that there are reasonably accurate population data available and that the land area of the geographic units, either surface or inhabitable, is known. Both concentration and distribution measures depend upon precise boundary delineations.

When concentration and distribution changes are calculated, possible changes in boundaries must be considered. MSA boundaries may change because of the addition of new counties, making it impossible to measure decade-to-decade change unless the boundaries are standardized. City boundaries are altered as the result of annexation, making standard boundary comparisons for two or more time periods difficult if not impossible. Regional, divisional, and state boundaries are useful because they remain constant over time. The tracting, including block numbering areas, for all areas of the United States for the 1990 census should facilitate geographic comparisons over time.

In order to calculate statistics for concentration and distribution, absolute numbers and their appropriate percentages are assigned to the geographic units of interest. For example, the population of the Middle Atlantic census division of the United States, which is composed of New York, New Jersey, and Pennsylvania, contained 38.1 million persons in 1993 or 14.8 percent of the total U.S. population. These data could be further refined to include, for example, only persons 55 years old and over to reflect the size of the potential market for supplemental health insurance. Or one could focus on the population of households with children age ten and younger as an indication of the size of the child care market.

Measures of Change

The last measurement issue involves the calculation of rates of change. Demographers and other users of demographic data often wish to describe or analyze changes in population size, concentration, or distribution for two or more time periods. Several options are available, and the method employed depends on the needs of the analyst. Initially, absolute differences—simply taking one number and subtracting the other—may be used to indicate numerical change. If more than two time intervals are being studied, then multiple differences may be generated, including measures for the entire time span as well as for each of the time segments comprising that span. The advantage of decomposing longer time intervals into shorter components is that the differences between and among component parts may reveal patterns not apprent for the total time span. For example, a population may have increased by 5 million persons over the three decades being studied, although virtually all growth took place over the most recent decade.

Proportional and percentage change measures are useful as well. A choice of the base population must be made, and this affects the interpretation of figures derived. If there are two time periods and the difference in the two figures—for example, the 1990 total minus the 1980 total—is the numerator, then choosing the 1980 figure as the base for rate calculation results in a figure of percentage change, either positive or negative, since 1980. However, if the 1990 figure is chosen as the base, then the statistic generated is the percentage of the 1990 population that was added (or subtracted) during the decade of the 1980s. In rapidly changing areas, the two rates may be quite different, perhaps resulting in two sets of conflicting conclusions.

It is important to use both absolute and relative measures in business planning. Looking at state comparisons, suppose the question concerns which state grew the fastest during the 1980s. Change in size is being measured in this case. In drawing conclusions on growth, two answers are correct: California with an increase of 6 million persons and Alaska with an increase in population of 36.8 percent (U.S. Bureau of the Census 1994, Table 26). Even though the absolute population increase for Alaska was only 148,000 persons during the decade, the Alaskan base population was so small (402,000) in 1980 that it yielded the nation's largest percentage of growth. It is only when the changes in population size and proportion are compared that meaningful information can be produced. The selection of a measure is predicated upon and limited by the specific use intended.

Counting the Population

Several methodological issues must be addressed in "counting" the population. The first issue concerns who is to be counted. Censuses, the most comprehensive efforts to count populations, are designed to enumerate every individual within the population. The U.S. Bureau of the Census attempts to count everyone who resides in the United States, regardless of his or her legal status, in the decennial census. Certain U.S. citizens residing abroad (e.g., U.S. military personnel and members of diplomatic missions) are also enumerated.

Second, the assigned geographic location of individuals is also important, and people generally are counted at their usual place of residence. *Place of residence* is defined as the location where the individual usually sleeps and eats. The usual place of residence is easy to establish for the vast majority of the population, although for subpopulations such as college students, migrant workers, persons with two or more residences, and the homeless, the task is much more difficult. While college students are assigned to the location of their educational institution, the determination of a usual residence for the remaining groups involves the application of specific rules, enumerator judgment, and special enumeration techniques. Greater detail regarding these issues can be found in Robey (1989).

Third, the distinction between an individual's usual place of residence (nighttime) and his workplace location (daytime) is significant given the vast differences between the two populations. Downtown areas in many U.S. cities teem with people during working hours only to become virtual ghost towns in the evening. The opposite is often true for residential areas. In many situations, data on the location of the daytime population are more useful than residence information, as in the case of restaurants catering to the lunch-time market. Traffic flow data, used to measure the passage of persons from home to work and back, become important for other business decisions. The ability to provide at least minimal service to all areas requires either a count or an estimate of these distinct populations. Daytime populations can be estimated using Census Bureau information on daily commuting patterns. Box 8.2 discusses the difference between daytime and nighttime populations for a specific census tract in suburban Omaha, Nebraska.

The fourth issue relates to the coverage of the enumeration. As specified above, an enumeration implies that everyone within the specified population has been counted. While censuses conducted in the United States come very close to full coverage, some portion of the population is inevitably missed. An evaluation of the 1990 census indicated that, while about 99 percent of the white population was accounted for, only 94 percent of the African-American population was counted. Furthermore, the undercount for African-American males between the ages of 25 and 54 was estimated to be about 15 percent. Some other subpopulations, such as the homeless, have even higher undercount rates.

Box 8.2

Daytime and Nighttime Population Comparisons

Census Tract 74.07 designates an area in suburban Omaha that contains a limited number of employment opportunities. Therefore, most of the working population can be assumed to work outside of tract 74.07. 1990 Census of Population and Housing data indicated the following characteristics of the tract:

Tract 74.07

Population	3,380
Workers Age 16 and Over	1,973
Workers as Percent of Total Population	58.4%
Persons Working at Home	30

While the nighttime population (not accounting for persons working at night) is 3,380, the daytime population is estimated to be 1,377. This assumes that all persons who are not employed are at home and that nearly everyone works in the daytime. The latter is probably a reasonable assumption given that this is a white-collar, upper-middle-class suburb. Clearly, many persons will be away from their residences for any number of reasons on any given day, conservatively reducing the daytime population to less than 1,000. The reduction of greater than two thirds of the population presents an entirely different market area profile than that shown by the enumerated population.

Census Tract 6 in Omaha is located closer to places of employment and contains a lower percentage of employed persons. Data from the 1990 Census of Population and Housing showed:

Tract 6

Population	1,801
Workers Age 16 and Over	562
Workers as Percent of Total Population	31.2%
Persons Working at Home	0

Box 8.2 continued

The smaller percentage of the population identified as workers means that, all other factors being equal, a larger percent of the enumerated population is at home during the day than in tract 74.07. However, even in tract 6 the population is considerably changed by economic activities and the resident count is not necessarily a good indication of market potential. Finally, the enumerated population in tract 74.07 is 1.87 times as large as that of tract 6 (3,380/1,801). Nevertheless, tract 74.07 is only 1.19 times as large when workers working outside the home are considered. In terms of the potential for products and services aimed at the daytime population, the markets are more comparable than they appeared at first glance.

The determination of what constitutes a count is the fifth important issue. Although an actual census takes place only once every ten years in the United States (special censuses are an exception), size data are available during intercensal periods for many geographic units at regular intervals through the production of population estimates and projections. These "synthetic data," as they are sometimes called, carry with them unique measurement concerns, some of which are addressed in Chapter 10. Population estimates and projections are usually produced by combining data from the most recent census, or most recent population estimates, with the factors that account for population change (births, deaths, and migrants), "symptomatic" data (e.g., housing starts and utility connections), and assumptions about likely demographic change. Using these methods, data on population size, and in some instances population characteristics, for the recent past and the future are produced. Population estimates and projections are viewed as surrogates for enumeration data, and business planners must rely on these calculated figures during intercensal periods. In many instances, however, synthetic data contain relatively large and often unknown amounts of error.

Finally, every population count must have a date attached to it. Decennial census counts refer to April 1 of years that end in zero, since that is the day the population is officially enumerated. Population estimates usually refer to July 1 (i.e., midyear) for the year in question, or in some instances December 31 (i.e., the end of year). Such a distinction, of course, may be crucial to an area undergoing rapid population change. Other dates can be chosen as long as they are clearly specified. Comparing two populations whose counts occurred at different dates may be risky, especially if one of the dates follows a significant demographic event, or if substantial continuing population growth or decline has been observed.

TRENDS IN SIZE, CONCENTRATION, AND DISTRIBUTION

Chapter 2 provided an overview of demographic change in the United States, including some information on size and distribution. In this section, detailed data are

Figure 8.1
U. S. Population Growth: 1900–2010

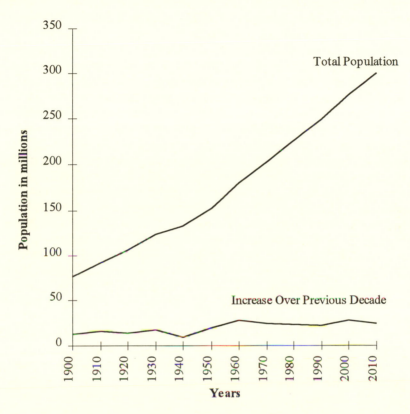

Source: U.S. Bureau of the Census (1994). *Statistical Abstract of the United States*, *1994*. Washington, DC: U.S. Government Printing Office, Table 1.

presented for a more complete picture of historical trends and likely future historical developments for these three important demographic components. Figure 8.1 depicts trends and projections for U.S. population growth. From 1900 to 2010 the population of the United States is projected to grow by about 225 million persons (300 percent). Similarly, an increase in density from 25.6 to 84.6 persons per square mile is expected. As stated in Chapter 2, the rate of population growth is slowing, although absolute numbers will continue to rise. It should be noted, however, that the 1990s and 2000s decades are projected to produce two of the three periods of largest absolute growth in U.S. history, adding 27.5 and 24.2 million persons, respectively. Clearly, many consumer markets in the United States will continue to grow as the result of this population increase.

Figure 8.2 presents population size data for the United States and for regions and divisions. (The reader is referred to Figure 7.3 in Chapter 7, which specifies the boundaries of these geographic units.) The period of time covered is 1970 to 1993. As can be seen in Figure 8.2, the population of the United States increased by nearly 56 million persons (26.9 percent) over the 23 year time interval. However, wide regional differences in growth are apparent. The West region grew by 21.2 million (or about 38 percent of all U.S. population growth). At the same time, the Northeast region grew by only 2.3 million persons, or 5 percent. Divisional variation (recall that there are four regions and nine divisions) is even greater (data not shown), and the range in growth percentages is from 2.4 percent for the New England division to 78.3 percent for the Mountain division.

Divisional "markets" changed considerably between 1970 and 1993. All of the divisions were "large," but as the result of differential growth rates their relative sizes changed over the interval. For example, the Middle Atlantic division was second in size only to the New England and East North Central divisions in 1970. It was also nearly 11 million persons larger than the Pacific division. By 1993, the Pacific and South Atlantic divisions were larger, with the Pacific division's increase numbering nearly 15 million persons.

Table 8.1 provides data on population size and growth for the 15 largest CMSAs and MSAs in the United States. A CMSA includes two or more contiguous MSAs that have strong social and economic ties. CMSAs varied in size in 1990 from nearly 20 million persons to only about 2.5 million. Together, the number of persons living in CMSAs totaled around 94 million persons, or about 37 percent of the entire U.S. population. CMSAs also exhibit considerably different rates of growth. Two (Detroit and Cleveland) lost population during the 1980s, while five (Los Angeles, Dallas-Ft. Worth, Miami, Seattle, and Atlanta) recorded growth rates in excess of 20 percent. High-growth CMSAs characterize the South and West regions, while slower growing CMSAs tend to be located in the Northeast and the Midwest. Without question, these CMSAs represent the largest markets for products, services, advertising, and labor. The size and growth rates for these markets, independent of those for the United States as a whole, have implications for local, regional, and national business strategies.

Data for the nation's 15 largest cities in 1992 are presented in Table 8.2. Together they totaled about 25 million residents, or approximately 9 percent of the total U.S. population. The cities range in size from 7.3 million (New York) to 661,000 (Jacksonville, FL), with only three cities exceeding 2 million persons. Six of the 15 largest cities have populations under 1 million. New York, by far the largest city, is more then twice the size of Los Angeles and 11 times the size of Jacksonville. To some extent these cities represent independent markets, although they also influence the larger areas of which they are a part.

When demographers assess the size of a market, they typically do so with respect to the total population or a segment of the population specified by some factor such as age (e.g., size of the population aged 60 and over in city X). It is possible to rank markets not only on the basis of total size but in terms of specific characteristics

Figure 8.2
Regional Population Growth: 1970–1993

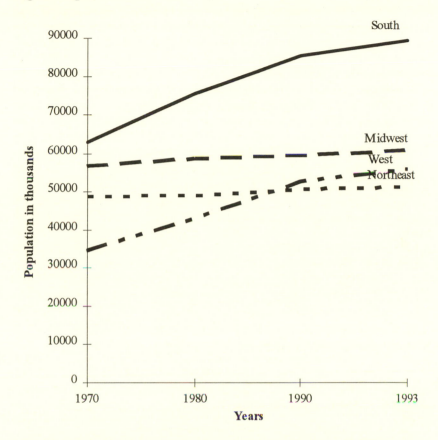

Source : U.S. Bureau of the Census (1994). *Statistical Abstract of the United States, 1994* .
    Washington, DC: U. S. Government Printing Office, Table 26.

(e.g., labor force employed in technical fields). As an example, Table 8.3 presents
data on the U.S. market and ranks the foreign-born population by place of birth.
Assuming that country of birth, along with characteristics such as language and
culture, are important for business reasons (e.g., targeting ethnic markets for food
products) the data in the table become very useful.

The foreign-born population is dominated by those from Mexico. The 4.29
million shown in the table represent 22 percent of the total foreign-born population
(19.8 million) residing in the United States. These 19.8 million persons comprise
about eight percent of the total U.S. population. Since most business decisions are
made at subnational levels of geography, an examination of data for states, counties,

Table 8.1
Population and Population Growth for the Fifteen Largest U.S. Consolidated Metropolitan Statistical Areas: 1980–1990

Consolidated Metropolitan Statistical Area	1980	1990	Percent Growth 1980-1990
New York-Northern New Jersey-Long Island, NY-NJ-CT-PA CMSA	18,906[a]	19,550	3.4%
Los Angeles-Riverside-Orange County, CA CMSA	11,498	14,542	26.4
Chicago-Gary-Kenosha, IL-IN-WI CMSA	8,115	8,240	1.5
Washington-Baltimore, DC-MD-VA-WV CMSA	5,791	6,727	16.2
San Francisco-Oakland-San Jose, CMSA	5,368	6,253	16.5
Philadelphia-Wilmington-Atlantic City, PA-NJ-DE-MD CMSA	5,649	5,893	4.3
Boston-Worcester-Lawrence, MA-NH-ME-CT CMSA	5,152	5,455	6.5
Detroit-Ann Arbor-Flint, MI CMSA	5,293	5,187	-2.0
Dallas-Ft. Worth, TX CMSA	3,046	4,037	32.5
Houston-Galveston-Brazoria, TX CMSA	3,118	3,731	19.7
Miami-Fort Lauderdale, FL CMSA	2,644	3,193	20.8
Seattle-Tacoma-Bremerto, WA CMSA	2,409	2,970	23.3
Atlanta, GA MSA	2,233	2,960	32.5
Cleveland-Akron, OH CMSA	2,938	2,860	-2.7
Minneapolis-St. Paul, MN-WI MSA	2,198	2,539	15.5

[a]Numbers in 1,000s.
[b]Data for Atlanta and Minneapolis are for MSAs only.

Note: 1990 MSA boundaries have been used for comparison purposes.

Source: U.S. Bureau of the Census (1994). *Statistical Abstract of the United States 1994*. Washington, DC: U.S. Government Printing Office, Table 42.

tracts, and block groups can provide information on the specific locations of this population.

Table 8.4 extends the notion of examining the size of specific populations, and focuses on the fifteen states with the largest nursing home populations. Assuming that the size of the nursing home population is valuable for some business reason (e.g., the marketing of medical supplies) then these data become valuable.

As can be seen, California contains by far the largest nursing home population, and only four states contain 100,000 or more nursing home residents. It is somewhat surprising that Florida has nearly 70,000 fewer nursing home residents than California. This ranking does not simply reflect differences in overall population

Table 8.2
Fifteen Largest U.S. Cities (1992)

City	1992 Population
New York NY	7,312[a]
Los Angeles, CA	3,490
Chicago, IL	2,768
Houston, TX	1,690
Philadelphia, PA	1,553
San Diego, CA	1,149
Dallas, TX	1,022
Phoenix, AZ	1,012
Detroit, MI	1,012
San Antonio, TX	966
San Jose, CA	801
Indianapolis, IN	747
San Francisco, CA	729
Baltimore, MD	726
Jacksonville, FL	661

[a]Population in 1,000s.

Source: U.S. Bureau of the Census (1994). *Statistical Abstract of the United States 1994*. Washington, DC: U.S. Government Printing Office, Table 46.

Table 8.3
U.S. Foreign-Born Population by Place of Birth: 1990

Country or Area of Birth	Population
Mexico	4,298[a]
Caribbean	1,938
Philippines	913
Cuba	737
Canada	745
Germany	712
United Kingdom	640
Italy	581
Korea	568
Vietnam	543
China	530

[a]Population in 1,000s

Source: U.S. Bureau of the Census (1994). *Statistical Abstract of the United States 1994*. Washington, DC: U.S. Government Printing Office, Table 54.

Table 8.4
Fifteen States with the Largest Nursing Home Populations: 1990

State	Population
California	148,362
New York	126,175
Pennsylvania	106,454
Texas	101,005
Ohio	93,769
Illinois	93,662
Florida	80,298
Michigan	57,622
Massachusetts	55,662
Missouri	52,060
Indiana	50,845
Wisconsin	50,345
New Jersey	47,054
Minnesota	47,051
North Carolina	47,014

Source: U.S. Bureau of the Census (1994). *Statistical Abstract of the United States 1994*. Washington, DC: U.S. Government Printing Office, Table 84.

size, however, it reflects the variation in living arrangements for the senior population between the two states.

Data on population concentration and growth for selected U.S. countries are presented in Table 8.5. The left panel lists the ten most densely populated U.S. counties, while the right panel contains the ten fastest growing counties (in percentage terms). Population density in the United States in 1993 was 70.3 persons per square mile. Four of the five New York City counties (boroughs) are also the nation's four most densely populated counties. The Manhattan borough of New York City has a density in excess of 52,000 persons per square mile! With the exception of San Francisco county, all of the densely populated counties are located on the east coast.

All the counties in the right panel at least doubled their populations between 1980 and 1992, and Flagler County, Florida, grew by more than 200 percent. Six of these ten counties are in Florida and Georgia and only two are in states outside the South (one each in Nevada and Colorado).

Population density and growth for cities of 200,000 or more population are examined in Table 8.6. New York City is made up of five boroughs, thus the lower density figure. All but one city on this list has a density of 10,000 or more persons per square mile. More geographic diversity is represented by these figures than those in Table 8.5.

Table 8.5
Ten Densest (Persons Per Square Mile) and Ten Fastest Growing Counties: 1980–1992

County	Density (1992)	County	Percent Growth 1980-1992
New York, NY	52,432	Flagler, FL	207.7%
Kings, NY	32,428	Douglas, CO	191.4
Bronx, NY	28,443	Camden, GA	181.7
Queens, NY	17,834	Matanuska-Susitna, AK	152.2
San Francisco, CA	15,609	Hernando, FL	146.5
Hudson, NJ	11,883	Osceola, FL	141.9
Philadelphia, PA	11,492	Fayette, GA	140.0
Suffolk, MA	10,926	Gwinneth, GA	134.9
District of Columbia	9,531	Dawson, GA	116.5
Baltimore, MD	8,986	Elko, NV	116.3

ᵃIndependent city.

Source: U.S. Bureau of the Census (1994). *County and City Data Book. 1994.* Washington, DC: U.S. Government Printing Office, Table 1.

Table 8.6
Ten Most Densely Populated Cities (1992) and Ten Fastest Growing Cities of 200,000 or More: 1980–1992

City	Population per Square Mile (1992)	City	Percent Growth 1980-1992
New York, NY	23,671	Mesa, AZ	94.6%
San Francisco, CA	15,609	Las Vegas, NV	79.5
Jersey City, NJ	15,341	Fresno, CA	72.9
Chicago, IL	12,185	Arlington, TX	72.3
Philadelphia, PA	11,492	Virginia Beach, VA	59.1
Boston, MA	11,398	Aurora, CO	51.1
Newark, NJ	11,254	Stockton, CA	48.1
Santa Ana, CA	10,628	Raleigh, NC	46.8
Miami, FL	10,309	Austin, TX	42.3
Washington, DC	9,531	Santa Ana, CA	41.2

Source: U.S. Bureau of the Census (1994). *County and City Data Book. 1994.* Washington, DC: U.S. Government Printing Office, Table 3.

With respect to growth rates, there is also considerable geographic diversity, although five of the fastest growing cities are in the West (three in California). These cities are already large, and therefore growth rates of this magnitude represent considerable marketplace expansion.

Data for Florida cities showing size, growth rates, and density, three key components to assessing market potential, are shown in Table 8.7. As can be seen, there is a considerable range in sizes for those cities, from 367,016 (Miami) to 35,587 (Altamonte Springs). However the rank order for size is a poor predictor of growth during the 1980s. Altamonte Springs recorded the fastest growth rate over the interval (68.6 percent), while Miami grew by only 5.9 percent. Ft. Lauderdale actually lost population. Miami recorded the densest population, followed by Ft. Lauderdale.

If size is the only criterion for marketplace selection, then Miami is the easy choice in Florida. However, if high growth is emphasized, a shift to Altamonte Springs or Tallahassee would be appropriate, while Ft. Lauderdale and Tampa should be avoided.

Table 8.7
Total Population, Density, Population Change for Ten Florida Cities: 1980–1990

City	1980 Population	1990 Population	Percent Change 1980-1992	Density[a] 1992
Altamonte Springs	22,028	35,587	68.6%	4,187[b]
Boca Raton	49,505	64,338	30.1	2,365
Clearwater	85,528	98,121	15.2	3,941
Daytona Beach	54,176	64,634	19.3	2,007
Ft. Lauderdale	153,279	148,524	-3.1	4,730
Melbourne	46,497	64,276	38.1	2,240
Miami	346,865	367,016	5.9	10,309
Orlando	128,291	174,215	35.8	2,589
Tallahassee	81,548	130,357	59.9	2,059
Tampa	271,523	284,737	4.8	2,619

[a]Per square mile.
[b]Population estimate.

Source: U.S. Bureau of the Census (1994). *County and City Data Book. 1994*. Washington, DC: U.S. Government Printing Office, Table C.

CONCLUSIONS

Population size, concentration and distribution are important factors in business decision making. Without a market of adequate size, business ventures either fail, are forced to relocate, or must change the way in which they market their products. Data on population concentration and distribution affect a number of business decisions as well. Distribution systems, such as those created by *Wal-Mart* and *K-Mart*, have been developed in response to the dispersion of customers, with particular attention paid to future population growth and distribution. Companies such as *Mutual of Omaha* allocate sales resources based on the distribution of their customers, again with attention paid to future customer base growth. Professional sports teams focus on both the size of the near market (for game attendance) as well as the potential television market before deciding if and where to relocate. Combined with data on competitor size and distribution, data on population size and distribution help drive decisions regarding location, expansion, and advertising. The size and distribution of the senior population with respect to the market for specialized health services is discussed in Box 8.3.

Box 8.3

The Size and Distribution of the Hypertensive Market

The size and distribution of the total population without respect to characteristics (e.g., age) is usually of limited value in business planning. This fact is clearly apparent when examining the market potential for health services. The senior population utilizes a great deal more services than the younger population. In particular, about 70 percent of the population age 75 and over in the United States has hypertension, or high blood pressure. In the younger population, the prevalence of hypertension is much lower (e.g., 6 percent for 20 to 24 year olds, 16 percent for 35 to 44 year olds, and 46 percent for 55 to 64 olds). The table below contains total population and age specific data for the six states with a population of at least 10 million in 1993. These six states contained about 40 percent of the U.S. population and 39 percent of the population age 75 and over. The data are in 1,000s.

State	Population	(Percent of U.S.)	Age 75 and Over	(Percent of U.S.)
New York	18,197	(7.1)	1,038	(7.3)
Illinois	11,697	(4.5)	655	(4.6)
Florida	13,679	(5.3)	1,103	(7.8)
Texas	18,031	(7.0)	772	(5.5)
California	31,211	(12.1)	1,383	(9.8)
Ohio	11,091	(4.3)	627	(4.4)

The distribution of the population age 75 and over is clearly different than that for the total population. Texas and California have fewer than expected older persons, based on the percentage comparison for the two columns. On the other hand, Florida has more than expected number of persons age 75 and over.

If the figure of 70 percent for share of total population were applied to generate the number of hypertensives, the following number of "expected" hypertensive persons would be generated for the six states under analysis.

Box 8.3 continued

New York	727,000
Illinois	458,000
Florida	772,000
Texas	540,000
California	968,000
Ohio	439,000

As can be seen, the concentration of hypertensives is much different from the concentration of population. All other factors being equal, Florida emerges as the second strongest overall market and, because of the high concentration of persons 75 years and over in specific substate locations, it may well be the best market. The Texas market is not nearly as good as it appeared when examining total population data alone.

The same type of simple analysis can be done for substate geographic areas such as counties and census tracts.

REFERENCES

Bogue, Donald J. (1985). *The Population of the United States*. New York: Free Press.
Robey, Bryant (1989). *Two Hundred Years and Counting: The 1990 Census*. Population Bulletin Vol. 44, No. 1. Washington, DC: Population Reference Bureau.
U.S. Bureau of the Census (1994). *Statistical Abstract of the United States, 1994*. Washington, DC: U.S. Government Printing Office.

SUGGESTED READINGS/RESOURCES

American Business Lists (Frequent updates). Lists: 94 million households, 10 million U.S. businesses and 1 million Canadian businesses, among others.
U.S. Bureau of the Census (Annual). *Statistical Abstract of the United States*. Washington, DC: U.S. Government Printing Office.
U.S. Bureau of the Census (Periodic publications). *State and Metropolitan Area Data Book*. Washington, DC: U.S. Government Printing Office.
U.S. Bureau of the Census (Periodic publications). *County and City Data Book*. Washington, DC: U.S. Government Printing Office.

Chapter 9

Population Composition

INTRODUCTION

For business planning purposes, the most important information required about a market, after its size, is its demographic composition. Population counts can tell how many of us there are, but indicators of composition tell us what we are like. An analysis of population composition involves the interesting facts about a market area, the characteristics that every business planner must become familiar with in order to make intelligent decisions. An area's age distribution, racial composition, income level, and dominant religion, for example, are the types of characteristics that give a population its "personality." When the press reports that America is becoming much older as a nation, or that in 2050 today's minority populations will constitute a numerical majority, these developments reflect the changing population composition.

An understanding of the composition of an area's population is essential for business planning. It may be of passing interest that a population is 15 percent elderly, 40 percent African-American, mostly at a working-class income level, reports an average educational level of high school graduate, and has an average family size of 3.5. When compositional traits are related to consumer behavior, however, they go beyond description and become powerful predictors of the consumption of goods and services. Information on the current number of residents is a good starting point, but information on age, racial composition or marital status, for example, can be combined with psychographic data to generate sales forecasts, financial projections, and the lifetime value of a customer. While the current demographic composition of a market may indicate a relatively low demand for a specific service, subsequent compositional change may result in a much different level of demand in the future.

Business planners are often concerned about the compositional nature of a variety of different groups and geographies within the population. The population whose composition is being examined may be the consumer population (potential customers), the customer population (existing customers), the labor force, decision makers, or some other segment of the population. It is also likely to be linked to a particular geography, such as a county, zip code, or census tract. The analyst will typically be studying a specific subpopulation within a specific geographic area.

COMPOSITIONAL ATTRIBUTES

Demographers divide compositional attributes into two categories: biosocial characteristics and sociocultural characteristics. *Biosocial* characteristics are those that have an underlying biological or physical component. They tend to be "ascribed" characteristics, present at birth and not subject to deliberate change. Biosocial factors include age, sex, race, and ethnicity. With the exception of ethnicity, all are rooted squarely in biology. Ethnicity has its basis in a common cultural heritage, although marriage within ethnic groups typically results in the development of a gene pool that includes common physical characteristics.

These biosocial factors also have significant social connotations in that there are behaviors associated with persons who have various combinations of ascribed characteristics. For example, by virtue of being biologically female rather than male, women purchase a distinct set of products and services. Senior citizens purchase different products than teenagers. Similarly, African-Americans display different buyer behavior patterns than do whites or Hispanics.

Sociocultural characteristics, on the other hand, are a reflection of the individual's position within the social system. Sociocultural factors, in U.S. society at least, are primarily "achieved" rather than ascribed. These are not traits with which one is born but ones that are achieved either voluntarily or involuntarily. Unlike biosocial factors, these traits are often amenable to change. The most frequently utilized sociocultural factors are marital status/living arrangements/family structure, income, education, and occupation/industry. Religious characteristics are sometimes considered under this category and housing characteristics and type of community may also be included under this heading. Each important compositional variable is discussed in turn in the sections that follow.

Biosocial Characteristics

Age. Age is measured in terms of years since birth lived by the individual. It is usually reported in whole years, except in the case of infants whose age may be recorded in months. In obtaining data on age, individuals may be asked to disclose their ages as of their last birthday or simply to provide their date of birth. In the latter case, exact age is derived by subtracting the birth date from the current date or from some reference date. For example, a person born on October 31, 1970, was considered to be 19 years old in the 1990 census, the date of reference being April 1, 1990.

Age data in the United States are of relatively high quality, although there is some evidence that survey respondents are not always truthful in reporting their ages. Age "heaping" occurs for milestone ages such as 21, 62, 65, 100, and ages that end in zero. There also are some differences in age determination from culture to culture, which may have growing implications in an increasingly multicultural society. In some cultures years are added at the start of the birth year—for example, Chinese calculations would place a newborn infant at age one, with the infant turning two at the beginning of her second year. Some societies may record an actual birth date and also an "official" birth date at the time the birth was registered with the authorities.

While age data are gathered in single years, they are typically reported by intervals for populations. Age intervals are usually five years in length with the exception of the youngest grouping (under age 5) and oldest grouping (age 85 and over). Age data are generally aggregated for a specific geographic unit such as a zip code, census tract, or market area. Further aggregations can be made simply by summing the totals for smaller units. For analytical purposes, one of the most common practices in assessing the relative characteristics of various market areas is to compare age structures.

Sex. The sex of an individual is perhaps the most straightforward attribute to measure, given that there are only two possible choices. Distinctions made on the basis of sex are important in all societies, and many aspects of social structure reflect the relative size and importance of the male and female populations within the society. For product planning and marketing, male/female preference differences in terms of products (and even brands) are an important consideration.

Race and Ethnicity. Race and ethnicity are at the same time biologically determined and socially constructed. Racial identity is derived from physical characteristics such as skin color or facial features *that are recognized as distinctive by the particular society*. Ethnic identification, on the other hand, is based on a common cultural heritage. Racial or ethnic identification is less clear than that for age or sex because the guidelines for placement in a category are not as well defined. In the United States, this lack of clarity reflects the fact that millions of Americans are of mixed parentage. Many individuals may not even know their historical racial background; when they identify themselves as African-American or Asian, for example, placement in that group may be as much a product of historical association as one of biological distinction. The same can be said for ethnic identification, where historical association plays an even bigger role.

The major racial groups recognized by the federal government for reporting purposes include whites, African-Americans, Asians and Pacific Islanders, and native Americans (i.e., Indians and "Eskimos"). As U.S. society has become more multicultural, it is increasingly possible to be a member of two groups.

Ethnic identification requires a person to specify ancestry or origin, such as Spanish/Hispanic, Italian, German, or Thai. Subgroup totals (e.g., for Cuban-Americans, Mexican-Americans, and Puerto Ricans) are sometimes summed and presented as an aggregate such as figures for the Spanish-origin (Hispanic) population. National origin groups may or may not be considered ethnic groups, depending on the extent to which they have taken on subcultural characteristics within a society. Box 9.1 presents a discussion of how racial/ethnic categories may be changed in the future.

Box 9.1
Categorizing Racial and Ethnic Groups

Professional demographers and the business community have shown a growing concern over the way in which race and ethnicity have been defined. The federal government has historically established the guidelines for racial categorization. For reporting purposes, individuals self-identify only one racial and one ethnicity category, although in the census and many surveys racial and ethnic identity for all members of a household is reported by one member of that household. Given the large degree of intermarriage among racial and ethnic groups, selecting only one category masks the level of intermarriage and subsequent racial diversity. For business analysts, racial and ethnic categorization is an important issue in the targeting and retention of customers. Moreover, these classifications have important personnel and human resources management implications.

As of this writing, a test of new racial and ethnic groupings is being planned by the Bureau of the Census for June 1996. The purpose of the test is to determine if current racial and ethnic identification methods should be altered in the 2000 census. The proposed changes reflect the fact that respondents are confused by the word ethnicity and that "ancestry" and "ethnic origin" are more user-friendly terms.

The 1996 test will examine the relative effectiveness of using multiracial or biracial categories, allowing respondents to check more than one category, and rearranging the order in which the questions are asked. While changes in the way we measure race and ethnicity are clearly needed by the business community, changes that might be made in the 2000 census would limit the comparability of these data to data collected in previous censuses and surveys. If changes in the racial and ethnic categories of the 2000 census are announced in 1997, businesses must determine what effect the change would have on customer, prospect, employee, and market data and be prepared to adjust to the new system.

Source: Susan Caleche (1996). "U.S. Ponders Its Race and Ethnic Categories for 2000 Census." *Population Today*, Vol. 24, No. 1 Washington, DC: Population Reference Bureau.

Sociocultural Characteristics

Marital Status/Living Arrangements/Family Structure. Marital status, living arrangements, and family structure are all ways of looking at household characteristics and are discussed collectively in this section. Historically, marital status has been the primary factor on which a determination of family status was made. However, as the traditional family has given way to new household organizational structures, other bases for describing household characteristics have become necessary.

Marital status is generally grouped into four or five categories: single, married, widowed, or divorced, with a category for the "separated" sometimes employed. Researchers sometimes collect information on marital history, particularly in view of the changing marriage patterns within U.S. society. Age at first (and subsequent) marriages may be determined, and the number of marriages and divorces may be specified, along with the timing of these events.

Although registries are maintained on the number of marriages and divorces by various levels of government (see Chapter 3), censuses or surveys are needed to determine the marital status of the population at a particular point in time. The decennial census collects information on marital status every ten years and these data are supplemented by means of sample surveys such as the Current Population Survey.

The determination of "living arrangements" requires several pieces of information. First, the grouping of the population into households must take place. A *household* is made up of one or more persons living in a housing unit, with a *housing unit* defined as one or more rooms that comprise separate living quarters. Individual apartments and duplex halves are separate housing units, while dormitories and military barracks are not. Dormitories and military barracks are considered *group quarters* and persons living in group quarters are enumerated separately. The population within housing units is subsequently categorized according to whether individuals are living alone, living with unrelated individuals, or living in one of the many "related individual" combinations.

Establishing whether or not persons in a housing unit constitute a family is also an important consideration. A *family* is defined, for statistical purposes, as two or more persons related by blood, marriage, or adoption who live together. Information on family status is obtained through the administration of censuses and surveys. If the data obtained meet the family definition requirements, those persons are considered a family. Two unrelated persons living in the same housing unit are designated as a household; if they are related they would be classified as both a household and family. Households are thus subdivided between family and nonfamily categories.

From a business planning perspective, these distinctions are important for a number of reasons. Whether the unit used for analysis is a household or a family depends on the circumstances. For example, median household incomes are likely to differ from median family incomes. Whether members of a household are "related" by marriage, blood, friendship, convenience or some other basis has important consumer behavior implications.

Community Type. The U.S. population is divided in terms of community of residence into metropolitan, nonmetropolitan, urban, and rural categories (see Chapter 7 on geographic units for a discussion of these concepts). These categories are further divided into subcategories, for example, urban into such subcategories as central city, suburb, and urbanized area, and rural into farm and nonfarm subcategories.

The U.S. Bureau of the Census is one of the few organizations that collects information on type of residence, primarily through the decennial census and sample surveys in between census years. However, the differences in consumer behavior between urban and rural populations are more significant than this lack of attention warrants.

Income. Income statistics generally refer to income accumulated during the previous year. Income usually refers to money earned from all sources. "Unearned" income, such as that received from investments, interest, and social transfer programs, may be added into total income and/or appear as a separate category. Data collection may focus on individual income or refer to household or family income. If the income reference is the family or household, all members of the household or family are included. Some surveys may require a respondent to disclose the source of the income (e.g., wages and salaries, dividends, royalty income, or income from estates and trusts) for the individual and/or the family/household.

A number of different income measures might be utilized for business planning purposes. These include median household (or family) income and per capita income. The amount of disposable or discretionary income is often determined by business planners. The level of poverty within a population is also used as a measure of economic well-being. Since averages are often misleading, the planner must also consider the distribution of income within the population under study.

Income is clearly a powerful predictor of consumer behavior. Not only does the amount of income serve as the most serious constraint on expenditures, but income level also influences the attitudes, preferences, and lifestyles of individuals and families.

Educational Level. Educational level is measured in terms of current educational attainment (i.e., completed years of school and/or degrees earned). Persons may be asked to report the number of years of schooling they have completed (e.g., completion of high school equals 12 years and college graduation equals 16 years). Alternatively, respondents may be asked to report the degrees they have completed (e.g., associate degree, masters degree). The educational attainment of a population is typically expressed in mean or median years, although the distribution of years of education completed by a population is often most important.

Like income, education is an important predictor of consumer behavior. Not only is there a correlation between education and income, but education, even more than income, is an important predictor of lifestyle and, therefore, of purchasing behavior.

Work Status/Occupation/Industry. Work status, occupation, and industry data all relate to one's position in the labor force. These data are collected through a variety of sources. "Work status" includes information on labor force participation, employment history, and episodes of unemployment. For individuals who are employed, additional information on the number of hours worked may be collected. Part-time and full-time classifications may be used based on the number of hours per week and weeks per year worked.

"Occupation" refers to the kind of work a person normally does. Examples of specific occupations include registered nurse, gasoline engine assembler, and cake icer. The hundreds of recognized occupations are often aggregated into nine or ten major occupational groupings, such as professional and technical, sales, and managerial. "Industry" refers to the business or industry where the occupation is held, such as health care or publishing.

The Bureau of Labor Statistics within the U.S. Department of Labor has primary responsibility for monitoring the occupational makeup of the U.S. population. Occupation and industry data from individuals and businesses are assigned code numbers developed for the Standard Industrial Classification (SIC) listing and the Dictionary of Occupational Titles (DOC). SIC and DOC data for market areas are particularly valuable in that they provide information regarding where people work and what they do. Both the SIC and DOC codes are currently being revised and may be available in a more meaningful form by the time this book is published.

Religion. Religious characteristics are one of the few compositional traits for which little information is collected in the United States. Questions regarding religious affiliation or levels of religiosity are not standard items in censuses and government-sponsored surveys because of public sensitivity toward government interference in religion. Data on religion are sometimes collected, however, by means of sample surveys. The types of questions usually asked concern religious affiliation (e.g., Roman Catholic), attendance (e.g., times per month), and religiosity, or depth of beliefs.

The usefulness of religious classification in U.S. society has been questioned because of the limited level of participation of Americans in organized religion. Although identification with a particular denomination is still common (Russell 1993), the business implications of these affiliations are not immediately obvious. Except for specific situations such as the sales of religious objects or the promotion of religion-oriented programs, knowledge of the religious composition of the population is likely to be less important to business planners than most other compositional characteristics.

Housing. Housing information, it can be argued, is a reflection of the level of economic well-being of the population. The decennial census, along with Census Bureau surveys such as the American Housing Survey, collects extensive housing data. The questions asked range from those related to home value to specific housing unit attributes such as type of heating. Because of the long-standing interest in the quality of housing on the part of the federal government, the housing data collected through the decennial census is both extensive and detailed.

MEASURES OF COMPOSITIONAL VARIATION

Descriptive Measures

The most common measures of compositional variation are descriptive and are presented in terms of simple *percentages or proportions*. These measures include simple data presentations, such as 15 percent of the population in market area X live below the poverty level, 74 percent of the population is non-Hispanic white, and females account for 52 percent of the population. When using percentage distribution information, it is generally better to include data for several categories (perhaps the entire distribution), even though the focus may be on only one level of aggregation. This will give the analyst a more complete picture of the conditions being addressed.

Rates and *ratios* are frequently utilized to measure compositional variation. The term "rate" applies to the number of demographic events in a given period of time divided by the population at risk during that period. Thus, we could characterize the number of deaths within a population divided by the total number in the population as the "death rate." In demographic analyses the "population-at- risk" may have to be approximated. The time period covered in the calculation of rates is typically one year and the rate is usually expressed per 100; 1,000; or 100,000 of the population. Percentages are often referred to as rates in common usage—e.g., a 40 percent illiteracy rate. A figure like the illiteracy rate is simply the percent of persons in a given population subgroup who are classified as illiterate.

Demographers sometimes distinguish "rates" from "probabilities." In calculating rates, the denominator is typically the population at the midpoint of the period under study (or the average population during that period). Probabilities, on the other hand, are based on the population at the beginning of the period—that is, the population considered to be at risk for experiencing the event during the period.

Summary measures such as means and medians are also utilized for measuring compositional attributes. The mean refers to the arithmetic average and the median to the midpoint of a distribution. For most purposes it is better to rely on the median, although the use of both statistics in conjunction is the best approach. The data user should keep in mind that a given mean or median may be the result of an infinite number of combinations of data distributions. Utilizing the mean or median without analyzing the distribution from which the figures are derived may result in an incomplete or even erroneous interpretation. This is particularly important when examining income and age distributions. Some examples of measures commonly used by demographers are presented below.

Dependency Ratio. Dependency ratios are utilized to characterize a population in terms of its "dependent" population (Bogue 1969, pp. 154–156). A dependency ratio is the quotient of an area's dependent population divided by its supporting population. The dependent population refers to those under 18 years of age and those over 65—that is, those dependent on the working population. The working or support population is usually considered to be those individuals between the ages of 18 (or 20) and 64.

The youth dependency ratio for the United States in 1950 can be calculated as follows:

$$\frac{\text{number of persons under age 20}}{\text{number of persons 20–64}} = \frac{51,000,000}{87,327,000} = 0.58.$$

This ratio of 0.58 converts to 1.72 persons of approximate working age for every person under age 20. By the year 2000, this ratio will shrink to 0.47, or 2.12 persons of working age for each person under age 20.

The aged dependency ratio for 1950 can be calculated as follows:

$$\frac{\text{number of persons aged 65 and over}}{\text{number of persons 20–64}} = \frac{12,270,000}{87,327,000} = 0.14.$$

This converts to 7.14 persons of approximate working age for each person age 65 and over. By the year 2000 this ratio is expected to increase to 0.40, meaning there will be only 2.50 persons of approximate working age for each person age 65 and over (U.S. Bureau of the Census 1995, Table 36). The anticipated change in the age dependency ratio illustrates the increasing impact of the elderly on the Social Security system, Medicare, and other programs specific to the older population.

The total dependency ratio takes the sum of both dependent populations (under age 20 and over age 65) and divides by the number of persons aged 20 to 64. In 1950, the total dependency ratio for the U.S. populations was 0.72, or 1.39 persons of working age for every person under age 20 or over age 64. In 2000, the total dependency ratio will be 0.69, or 1.45 when inverted. As can be seen, the total dependency ratio is virtually the same for both years, despite the substantial rise in the median age of the population. The increase in the older population will be offset by a decrease in the younger population.

Dependency ratios exhibit considerable variability across geographic areas. For example, in 1990 the youth dependency ratios for Tallahassee and St. Petersburg, Florida, were 0.27 and 0.34, respectively. In contrast, the aged dependency ratios were 0.12 and 0.38, respectively (U.S. Bureau of the Census 1993, Table 169). In other words, St. Petersburg had approximately three working age residents for every person age 65 and over, while Tallahassee had more than eight!

Sex Ratio. The sex ratio is used to specify the relative proportions of males and females within a population. The sex ratio is calculated by dividing the total number of males by the total number of females and multiplying by 100. The product represents the number of males for every 100 females in the population. For 1990, the sex ratio calculation for all ages in the United States was as follows:

$$\frac{\text{Males } (121,239,000)}{\text{Females } (127,471,000)} = 0.95 \text{ x } 100 \text{ (or 95 men for every 100 women)}.$$

The sex ratio is a useful indicator for assessing the characteristics of the population since it can reflect a number of factors. A high sex ratio—that is, an "excess" of males—could indicate a very young population, since more males are born than females. This is often the case, in fact, in developing countries with high birth rates. A low sex ratio or an excess of females often indicates an older population. Perhaps more importantly, a low sex ratio may imply poor economic conditions, since it could reflect the selective outmigration of residents in the productive age ranges. Thus, some rural communities have low sex ratios because young persons have left the community for economic opportunities elsewhere.

Since the age distribution of males is usually different from that of females, the overall sex ratio may mask some important information. For persons under age five in the United States today, there are 105 males for every 100 females. At ages 25 to 29, the sex ratio decreases to 100, representing parity between the sexes. For each successive age category the excess of females over males grows and, for ages 75 and over, there are 182 women for every 100 men.

Sex ratios can show even more variability at smaller units of geography. In Florida, for example, the ratio of males to females was 0.94 in 1990, and 0.74 for the age groups 65 and over (U.S. Bureau of the Census 1993, Table 20). In St. Petersburg the sex ratio for the total population was 0.86 in 1990. The state of Utah, on the other hand, exhibited the unusual pattern of sex ratios for the age intervals 10 to 14, 15 to 19, 20 to 24, and 25 to 29 of 1.06, 1.00, 0.98, and 1.02, respectively. This pattern reflects the fact that many males in their late teens and early twenties leave the state to perform missionary work for the Mormon church.

Analytical Techniques

Population Pyramids. Population distributions are sometimes presented visually in the form of population pyramids. The age/sex distribution for males and females within a population is usually presented in a series of stacked bars. Each bar represents the percentage of the total population in that age interval, although absolute numbers may be used as well. On the left side of the stacked bars are the percentages or numbers for males and on the right those for females. Analysts can determine a lot about a population simply by examining its pyramid. Pyramids that are "bottom heavy" have younger age structures, while older age structures demonstrate more constant age-to-age percentages. Other combinations of characteristics (e.g., age and race) could also be used (Newell 1987, pp. 25–26; Pressat 1972, pp. 263–276).

Figures 9.1 and 9.2 present population pyramids using absolute numbers for St. Petersburg and Tallahassee, Florida, for 1990, created by a readily available computer software package. As can be seen, the age distributions of the two cities are markedly different. St. Petersburg contains fewer persons aged 0 to 4 than it does persons aged 65 to 69. It also contains more females than males. Tallahassee, on the other hand, has a much younger population; there are relatively few persons aged 65 and over. Moreover, to the extent that Tallahassee is a college town (Florida State and Florida A&M universities are located there), there is a bulge in the pyramid at ages 20 to 24. A great deal can be learned about both populations just by examining their population pyramids.

Cohort Analysis. A second method used to examine compositional data is cohort analysis. A "cohort" is a group of persons within a population with a common characteristic. This characteristic could be any one that an analyst finds valuable for creating a population segment for analysis. For example, military personnel exposed to Agent Orange during the Viet Nam war, persons who bought a new Mercedes 190E in 1989, or persons born during a particular time interval might be identified as a cohorts of interest.

Age is the most frequent basis for cohort identification used by demographers. Age cohorts are delineated by grouping persons who were born within a certain range of years. The U.S. cohort aged 46 to 50 in 1996, which contains the oldest of the "baby boomers," is made up of persons who were born between 1946 and 1950. The so-called "notch" cohort, born between 1917 and 1920, has received recent attention because of its unique status with regard to Social Security benefits.

Figure 9.1
Population Pyramid, Tallahassee, Florida, 1990

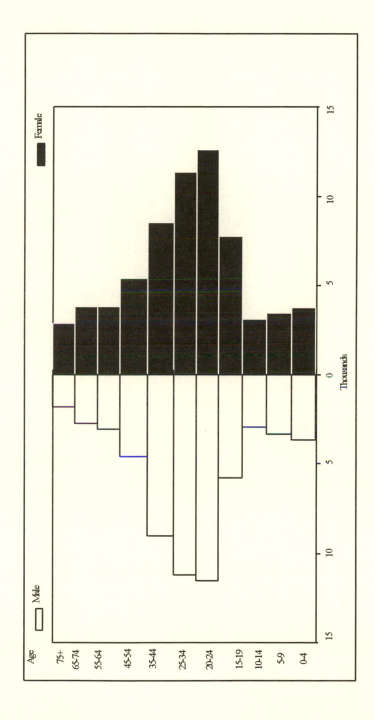

Figure 9.2
Population Pyramid, St. Petersburg, Florida, 1990

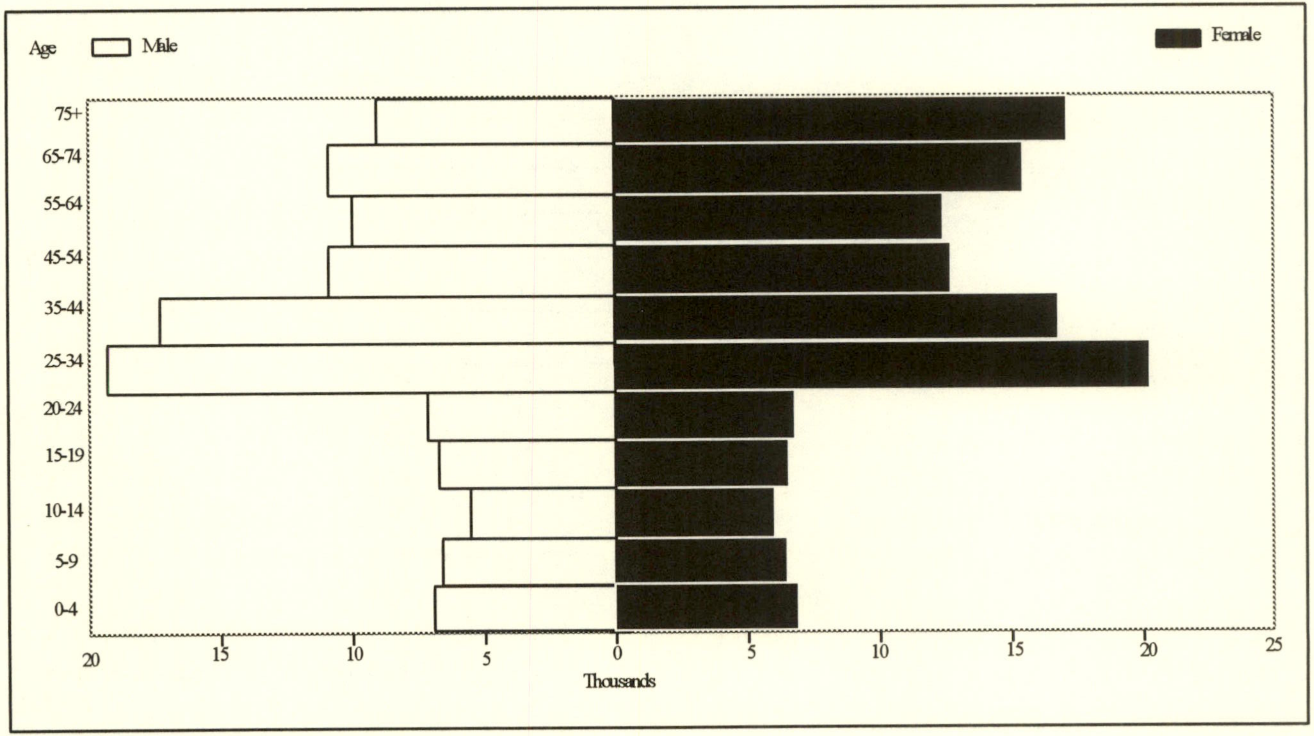

Age

Male

Female

75+
65-74
55-64
45-54
35-44
25-34
20-24
15-19
10-14
5-9
0-4

20   15   10   5   0   5   10   15   20   25

Thousands

Cohort analysis typically involves following a cohort over time to determine changes in its characteristics. For example, one might want to measure the consequences of exposure to toxic materials, track shifts in buying patterns of household appliances, determine whether or not repeat buying took place, or monitor trends in disposable income. It is assumed, although not always correctly, that persons within a cohort share experiences and behavior because of their common characteristic.

Cohort identification and analysis are sometimes used to ascribe experiences and behavior patterns to a cohort when individual data are not available. Cohort analysis can range from simply measuring the number and proportion of persons in various age groupings over time to determining the ways in which cohort experiences affect different types of behavior (Glenn 1977; Hobcraft, Menkin, and Preston 1982; Rentz, Reynolds, and Stout 1983; Reynolds and Rentz 1981). Cohort-to-cohort comparisons allow an assessment of change in cohort behavior over time.

Studying the transition of a cohort from one period to the next involves the use of mortality data and survival analysis techniques. For example, the cohort of individuals aged 65 to 69 in 1995 is composed of those persons aged 60 to 64 in 1990, minus those who died during the 1990 to 1995 time interval (not accounting for any migration). The observed changes in cohort size and characteristics tell the analyst a great deal about consumer patterns that are likely to characterize this cohort in the future.

Cohort analysts must consider the fact that population change is affected by factors other than mortality. Persons are added at the youngest ages as a result of births occurring to the population and this establishes the initial size of the cohort. Once a cohort is born, the cohort's population may be added to by immigration or subtracted from by emigration. Factoring immigration and emigration into the analysis, however, somewhat violates the "spirit" of cohort analysis and may complicate the comparison over time.

Standardization. Business analysts often desire to compare two or more populations with regard to one or more characteristics. Since the sizes and composition of populations are likely to vary, some method of *standardization* is necessary to ensure that appropriate comparisons are being made. If the data are not standardized, incorrect conclusions could easily be drawn. A good example of this would be a comparison of death rates by state. Florida reports one of the highest death rates among the 50 states, making it appear to have an "unhealthy" environment. However, if state death rates are statistically adjusted (standardized) to account for the fact that Florida has an older age distribution, Florida turns out to be one of the "healthiest" states.

A simple form of standardization involves the use of rates. The number of events per 1,000 residents provides a typical example, as in 10 births per thousand people for one population and 15 births per thousand for a second. The use of percentages, for example, 45 percent of the market prefers Brand X, is another way of generating a rate. The percentage, of course, is simply the rate per 100 persons. As with the Florida example above, rates are most useful in comparisons if similar populations are being examined.

There are a number of other ways in which analysts can standardize populations under study. The first of these is through a "homogenization" process whereby apples are compared to apples and not oranges or bananas. In this case, the analyst would segregate the populations under study into the categories of interest, for example, all those 65 and over. Then, the characteristics of the elderly in one population could be compared to those of the elderly in another population, thereby homogenizing the subgroups being analyzed.

A more complex form of standardization involves the statistical standardization of populations under study. For this procedure a "standard" population is chosen as the benchmark for calculating rates, then the observed cases for the two populations are applied to this standard population. For example, if the population of Florida were standardized to resemble that of the United States in terms of age, we would find that the death rate is actually relatively low. The apparent high rate is due to the excess of residents in the older age groups where most of the deaths are concentrated. In this case the national population structure is used as the standard, although the standard population could be that for one of the populations in the comparison. Thus, standardization allows the analyst to adjust the rate of the comparison population to reflect the rate if both populations had similar population structures.

The use of a standard population allows differences in age, sex, and other characteristics to be held constant for purposes of analysis. Age and sex are probably the most frequently utilized bases for standardization. However, there are circumstances when characteristics like race, marital status, or housing type might be held constant. For business planning purposes, analysts often use standardization to control for differences in income levels or educational achievement. For example, the fact that the number of luxury automobiles is higher within Population A than within Population B might lead one to conclude that the preference for luxury cars in Population A is higher. Simply standardizing the populations to take income into account may reveal that, among those at comparable income levels, the preference for luxury cars within Population B is actually higher.

Another form of standardization involves stratification of the populations under study. Like the other approaches identified, stratification involves segmenting the populations being compared in such a way that comparisons are meaningful. For example, if the two populations being compared are dissimilar in terms of racial characteristics, it may be worthwhile to stratify the populations by race. Thus, whites within one population would be compared to whites in the other, as would African-Americans, Hispanics, or whatever other racial or ethnic groups are of significance. This stratification approach could be taken with almost any demographic attribute of a population.

More recent advances in standardization techniques have applied log linear models to the same sets of data (e.g., Clogg and Eliason 1988; Xie 1989). Log linear analysis addresses some of the shortcomings in traditional standardization techniques and allows for the isolation and identification of the effect of age structure and other variables on the rates under study. Pol and Pak (1995, 1996) have used these techniques for segmenting the fast food and health care markets.

TRENDS IN POPULATION COMPOSITION

During the last part of the twentieth century, the United States has experienced a number of significant demographic trends. Changes in the age structure, shifts in family type, and growing diversity have made an understanding of the changing composition of the population more important than ever for business planning. The most significant trends were discussed in detail in Chapter 2. Trends for each of the compositional attributes are summarized below.

Age Distribution

The changing age distribution of the U.S. population has been one of the major news stories of the last quarter of the twentieth century. The aging of the nation's population has already had major implications for businesses of all types. The median age of the U.S. population has steadily increased since records have been kept. In 1990 the median age of the population was 32.8, up from 30.0 in 1980. By 2000 the median age is projected to be 35.7, representing by far the largest increase ever over one decade in the United States. This means that one half of the population will be 35 or over in 2000, a phenomenon that few other societies have experienced.

It is more important to focus on components of the age structure rather than simply observe one summary statistic. Population "growth" at the middle ages (e.g., age 50 to 54) is currently faster than that at the younger ages due to the movement of baby boomers into the middle age range. Several younger groups, in fact, will experience a net loss of population into the twenty-first century.

While the overall population distribution is shifting upward and creating an increasingly top-heavy age distribution, the major force for aging will be the huge baby boom cohort (78 million) as it moves into the 45–65 age bracket. While all older age groups will increase significantly in numbers, the 85 and over age group will grow faster than every other cohort. As a result of these differential growth rates by age, the age structure in 2010 will be noticeably different from that in the mid-1990s. The share of the population made up of persons aged 55 and over will increase from 21 percent to 25 percent. Those under 18 are expected to account for only 24 percent of the U.S. population in 2010 (compared to 26 percent in 1990) (see Table 9.1). Boxes 9.2 and 9.3 focus on compositional change.

Box 9.2

The Changing U.S. Population Composition and Demographic "Firsts"

Throughout U.S. history demographic change has been a slowly evolving process. Although there has been the occasional "spike" on the demographic radar screen, fertility, mortality and migration rates typically change slowly over time. Thus, the likelihood of major change occurring rapidly in our society is low and the occurrence

Box 9.2 continued

of unexpected situations is rare.

The demographic events of the second half of the twentieth century, however, have generated a number of unprecedented developments—demographic "firsts"—in U.S. society. We are confronted with many situations that may have been experienced only to a limited extent in other societies and some that are totally unknown elsewhere. Some of these developments are so unexpected that even the market does not know how to respond to them. Who would have predicted that large numbers of "forty-something" women would start having babies, that 60-year-old children taking care of 80-year-old parents would be common, or that teenage children would be giving their parents "dating" lessons?

Many of these unprecedented situations are a function of the aging trend that is affecting U.S. society. While the United States is not the first country to experience this process—the Scandinavian countries have already been through it—the magnitude of the situation in terms of numbers is much different. The 31 million elderly Americans in 1990 constituted a larger group than the combined populations of Sweden, Norway, Denmark, and Finland!

Yet it is the characteristics of the population rather than their numbers that are so unprecedented. This aging process means that, today, over one half of our population is over 35, a significant factor in a "youth-oriented" society. Because of the increased longevity of American seniors, we now have elderly citizens living so long they exhaust their financial resources before they die. This has an obvious impact on inheritance, where either there is nothing left to pass down to their heirs or the heirs themselves are elderly at the time of their parents' deaths. Indeed, we now have many elderly parents being cared for by their elderly children. Or alternatively, there is the "sandwich" generation of middle-aged adults who are simultaneously caring for their children and their parents.

Many of these "firsts" also stem from changes in the American family, particularly with regard to marital status. Historically, almost all Americans married (and some several times). That is no longer the case and we now find an unprecedented situation in which over 25 percent of the "middle-aged" population (i.e., those 45–65) is not married. Among those who have married, the numbers of widowed and divorced are at record levels, prompting some to identify a "postmarital" cohort.

The decline in marriage rates, coupled with later marriage for those who do marry, has created a large bachelor/bachelorette cohort in U.S. society. Thus, there are unprecedented numbers of "thirty-something" males and females who have never married. The emergence of a significant young, professional, and single population is certainly a new development in U.S. society. There is also a new and unprecedented cohort of first-time mothers in their 30s and 40s. Childbearing in this age group is not new; what is new is the fact that they have had no children at a younger age.

This trend has also affected living arrangements. Barely one fourth of the nation's households could be considered "traditional," with mother, father, and 2.1 children. Large numbers of new living arrangements have emerged, including cohabitative arrangements and same-sex marriages. More than one fourth of all U.S. households are one-person households. The size of this population living alone is remarkable, being greater than the entire population of Canada. The number of children born out of wedlock every year is at record levels and the proportion of children not living with both

---

Box 9.2 continued

their natural parents is staggering. Single-parent households are the fastest growing household type, and father-only households have become common. Nevertheless, the number of children growing up without a father present has become a national scandal.

One other "new" development discussed earlier has been the high level of immigration. Large numbers of immigrants are not unprecedented, but ethnic and minority groups have never accounted for 25 percent of the population or 40 percent of American children. The types and characteristics of today's immigrants also create an unprecedented situation. Past waves of immigrants were eager to become Americanized at the expense of their native cultures; today's are not. For the first time, there are large ethnic communities within our society that are to a greater or lesser extent resisting assimilation. These immigrants may be settling the debate over whether the United States is a melting pot or a salad bowl—in favor of the latter.

These and related demographic firsts present a challenge to business analysts and decision makers in virtually every industry. New groups of consumers are created and the old perspectives on consumer behavior no longer have validity. There is no indication that this situation is going to stabilize in the foreseeable future, requiring business analysts to become even more sophisticated in demographic analysis.

Table 9.1
Age Distribution in the United States: 1990–2010 (Projected)
(In Millions)

Age Category	1990	2000	2010
Under 5	18.8	19.4	20.0
5 to 13	31.8	36.5	36.2
14 to 17	13.3	15.8	17.4
18 to 24	26.9	25.9	30.2
25 to 34	43.2	38.2	38.2
35 to 44	37.4	45.1	39.7
45 to 54	25.1	36.1	44.1
55 to 64	21.1	23.7	34.6
65 to 74	18.0	18.6	21.0
75 to 84	10.0	12.4	13.2
85 and over	3.0	4.3	5.9

Source: U.S. Bureau of the Census (Middle Series Projection) (1993). *Current Population Reports*, P25-1104. Washington, DC: U.S. Government Printing Office.

Box 9.3
The Special Case of the Baby Boomers

The major demographic event of the second half of the twentieth century in America has been the emergence of the huge "baby boom" cohort. Totaling 78 million people, the baby boomers represent the largest generation ever within the U.S. population. This cohort of individuals born between 1946 and 1964 is unique in that they far exceed successive generations in numbers; even the baby boomlet they spawned equals only 72 million individuals.

Perhaps more important, baby boomers are unique in terms of the circumstances of their birth and the characteristics they have subsequently developed. Baby boomers are probably the first American generation that can be distinguished from their parents in significant ways. This cohort was born into a world of comparative stability and unprecedented affluence. This situation has created a generation that is used to acquiring whatever it wants and generally having things its way.

This environment has spawned a new type of consumer. Baby boomers are well educated and well informed. They are interested in participating in any decision making related to their lives, from choice of their children's schools to decisions concerning their medical treatment. They are used to being in control and, as such, become very demanding consumers. They are used to having things in working order and are very concerned about quality. Baby boomers are determined to get what they pay for. Boomers want quality, reasonable costs, convenience, and personal service. They want it all.

The large baby boom cohort has already reshaped many U.S. industries and, as it enters "middle age," it is likely to have an even greater impact on the American landscape. It has already influenced major change in health care and, as boomers become the major consumers of health services over the next two decades, they are likely to further modify the industry. Baby boomers are effecting the same kinds of changes in other industries.

Baby boomers are unlike any previous generation in terms of lifestyles, attitudes *and* consumer behavior, and cannot be expected to "age" in the same way as their forefathers. Boomers cannot be lumped into the "mature market" category any more than they could have been considered typical young adults. Rather than becoming the well-documented fifty-something consumer, boomers are likely to constitute a new and different older adult market segment. Their backgrounds and their lifestyles mean that marketers are going to have to rethink their notion of the middle-aged consumer. In fact, a new term—"midyouth"—has already been coined to describe this generation of consumers.

For more information on baby boomers as consumers see Cheryl Russell, "The Baby Boom Turns 50," *American Demographics*, December, 1995.

Sex Distribution

An automatic accompaniment to the aging of America has been the "feminization" of the U.S. population. Generally speaking, the older the population, the greater the "excess" of females. Although more males are born than females in the United States and other industrialized countries, as discussed in Chapter 6 developed nations are typically characterized by an excess of females over males. For every age cohort over 30, females outnumber males. By the time we are considered elderly, females outnumber males as much as two to one.

Males outnumbered females in the United States at the beginning of the twentieth century, principally due to the level of maternal mortality and the effects of immigration. In fact, males outnumbered females until 1950. As a result of the demographic transition to an older population, however, the number of females began to exceed the number of males after that year The data in Table 9.2 show the sex distribution in the United States for three different time periods. In 1990 there were approximately 95 males for every 100 females in the U.S. population. By 2010, demographers are projecting a sex ratio of 96 males for every 100 females. There will be an "excess" of 6.1 million females in 2010 compared to 6.3 million in 1990. Although the population will continue to age, high levels of immigration (and the subsequent high fertility levels of immigrant populations) will temporarily retard the growth in the excess of females.

Table 9.2
Sex Distribution in the United States: 1990 to 2010
(In Millions)

Sex	1990	2000	2010
Male	121.2	135.1	147.2
Female	127.5	141.4	153.2

Source: U.S. Bureau of the Census (Middle Series Projection) (1993). *Current Population Reports*, P25-1104. Washington, DC: U.S. Government Printing Office.

Race/Ethnicity

As noted in Chapter 2, one of the major current demographic developments is the growing numerical significance of racial and ethnic minorities within the U.S. population. America has once again become a nation of immigrants, with the numbers of newcomers from foreign lands equaling historic highs. Long-established ethnic and racial minorities are growing at faster rates than are native-born whites. This growing racial and ethnic diversity is expected to continue for the foreseeable future and some demographers predict that minority group members will constitute nearly 40 percent of the U.S. population by 2025 (U.S. Bureau of the Census 1995, Table 25).

As a result of this trend, the visibility of non-Hispanic whites in the U.S.

population is decreasing. Non-Hispanic whites accounted for 80 percent of the U.S. population in 1980, 76 percent in 1990, and a projected 72 percent in 2000. By 2025, non-Hispanic whites are projected to make up only around 62 percent of the U.S. population. By 2000 over one third of American children under age 5 will be members of minority groups.

In 1990 African-Americans comprised 12.1 percent of the U.S. population, while Asians and Pacific Islanders comprised 3.7 percent. Hispanics, who are also counted within the racial groupings, accounted for 9.0 percent of the population. By 2010 African-Americans are expected to account for 12.5 percent of the population, Asians and Pacific Islanders for 6.4 percent, and Hispanics for 12.9 percent.

Thus, the American population will be increasingly characterized by a relatively smaller and older white population and a relatively larger and younger nonwhite and Hispanic population. These trends assume that the level of immigration will remain constant and that the fertility rates for the nonwhite population will remain higher than those for the white population during this time span (see Figure 9.3).

Marital Status/Living Arrangements/Family Structure

Traditionally, Americans have married at a higher rate than any other industrialized country. Since the 1970s, however, significant shifts in marital status have been recorded. In 1990, 63.7 percent of the adult resident United States population was married, down from 69.3 percent in 1980. Historically, some 95 percent of American adults eventually got married. By 1990, this figure was down to 91 percent for women and 89 percent for men. The nonmarried figures are much higher for African-Americans and certain ethnic groups. Today, more than 25 percent of those considered "middle aged" are not married, a situation unprecedented in any modern society.

The number and proportion of single (i.e., never married) Americans were at record levels of 40.4 million and 20.6 percent, respectively, in 1990. The number and proportion of those divorced were also both at record levels. Although the number of widows increased between 1980 and 1990, widows declined as a proportion of the population. The number of unmarried women in U.S. society (44.3 million in 1990) is substantial by historical standards, with the unmarried accounting for 44 percent of women over 15 compared to 30 percent only a decade before. Fewer people are marrying in the United States today and those that are are marrying at an older age (Spain and Bianchi 1996; Tucker and Mitchell-Kernan 1995).

The number of households in the United States is expected to grow steadily through 2010 and beyond, from 91.9 million in 1990 to 114.6 million in 2010, an increase of 24.6 percent. However, growth in the component parts will be uneven, with single-parent households expected to grow considerably faster than the average.

Married couple households with children, reversing the recent trend, are also expected to grow slightly faster than average. Household types expected to lag

Figure 9.3
Changing Racial and Ethnic Distribution: 1980 to 2050

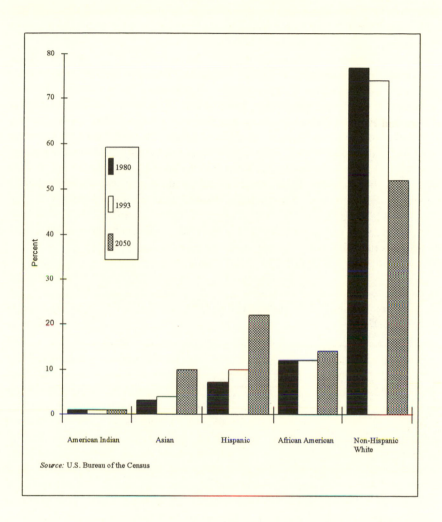

Source: U.S. Bureau of the Census

behind the others in growth are married couple households without children and nonfamily households. One-person households grew phenomenally (+69 percent) during the 1970s, but increased more slowly during the 1980s. However, the 26 percent increase recorded for one-person households was still well above the average of 16 percent growth in all households.

The trend toward smaller household sizes is expected to continue. The average household contained 2.76 persons in 1980, and this figure fell to 2.63 in 1990. For family households, these figures were 3.29 and 3.17, respectively. While the rate of decline in both household and family size is likely to slow, the size of both will continue to shrink for the foreseeable future.

Income Distribution

Income levels in the United States have continued to grow steadily for decades, although in constant dollars income has declined from its 1989 peak (median household income = $34,445 in 1994 dollars). In 1994 personal per capita income was $16,555 according to the U.S. Bureau of Economic Analysis. As can be seen in Table 9.4 median household income in 1994 was $32,264. In 1994, median household income was fairly evenly distributed among the various income categories. The lowest proportion in any income interval was 9.5 percent for the $10,000–14,999 interval. The largest proportions were in the $15,000–24,999, $35,000–49,999, and $50,000–$74,999 intervals, with about 16 percent of the households in each.

Table 9.3
Marital Status in the United States: 1990 to 1994
(In Millions)

Sex	1970		1980		1990		1994	
Never Married	21.4	(16.2)	32.3	(20.3)	40.4	(22.2)	44.2	(23.3)
Married	95.0	(71.7)	104.6	(65.5)	112.6	(61.9)	115.1	(60.6)
Widowed	11.8	(8.9)	12.7	(8.0)	13.8	(7.6)	13.3	(7.0)
Divorced	4.3	(3.2)	9.9	(6.2)	15.1	(8.3)	17.4	(9.2)

Note: Figures in parentheses are percentages

Source: U.S. Bureau of the Census (1995). *Statistical Abstract of the United States, 1995*. Washington, DC: U.S. Government Printing Office, Table 58.

The income gap between the poorest Americans and the richest Americans has begun to widen once again, after a couple of decades of decreasing differentials between the top and bottom. Some observers predict that the middle class will be substantially thinned out by 2010. This projected bifurcation along income lines is partly a function of divergent educational levels and work skills. The baby boom cohort also has been financially weakened by virtue of its position as the "sandwich" generation.

Table 9.4
Household Income: 1994

Income Category	Percent of Households
Under $10,000	13.6
$10,000-14,999	9.5
$15,000-24,999	16.6
$25,000-34,999	14.1
$35,000-49,999	16.3
$50,000-74,999	16.5
Over $75,000	13.6
Median	$32,264

Source: U.S. Bureau of the Census (1996). "Income, Poverty and Valuation of Noncash Benefits: 1994."
   Current Population Reports, P61-189. Washington, DC: U.S. Government Printing Office, Table
   12.

Community Type

Since the nation's founding, the U.S. population has become increasing urban in
terms of residence. It was not until the 1920s, however, that the number of citizens
living in urban areas equaled that in rural areas. By the early 1950s, the number of
urbanites in America was double the number living in rural communities. In 1990,
over 187 million Americans resided in urban areas, compared to 61.7 million in rural
areas. Currently, the urban component of the American population is growing by
around 12 percent per decade, while the rural component's growth rate is less than
4 percent.

Education

A relatively high proportion of the U.S. population is enrolled in some type of
educational program. Despite concern over the school dropout rate, the overwhelming majority of school-aged children are enrolled in elementary or secondary
schools. The size of the elementary/secondary school age population has grown
steadily for several years, with continued growth anticipated into the next century.
During 1995, nearly 51 million children were enrolled in elementary or secondary
schools.

Similarly, the level of enrollment in higher education in the United States exceeds
that of most other countries. College enrollment has grown for several years and is
also expected to continue to increase into the twenty-first century. In 1995, 15
million Americans were enrolled (either full or part-time) in colleges and universi-

ties. This means that one out of every 12 U.S. residents 18 and older was enrolled in a higher education program.

Educational participation and attainment vary along a number of demographic dimensions. Educational attainment levels for the older population are lower on the average than those for the younger age cohorts. While approximately equal numbers of males and females are enrolled in elementary and secondary schools, the number of females enrolled in higher education is considerably larger than the number of males today. Ironically, males continue to be more likely to have college degrees than females.

Educational attainment by race and ethnic group favors the non-Hispanic white and Asian-American populations. Approximately 81 percent of whites age 25 and over had completed high school in 1992, compared to 61 percent of African-Americans, 82 percent of Asians and Pacific Islanders, and 51 percent of Hispanics. College degrees were held by 39 percent of Asian-Americans, 22 percent of whites, 12 percent of African-Americans, and 10 percent of Hispanics.

One trend that bears watching is the growing gap between the best educated and the worst educated in U.S. society. While educational levels continue to rise overall, a significant minority of poorly educated Americans has emerged. This bifurcation of the population along educational lines could have serious implications for the job market of the future, particularly the supply of skilled and semiskilled workers.

Labor Force/Occupation/Industry

Labor force participation rates in the United States. continue to run high (in excess of 60 percent of adults) and this trend is expected to extend into the foreseeable future. This has been boosted to a great extent by the growing involvement of women (including mothers of young children) in the labor force. At the same time, the number of older males in the workforce has been declining.

Demographic trends are having an impact on the workforce as it becomes increasingly older. Because of the age distribution, there is a labor force size gap between younger workers and older workers. As the baby boom ages, there are few people in the baby bust cohort to replace them in industry.

Continued high levels of female participation in the workforce are expected, including women with children at home. In 1990 many parts of the country reported that, in over 60 percent of the households with children, both parents (or the sole parent for one parent households) were in the workforce. As a result of these trends, child care has become a major issue (and a big business).

The changing age composition of the labor force is particularly critical for business planning. As a result of demographic changes, the future U.S. workforce will face a shortage of entry-level workers, increased ethnic and cultural diversity (along with more women), and an aging workforce (with likely lower productivity and less flexibility in terms of retraining and relocation). The projected shortage of entry-age workers is a reflection of the decrease in the population in the age groups at the lower end of the age distribution. Through the 1990s, the population aged 16 through 34 will decline both numerically and as a proportion of the workforce. On the other hand, the number of workers aged 35 to 54 will increase significantly during this decade. The numbers and proportion of workers aged 55 and over will remain essentially unchanged. However, as we enter the twenty-first century, the 55-to-64 age group will show an increase due to the aging of the baby boomers. The declining younger working-age population is already laying the groundwork for future problems for the Social Security and Medicare programs. (Figure 9.4 depicts age trends in the size of the labor force.)

The labor force is also changing in terms of its diversity. White males will have a declining presence in the workplace, as women and minority group members account for most of the new entrants into the workforce. A lowering of the average retirement age is also contributing to attrition among white males in the workforce. To a certain extent, the workers that will be dominant in the workforce of the future will be less educated than those of the past. Not only will there be differences in terms of cultural backgrounds, but today's workers bring a wide variety of lifestyles into the workplace and have different expectations with regard to employment.

As with education (and income), a growing gap is in evidence between the haves and have nots in terms of labor force skills. This will be reflected in wage levels and some predict that the subsequent income gap will result in the thinning of the middle class as the United States enters the twenty-first century. A related issue involves compensation for working women. Although the youngest cohort of women today experiences a smaller gap in income compared to same age males, the gap is still significant. To the extent that women continue to become heads of household, their lower relative income could ultimately have implications for their ability to purchase goods and services.

Religion

Despite the demographic changes of the twentieth century, most Americans consider themselves "Christian" in terms of religious affiliation (Kosmin and Lachman 1993). Christian denominations as a whole accounted for 86.2 percent of all Americans, with the largest denominations being Catholic (26.2 percent), Baptist (19.4 percent), and Methodist (8.0 percent). Only 4 percent of the population claims affiliation with a non-Christian religion (including agnostics); Jews account for by far the largest subgroup with 1.8 percent of the total population. Some 7.5 percent of the population reports having no religion.

While the distribution of Americans across the religious spectrum has remained surprisingly constant over time, certain demographic trends are operating to bring about change. The proportion of Americans describing themselves as Protestant has declined somewhat since the mid-1960s and has appeared to level off. The largest group of immigrants (Mexicans and other Hispanics) are traditionally Catholic in their religious affiliation. Their volume of immigration and their higher than average fertility rates are likely to boost the number of adherents to Catholicism in American society. A less dramatic trend is a function of growing immigration from Asia. Asian

Figure 9.4
Age Distribution of the Labor Force: 1979 to 2005

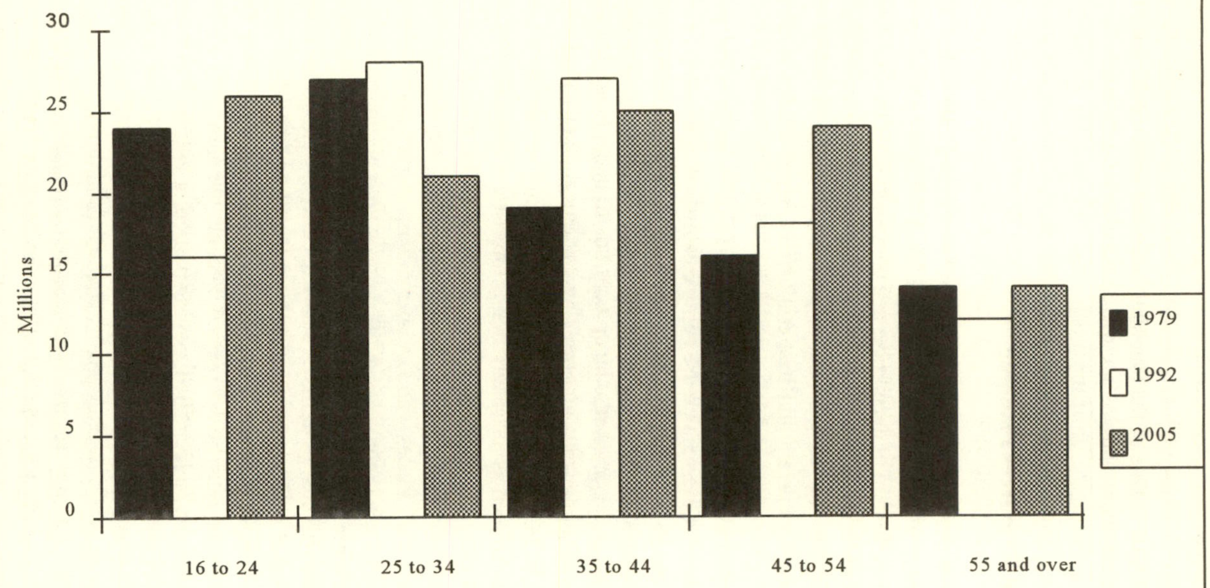

Source: U.S. Bureau of Labor

immigrants often report Buddhism or Hinduism as their religions, and this phenomenon is likely to result in significant proportional, if not numerical, increases in these religious congregations.

CHANGING POPULATION COMPOSITION: IMPLICATIONS FOR BUSINESS PLANNING

The data presented in this chapter reflect the major compositional changes that are taking place in the United States. Each of these changes, whether viewed at the national level or at the local market level, has numerous implications for business planning. The compositional snapshot presented here reflects both diversity and change. Substantial compositional change will continue to mark the U.S. population well into the future. Overall, the population is aging and, though the impact of additional persons reaching retirement age is important, the aging of baby boomers is likely to have the greatest effect on the U.S. business climate until well into the twenty-first century. The imbalance of males and females at the older age groups is likely to persist. Racial and ethnic diversity is likely to increase for the foreseeable future.

It must be remembered that compositional change occurring for the nation as a whole is not necessarily reflected in data for regions, counties, and smaller units of geography. Some areas (e.g., certain metropolitan counties in Florida) are maintaining a younger age structure due to consistent in-migration and high levels of fertility, while other areas (e.g., certain rural counties in Nebraska) are much older than the U.S. average. Some areas exhibit a high proportion of racial and ethnic minorities, while others have virtually no minority population at all. Each market area is different and must be evaluated on its own merits.

Compositional structure and change have a wide range of effects on markets and on the manner in which business is conducted. Population segments that are increasing in size represent new and/or expanding opportunities, while those segments experiencing population decline offer challenges to existing businesses. Though demographic trends do not tell the whole story of the way in which markets change—since psychographic and behavioral data are required as well—they do provide some hard information on the size and characteristics of market segments.

The tendency on the part of most businesses has been to follow the aging of the baby boom cohort. Some observers, in fact, argue that, by the end of the twentieth century, baby boomers will account for over one half of consumer expenditures. Evidence of baby boomer targeting can be seen in expanded options in minivans and the reintroduction of convertibles in the automobile market, the modification of resort services to accommodate the interest in physical fitness, and the introduction of health-oriented foods at both the grocery store and restaurant. The baby boomer market is changing, however, and these changes call for new business strategies. Today most baby boomers are married and are homeowners, and these facts alone have important implications for business.

Other age segments should not be ignored, however. While baby boomers number 78 million persons, the children of boomers are nearly as plentiful—72 million (Mitchell 1995). The teen, baby, and mature markets are being targeted by various industries. More recently, the children of the baby boomers (the so-called Generation X) have attracted attention from marketers. The teenage market is growing, with annual teenage spending estimated at between $30 and $50 billion (Zollo 1995). At the other end of the spectrum, the "senior" market is more affluent than ever—and more complex than previously thought. Marketing consultants knowledgeable on ways of reaching the mature market are in great demand.

Racial and ethnic diversity results in growing diversity in consumer behavior. African-Americans, Asian-Americans, and Hispanics all display distinctive patterns of expenditures, although significant differences exist within these broad categories themselves. Not only are racial and ethnic differences reflected in the products purchased, but subcultural preferences even extend to brands. Further, the marketing approach required for each of these groups (and often their component subgroups) must be determined.

The decreasing size of the American household and the decline of the family household are two trends that have serious implications for the manner in which consumers spend their money. The allocation of resources among housing, food, entertainment, and other items varies widely depending on the size and structure of the household. Indeed, trends in family characteristics have created whole new categories of consumers that did not exist in the past. These include thirty-something single men and women with substantial disposable income, along with a new category of consumers to target, the "postmarital" population—that is, those who are widowed or divorced.

Projections of compositional change tell business analysts a great deal about the future demand for goods and services. The changes documented in this chapter require monitoring over time in order for industry to position itself to respond to growth in some markets and decline in others. Box 9.4 focuses on the business implications of "excess" women, and Box 9.5 contains another biography of an applied demographer.

Box 9.4

Too Many Women?: The Implications of an "Excess" of Women

Observing that there is an "excess" of a certain segment of the population at the very least implies a value judgment. However, documenting that there are significantly more females than males in the United States has implications for businesses that engage in a wide range of activities. In 1990 there were about 95 men for every 100 women of all ages in the United States. But, the sex ratio varies considerably by age from 105 at the ages 0 to 4 to about 39 at the ages 85 and over. In other words, there are 259 women for every 100 men age 85 and over.

To the extent that women purchase, use, and dispose of products and services differently from men, sex ratios that deviate very much from 100 indicate that a one-sex-dominated market may exist. At the older ages, 65 and over, for example,

Box 9.4 continued

marketers, product developers, and managers must design a marketing mix appropriate for the specialized needs and interests of the older female population. The male market is not ignored, but it clearly is smaller. On the basis of size alone, clothing manufacturers, for example, would be best advised to position themselves in the female market, particularly if they can offer garments that meet the unique demands of an older population. Moreover, 40 percent of the female population age 65 and over live alone (and 52 percent of those 75 and over), providing further evidence that a unique market exists. In comparison, only 18 percent of the female population age 55 to 64 lives alone. Food and other products are purchased and consumed in small amounts, although frequency of purchases may decline as transportation problems surface. When factors such as income and education level are considered, this segment becomes even further segmented.

While the sex differential in life expectancy has narrowed somewhat in the last two decades (see Chapter 6), a large difference will continue to persist in the foreseeable future. As the U.S. population ages, the male/female numerical difference will widen and the issue of "excess females" will become even more important to business planners.

Box 9.5

Peter A. Morrison

The Varied Activities of an Independent Applied Demographer

As an applied demographer, I have always worn two hats—one through my affiliation with The RAND Corporation, the other as an independent demographer performing applied work through my own consulting firm. My work for RAND (a nonprofit institution whose mission is to improve public policy through research and analysis) typically has served the interests of federal agencies, acting within a changing demographic context. Interpreting that context and the constraints it may impose is the piece of the problem I typically handle—for example, analyzing the demographic makeup of Army families to anticipate their needs when soldiers must be deployed to some distant crisis zone.

Wearing my other hat, I consult for a wide array of clients whose concerns lie beyond the public policy realm. The range of such applications changes with the times. After the decennial census, for example, the calls for electoral redistricting begin. By the mid-1990s, business concerns were focused increasingly on globalization and the emergence of new consumer markets.

Although such outside assignments now absorb most of my professional time, I retain ties with my RAND colleagues, issue my publications through RAND, and field questions from the media on RAND's behalf. Occasionally, I involve a colleague in my work as an independent subcontractor. Over the years, I have developed something every independent applied demographer needs: an informal network of talent to call on for specialized tasks (e.g., data processing, statistical advice, etc.). Knowing whom to call on, where to get the data, and how to coordinate activities are part of the value I can add as an entrepreneur.

Box 9.5 continued

Clients engage me for distinctly different purposes. Lawyers, for example, need studies addressing issues to be resolved in an adversarial context. The question posed may be "Is the county's jury pool representative of its population's racial makeup?" or "Do the boundaries of an election district concentrate a particular minority group among adult voters?" or "What proportion of a city's present-day population was there five years ago (when milk wholesalers overcharged all consumers) as members of the injured 'class' in a class action lawsuit?" Not only do I address such questions, I also must craft a well-reasoned report on my findings and often defend my conclusions in court.

Local jurisdictions retain me to establish or realign the boundaries of their election districts. Such assignments call for both technical familiarity with small-area census data and an understanding of the legal requirements that apply.

Working with lawyers can be intellectually rewarding, for one can observe first-hand how purposes behind the law come to be fulfilled in practice. Concepts of fairness and equity often boil down to a question of comparing groups statistically—for example, whether applicants get hired or promoted at the same rate regardless of race. Devising and making such comparisons comes naturally to an applied demographer.

Outside the legal arena, I often get requests to clarify and explain demographic developments for business audiences concerned with the implications of forthcoming population shifts. For such public speaking requests, every applied demographer must have at the ready an all-purpose graphic presentation. I maintain an extensive collection of graphics covering various facets of population structure and change, along with implications organized around broad themes. This helps me to tailor presentations to particular audiences.

Ordinarily I devote several hours per week to fielding questions from news reporters and others seeking information, interpretation, or a referral to another source. Often, I am able to give a reporter some new slant on a story or a fuller appreciation of what's behind a demographic trend.

I often am asked to interpret the implications demographic and related social trends have for some consumer markets. Business clients understand their markets well enough; what's less apparent to them is how demographic changes in consumer units will play out in those markets. Here, the premium is on relevance—not simply documenting trends with data but offering useful insights into how they may affect a particular market.

Once, an association of paper shipping sack manufacturers retained me to present an overview of demographic developments relevant to their industry. My brief presentation featured several points any demographer would find obvious: the shrinking average size of families, the growth of one-person households, and more families reaching the "empty-nest" stage. The simple (but compelling) idea that demographic changes might gradually "miniaturize" consumer units prompted considerable discussion of the potential new uses for smaller paper shipping sacks in the future I had sketched. The data buttressing these points acted like a solvent poured down a clogged kitchen drain, dissolving an old stereotype of the traditional American family and inviting a fresh perspective on the bright future of *smaller* paper shipping sacks in the lives of American consumers!

REFERENCES

Barclay, George W. (1958). *Techniques of Population Analysis*. New York: Wiley.

Bogue, Donald J. (1969). *Principals of Demography*. New York: Wiley.

Caleche, Susan (1996). "U.S. Ponders Its Race and Ethnic Categories for 2000 Census." *Population Today*, Vol. 24, No. 1 Washington, DC: Population Reference Bureau.

Clogg, Clifford C., and Scott R. Eliason (1988). "A Flexible Procedure for Adjusting Rates and Properties, Including Statistical Methods for Group Comparisons." *American Sociological Review*, 53: 267–283.

Glenn Norval D. (1977). *Cohort Analysis*. Beverly Hills, CA: Sage.

Hobcraft, John, Jane Menken, and Samuel Preston (1982). "Age, Period and Cohort Effects in Demography: A Review." *Population Index*, 48 (Spring): 4–43.

Kosmin, Barry A., and Seymour P. Lachman (1993). *One Nation Under God–Religion in Contemporary Society*. New York: Harmony Books.

Mitchell, Susan (1995). "The Next Baby Boom." *American Demographics* (October): 22–31.

Newell, Colin (1987). *Methods and Models of Demography*. New York: Guilford.

Pol, Louis G., and Sukgoo Pak (1995). "Consumer Unit Types and Expenditures on Food Away From Home." *Journal of Consumer Affairs*, 29(2): 403–428.

Pol, Louis G., and Sukgoo Pak (1996). "Segmenting the Senior Care Market." *Health Marketing Quarterly*, 13(4): 63–77.

Pressat, Roland (1972). *Demographic Analysis*. New York: Aldine.

Rentz, Joseph O., Fred D. Reynolds, and Roy G. Stout (1983). "Analyzing Changing Consumption Patterns with Cohort Analysis." *Journal of Marketing Research*, 20(February): 12–22.

Reynolds, Fred D., and Joseph O. Rentz (1981). "Cohort Analysis: An Aid to Strategic Planning." *Journal of Marketing*, 45 (Summer): 62–70.

Russell, Cheryl (1993). *Master Trends*. New York: Plenum.

Russell, Cheryl (1995). "The Baby Boom Turns 50," *American Demographics*, December.

Santi, Lawrence L. (1988). "The Demographic Context of Recent Change in the Structure of American Households." *Demography*, 25 (November): 509–519.

Shryock, Henry S., and Jacob S. Siegel (with Edward Stockwell) (1976). *The Methods and Materials of Demography*. New York: Academic Press.

Spain, Daphne, and Suzanne Bianchi (1996). *Balancing Act*. New York: Russell Sage Foundation.

Sweet, Janus A., and Larry L. Bumpass (1987). *American Families and Households*. 1980 Census Monograph Series. New York: Russell Sage.

Tucker, M. Belinda, and Claudia Mitchell-Kernan (eds.) (1995). *The Decline in Marriage Among African Americans*. New York: Russell Sage Foundation.

U.S. Bureau of the Census (1975). *Historical Statistics of the United States, Colonial Times to 1970*. Washington, DC: U.S. Government Printing Office.

U.S. Bureau of the Census (1993). *1990 Census of Population. Social and Economic Characteristics, Florida*. Washington, DC: U.S. Government Printing Office.

U.S. Bureau of the Census (1995). *Statistical Abstract of the United States, 1995*. Washington, DC: U.S. Government Printing Office.

U.S. Bureau of the Census (1996). "Income, Poverty and Valuation of Noncash Benefits: 1994." *Current Population Reports*, P61-189. Washington, DC: U.S. Government Printing Office.

Xie, Yu (1989). "An Alternative Purging Method: Controlling the Composition-Dependent Interaction in an Analysis of Rates." *Demography*, 26 (November): 711–716.

Zollo, Peter (1995). "Talking to Teens." *American Demographics* (November): 22–28.

SUGGESTED READINGS

Ambry, Margaret (1989). *The Almanac of Consumer Markets*. Chicago: Probus.
Bennett, Claudette E. (1995). "The Black Population of the United States: March 1994 and 1993." *Current Population Reports*, Series P-20, No. 480. Washington, DC: U.S. Government Printing Office.
Danzinger, Sheldon (1995). *America Unequal*. New York: Russell Sage Foundation.
Gettentag, Marsha, and Paul F. Secord (1983). *Too Many Women?: The Sex Ratio Question*. Beverly Hills, CA: Sage.
Handler, Joel F. (1995). *The Poverty of Welfare Reform*. New Haven, CT: Yale University Press.
Hernandez, Donald J. (1992). "Studies in Household and Family Formation." *Current Population Studies*, Series P-23, No. 179. Washington, DC: U.S. Government Printing Office.
Levy, Frank (1987). *Dollars and Dreams: The Changing American Income Structure*. New York: Russell Sage.
Norton, Arthur J., and Louisa F. Miller. (1992). "Marriage, Divorce and Remarriage in the 1990s." *Current Population Reports*, Series P-23, No. 180. Washington, DC: U.S. Government Printing Office.
Soldo, Beth J., and Emily M. Agree (1988). "America's Elderly." *Population Bulletin*, Vol. 43, No. 3 (September). Washington, DC: Population Reference Bureau.
Spain, Daphne, and Suzanne M. Bianchi (1986). *American Women in Transition*. New York: Russell Sage Foundation.
Taeuber, Cynthia M. (1992). "Sixty-Five Plus in America." *Current Population Reports*, Series P-23, No. 178RV. Washington, DC: U.S. Government Printing Office.
Valdivieso, Rafael, and Cary Davis (1988). "U.S. Hispanics: Challenging Issues for the 1990s." *Population Trends and Public Policy*, No. 17 (December). Washington, DC: Population Reference Bureau.

Chapter 10

Estimates and Projections in Business Demography

INTRODUCTION

At the heart of demographically driven decision making are population estimates and projections, earlier referred to as synthetic data. In today's business environment current data are needed immediately and censuses, surveys, and registries often cannot provide all of the information required for the *most* recent time periods. Moreover, business planning is concerned with the future and, without demographic projections, future demographic conditions cannot be factored into the decision-making process.

Businesses have long recognized the inherent time and geographic limitations of censuses, surveys and registries and have demanded estimates and projections for time intervals and geographic units not covered by the established data collection systems. Historically, the federal government and state governments have produced some population estimates and projections as part of a cooperative program. More recently, private data vendors have increased the frequency of production of estimates and projections, the range of geographic units for which data are available, and the number of factors (e.g., income) that are estimated and/or projected. Today, many vendors can provide a current year estimate of median household income for a two-mile-diameter circle whose center is 72nd and Dodge Streets in Omaha, Nebraska. There are no census, survey or registration data for the current year on which to base that estimate.

Given the reliance on estimates and projections by business planners and the number of data vendors now in the market place, it is important to be aware of methodologies utilized for the estimates and projections. The overall goal of this chapter is to make readers better consumers of such data.

Population censuses are conducted every ten years and economic censuses every five years. In between censuses, national-level data collection efforts such as the Current Population Survey (CPS) produce reliable national and regional estimates of population characteristics. These data are not reliable, however, for many subnational needs because the sample size, about 54,000 households nationwide, is too small to generate reliable estimates and projections for subregional areas. Subsamples for small areas such as counties and census tracts are *so* small that the estimates that could be produced would be of no value. In addition, census bureau activities are slated for cutbacks, and the data-user community may be forced to rely on estimates and projections more than ever (Spar 1996). The challenge for data vendors is to produce the necessary data for the geographic units of interest while limiting the amount of error. The challenge for users is to be able to judge the quality of the data produced

Before proceeding any farther, the distinction between an estimate and a projection must be made clear. First, let us examine a simple population equation:

$$P_{1996} = P_{1990} + B_{1990-96} - D_{1990-96} \pm M_{1990-96};$$

where

$P_{1996} =$	population for a specific geographic unit (e.g., county) in 1996
$P_{1990} =$	population for that same geographic unit in 1990
$B_{1990-96} =$	births to residents of that geographic unit between 1990 and 1996
$D_{1990-96} =$	deaths to residents of that geographic unit between 1990 and 1996
$M_{1990-96} =$	net migration (inmigrants minus outmigrants) for that geographic unit between 1990 and 1996.

We are assuming that no census was conducted in 1996 and the last census was carried out in 1990. We also stipulate that we are producing the estimate in 1997, so the data needed (births, deaths, and net migrants) are for events that have already occurred. P_{1996} is considered an *estimate* because the date in question (e.g., July 1, 1996) is in the present or recent past *and* other historical data are used to derive the figure. That is, $B_{1990-96}$ and $D_{1990-96}$ can be measured by using vital registration data for births and deaths, and $M_{1990-96}$ can be estimated by using *symptomatic data* or making assumptions regarding the relationship between current migration patterns and those measured in the recent past. Symptomatic data include information such as school enrollment figures used as a basis for approximating the number of school age migrants.

A *projection* focuses on a date or dates in the future (e.g., July 1, 2000). The data used to calculate the projection might use population growth through July 1, 1996, incorporating assumptions about future changes in births, deaths, and migrants to derive the figure(s). Population projections are illustrative of figures produced given a baseline set of data and a set of assumptions which reflect possible changes over time. Moreover, projections are produced as a series; that is, more than one projection is produced by varying the set of assumptions. The range in projections provides a sense of confidence that can be placed in one figure that may be chosen as "best." Together, estimates and projections are referred to as synthetic data because they do not involve direct measurement and historical data and associated assumptions for production.

Demographic estimates and projections are available for a variety of geographic units. Three considerations are important in reviewing these data. The first is availability. In deciding to use demographic data in business decision making, it is essential that data be available for the time periods and units of geography required. The second consideration concerns the sources of the estimates and projections, given that there may be multiple sources of data to choose among. The third consideration, data quality, probably is the most important consideration. Data quality is a major concern because, while all estimates and projections contain some error, certain figures may be far better or far worse than others (Pittinger 1977). In a business world that relies more heavily than ever on demographic estimates and projections, an understanding of the quality limitations of these data cannot be overemphasized (Exter 1996). Decisions that are partly or largely based on seriously flawed data can lead to poor and sometimes disastrous outcomes. Box 10.1 provides a more detailed list of questions to ask when estimates and projections of demographic data are to be used.

Box 10.1
What to Look for in Population Estimates and Projections

Before buying or using any population estimates or projections one should consider:

1. Is the time frame reasonable? For the most part this concern is relevant to projections, although the time period since the last actual measurement (e.g., census) can be important for estimates as well. While projections can be reasonably accurate over some geographic units for 10 or 20 years, projections beyond 20 years should be seen simply as illustrations of numbers that would result if the assumptions underlying the projection held for more than 20 years, an unlikely assumption itself. More importantly, for most business users of projected data the number of years for which the projections can be considered reliable is limited for small areas due to subtle social, political, economic, and/or other changes. In high-growth areas, projections may only be reliable for two or three years. Therefore, the user should examine historical data and ascertain previous growth patterns and potential volatility before making judgments about the appropriateness of the time span of the projection.

2. Is the methodology clearly understood? The method used for generating the estimate or projection should be understood as clearly as possible. Some data providers make available on request very detailed descriptions of methodologies while others use the "black box" approach, arguing that the procedures utilized for producing the statistics are proprietary. Some methods *are* better than others, and just because the numbers "seem" reasonable does not mean that they are. Moreover, methods that work well at the national level generating little error may perform poorly for small units of geography.

3. Have tests been conducted to determine the method's accuracy? With respect to methodological tests, the user is encouraged to determine if the provider of the estimates and/or projections has performed accuracy tests. Estimates and projections can be compared to data derived from regular censuses, special censuses, surveys, and

Box 10.1 continued

administrative records to ascertain accuracy, and those in the business of producing demographic estimates and projections should be engaged in such comparisons. The user should make sure that the comparisons are for the same geographic units that will be employed. Users should determine if independent tests have been performed such as those by Tayman and Swanson (1995).

4. Are the geographic units reasonable? There are many nonstandard geographic units for which data are now available (e.g., two mile radius around a particular retail store). Because these units have no direct link to standard data sets (e.g., census data) and standard geographic units (e.g., block groups), the user should inquire about the methods and underlying assumptions for producing such data. Use of nonstandard units frequently requires that estimates or projections from a larger unit (e.g., county or zip code) be subdivided to fit the nonstandard boundaries. The methods of allocation can vary greatly and thus significantly affect the figures produced.

5. In recent years, the generation of estimates and projections has expanded beyond the simple production of data for age, sex, and race categories. Estimates and projections of income, households by type, school enrollment, and labor force, among others, are now routinely generated. While the methodologies used to produce total population estimates and projections have a relatively long history of testing and refinement, the "track record" for other types of data is not as well established. Users of these data are cautioned to carefully examine the methodologies employed (e.g., to produce an estimate of median household income for a two mile radius around a potential retail site), and to determine if that methodology involves too many unsubstantiated assumptions.

It should be recognized that bad estimates or projections are *not* better than no data at all. Frequently, other economic indicators can be used as substitutes for variables such as income (e.g., rent and selling prices of houses). These indicators are much more reliable because they are part of an ongoing data collection activity that has a sound and tested methodology. Given the costs associated with bad decisions, it is best to have a smaller selection of reasonably reliable data than a larger one containing a host of seriously flawed elements.

Population estimates and projections have a long history of use in the public sector. While census data have always been needed for reapportionment and restricting purposes, estimates and projections have been used for public sector planning and the allocation of resources by national, state and local governments. Until business users became more interested in these data, it was public sector users that guided most of the methodological and use issues. Clearly, the situation has changed and private sector demands for data are at least as strong as public sector demands. Private sector users should demand the same level of data quality that public sector users have demanded.

SOURCES OF ESTIMATES AND PROJECTIONS

The 1980s witnessed a boom in the number of public and private organizations producing estimates and projections. In the public sector, federal, state, and local governments expanded both the quantity and quality of population estimates and projections for a variety of standard geographic units. In the private sector, vendors produced population projections for standard geographic units and expanded data availability for customized, nonstandard geographic units (e.g., market areas) along with the number of factors being estimated and projected. The 1990s saw an expansion of these activities in both the public and private sectors.

Population estimates are produced at the national level by the U.S. Bureau of the Census and the states through a national-state cooperative program coordinated by the Bureau. Substate estimates by county are available from state data centers (see Appendix 1) as part of the federal-state cooperative program discussed in Chapter 3. Estimates by city and other subcounty areas are sometimes available through the state data centers. Other local organizations (e.g., regional planning groups) sometimes produce estimates for very small geographic units (e.g., census tracts). The availability of such locally produced data will vary from location to location.

A variety of demographically related data estimates are available through private vendors. For example, *Sales and Marketing Management* magazine publishes estimates of effective buying income, household expenditures by category and the number of business establishments and employees at the MSA, city, and county levels. CACI is a commercial data vendor that sells data on nearly 100 demographic variables for zip codes and other units of geography. The user can sometimes purchase customized data that fit the unit(s) of geography appropriate to the decision at hand. A brief description of some of the major data vendors and their products is offered in Box 10.2.

In the public sector, the U.S. Bureau of the Census produces national-level population projections by age, sex, race, and Hispanic origin, with the furthest projection year currently 2080. Projections are also produced for regions, divisions, and states, although the furthest year for which a projection is available for these subnational units is currently 2020. Given the 20-year rule-of-thumb discussed earlier, these data are more than adequate for most purposes.

At both the national and subnational levels, a series of projections are produced by adjusting assumptions regarding the three components of population change: fertility, mortality, and migration. Each component has three underlying assumptions (low, medium, and high), and the combination of these components and assumptions yields 30 different projections. At the national level, the middle series of the 30 projections is most often used by researchers and planners. Nevertheless, the assumptions underlying the middle series figures should be examined carefully before the data are used. Recent fluctuations in fertility rates and proposed changes in immigration law could render most, if not all, of the projections virtually useless. At the regional, divisional, and state levels, only four alternatives are available, with the first being judged as the preferred series. Again, assumptions must be studied carefully before the data are used. A list of contact telephone numbers, prices, and formats for state population projections can be found in Edmondson (1996).

The same type of projections are available from private sector data vendors for most levels of geography, including customized, nonstandard market areas. An advantage in using figures from private vendors is that projections data are published along with a number of other potentially useful variables. Another advantage is that these data may be available for "custom" time periods (e.g., one- or two-year projections). The primary disadvantage is that the quality of the projections for some variables is uncertain, since the methods utilized to produce the data may have not been rigorously tested.

Box 10.2
A Sample of Vendor Product Offerings

CACI Marketing Systems
Main Office: 1100 N. Glebe Rd.
Arlington, VA 22201
800-292-2224
Fax: 703-243-6272
West Coast Office: 3333 N. Torrey Pines Ct.
LaJolla, CA 92037
800-394-3690
Fax: 619-450-0463

CACI makes available a host of data products including current year demographics, five-year forecasts, sales potential, business data, consumer segmentation, and shopping center data. Current year demographics are available for over 30,000 residential zip codes, counties, and cities and include over 150 characteristics such as age, race, income, and households. They also make available the ACORN consumer classification system which places all households into geographic, socioeconomic, and demographic segments based on neighborhood of residence. It identifies, describes, and locates the market for almost any product or service. These products are available in paper form, diskette and CD-ROM. CACI's software Gold Standard solution with Scan/US combines current year demographics and five-year forecasts with geomarket analysis and mapping software. Included are built-in demographic summary reports, street level data, geographic boundaries, and highways.

Claritas
Main Sales Office: 1525 Wilson Blvd., Suite 1000
Arlington, VA 22209
703-812-2700 or 800-284-4868
Regional Offices:
Chicago—312-986-2650
Ithaca—607-257-5757
Los Angeles—213-954-3210
New York—212-789-7580

Claritas offers a broad range of powerful and easy-to-use precision marketing products. These products include PRIZM® lifestyle segmentation; PRIZM+4 microneighborhood

Box 10.2 continued

segmentation; annually updated small-area demographic data; express delivery of demographic reports; Compass PC-based market analysis and mapping system; and a new Windows-based family of target marketing and mapping software, Catalyst. Claritas also offers numerous specialized products such as Compass/Banking, demographic data defined by Yellow Pages geography, LifeP$YCLE life insurance usage segmentation, and The Market audit survey of consumers' financial product use. A new Claritas product, Workplace Prizm, offers marketplace profiles for both daytime and nighttime population. REZIDE, a national zip code encyclopedia, offers data compiled annually from the U.S. census and over 1,600 local government and private sources. Data are available in published reports as well as CD-ROM, magnetic tape, tape cartridges, and HD diskettes.

National Decision Systems/Equifax National Decision Systems
Corporate Headquarters: 5375 Mira Sorrenta Place, Suite 440
San Diego, CA 92121
800-866-6520
Fax 619-550-5800

NDS' "Pop-Facts Reports" provides reports based on over 1,200 demographic, socioeconomic and housing characteristics from the 1990 census, and also includes current-year estimates and five-year projections for selected variables, updated twice a year. "Financial Facts" provides current and historical deposit information for bank and thrift locations nationwide, along with market shares and trends. "Consumer Facts" provides current-year estimates and five-year projections on consumer spending for over 400 categories of products. "MicroVision" is a microgeographic consumer targeting system based on aggregate consumer demand data and zip + 4 geography, with annual updates. Consumers are assigned to one of 50 lifestyle segments, based on the actual demographic, socioeconomic and housing characteristics of the zip + 4. Segmentation data available for several vertical industries, including health care segmentation based on research by National Research Corporation. "Sparta-Site" is PC-based GIS software and database, operating in a Windows environment, interfacing Equifax's market data and NDS' demographic data with ESRI's ArcView GIS system. It allows the analyst to access, display, query, analyze, compare and output market information.

Strategic Mapping, Inc.
Corporate Headquarters: 3135 Kifer Road
Santa Clara, CA 95051
408-970-9600
FAX: 408-970-9999

Strategic Mapping (SMI), primarily a desktop mapping vendor, purchased Donnelly Marketing Information Services, one of the largest vendors of demographic data, in 1993. SMI produces a report, "AmericanProfile" which consists of profiles, updates, and trend data for a number of demographic attributes, including household-based estimates

Box 10.2 continued

and projections down to the street-level. "Market Potential" retail sales reports provide data by vertical industry. "BusinessLine" summarizes statistical reports for various industries. "Healthcare Statistical Reports" provide data on MDC/DRG forecasts, ambulatory care demand, physician characteristics and ICD-9 estimates. Atlas "MarketQuest," the successor of Donnelly's "Conquest" desktop analysis system, provides integrated analysis for site selection, target marketing, trade area analysis, media selection and customer profiling. "MarketQuest" incorporates the industry's only household-based demographic estimates and projections and couples them with its targeting, lifestyle segmentation and mapping modules.

Market Statistics
355 Park Avenue South
New York, NY 10010-1789
212-592-6246
Fax: 212-592-6259

Market Statistics specializes in updating demographic, economic, retail trade, and business-to-business data for all standard levels of geography and custom sales territories. They also offer a variety of PC mapping software packages for site selection, sales territory management, and demographic modeling. In addition, Market Statistics produces DART (Data Analysis and Reporting Tool)—a fast, easy-to-use data management package for searching, viewing, sorting, ranking, and analyzing data. They produce demographic retail sales and buying power index data for *Sales and Marketing Management* magazine. Their demographic data are also available on DIALOG—for over 40,000 U.S. zip codes and 100 demographic variables.

Urban Decision Systems
West Coast: 4676 Admiralty Way
Marina del Rey, CA 90292
800-633-9568
Fax: 310-827-2339

Urban Decisions Systems offers a full range of products and services, including demographic and business information in the form of reports, maps, graphs, publications, diskettes, and CD-ROM. Products offered include the MarketReporter™ site analysis system, ZIPBase™ zip code boundary files, MarketBase™ and MarketBase Life, daytime census data, traffic volumes, shopping center data on 34,000 centers, details on 380,000 restaurants, crime data, environmental data, and more. ZIP BASIC provides data on more than 50 variables for 32,000 U.S. zip codes, as well as a zip code boundary file.

Box 10.2 continued

Woods & Poole Economics, Inc.
1794 Columbia Road, NW, Suite 4
Washington, DC 20009-2805
800-786-1915

Woods & Poole Economics, Inc., specializes in detailed long-range projections for counties and metro areas. The Woods & Poole database contains more than 550 economic and demographic variables for every state, region, county, Metropolitan Statistical Area (MSA/PMSA/CMSA) and Designated Market Area (DMA) in the United States for every year from 1970 to 2020. This comprehensive database includes detailed population data by age, sex, and race; employment and earnings by industry; personal income, retail sales by kind of business; households by income bracket; and data on the number of households, their size, and their income. All of these variables are forecast for each year through 2020. Each year Woods & Poole updates its county database and makes a new long-range forecast. Special forecasts are available using Woods & Poole's regional model. The data are available in print as well as on diskette, magnetic tape and CD-ROM.

ESTIMATE AND PROJECTION METHODOLOGIES

Standard Methodologies

While most readers do not require a detailed understanding of all of the methodologies available for producing estimates and projections, some understanding of methodological differences is needed if one is going to be an informed consumer of various data products. Data users often need a continuous flow of historical information based on actual counts, estimates, and projections. Time series data are particularly important when frequent strategic changes are made and when there is continuous evaluation of strategies. In this continuous data acquisition mode, it is very important to understand the similarities and dissimilarities in data collection and production methods.

The simplest technique for producing both estimates and projections is *mathematical extrapolation* (Shryock and Siegel 1973, Chapter 23). Beginning with a series of historical data, rates of change (increase or decrease) are calculated on the assumption that these historical rates will continue into the future to some estimated projection year. For example, a 1996 estimate for a given county can be produced by calculating the 1980–1990 growth rate from census data and assuming that the rate of growth continued through 1996. If the rate of growth averaged 1 percent per year between 1980 and 1990, it could be assumed that the rate of growth for 1990 to 1996 was 1 percent per year. If enough past data points are available, differentiated weights can be applied, with the most recent data points receiving the greatest weight.

An example of the generation of a population estimate is available for Harris County Texas (Houston) for 1982 (Rives and Serow 1984, p. 43). The ratio of the 1980 Harris County population to the 1970 figure provides the growth ratio. Taking the natural log of this ratio and dividing by ten generates the annual growth rate. This rate is multiplied by the number of years for which the projection is generated, in this case two years and three months—April 1, 1980, to July 1, 1982. The exponential of this figure, using the base of the natural logarithm, produces a multiplier for the 1980 population that yields the 1982 estimate. The same principles are easy to apply in producing a 1996 estimate (using the 1980–1990 growth rates to start with). The same procedure can be used to produce a population projection. In this instance, the calculated growth rate is assumed to continue X years into the future. However, as the projection year gets further from the historical data, the continued growth assumption becomes more tenuous.

The key to this and related methods is the soundness of the assumption of continued rates of growth. For populations with relatively stable growth, estimates and short-term projections will be reasonably accurate. When the constant rate of growth assumption is questionable, either an "adjusted" growth rate must be found or a new method sought. In making projections for geographic areas that have had fluctuating or extremely high growth rates that cannot be maintained, the figures produced may contain large errors. Sometimes these methods can be improved by studying land use and carrying capacity, allowing the analyst to modify the growth rate assumption as areas become "built out" and substantial further growth becomes virtually impossible.

The *cohort component* technique is a more complex method for population projections. It is the most frequently used method of projecting the populations of nations, states, and, sometimes, smaller units of geography (Shryock and Siegel 1973, Chapters 23 and 24). The method begins with a base population, usually subdivided by age, sex, race, and ethnicity, and "ages" that population X years to the projected year(s). This process involves tracking the movement of age cohorts through the age structure. For example, the analyst might start with the population on April 1, 1990, and project it forward to April 1, 2000. As a result, the population age 15 to 19 in 1990 is 25 to 29 in 2000. In aging the population, some persons are subtracted due to mortality and out-migration. Persons are added through births and in-migration. The additions and subtractions to the base population are made by age, sex, race, and ethnic categories.

The key to the production of these data, again, is the underlying assumptions. Assumptions regarding fertility, mortality, and migration are based on historical data, making the accuracy of the projections subject to both known and unforeseen factors. This happened in 1988 when an unexpected rise in fertility in the United States made national population projections produced before 1988 too low. Another potential development, proposed legislation that would severely reduce the number of legal immigrants to the United States, could render many current projections too high. See Ahlberg (1993) and Ahlberg and Vaupel (1990) for a more detailed discussion of projection accuracy.

As stated earlier, the U.S. Bureau of the Census generates 30 alternative projections for the United States as a whole and four for regions, divisions, and states. For each series a different combination of fertility, mortality, and migration assumptions is utilized to produce different figures. The business analyst should carefully examine the underlying assumptions and select more than one series for comparison. By selecting multiple series, a better understanding of the "likely range of scenarios" will be derived.

Recent Methodological Developments

The population estimation method receiving the greatest attention in recent years is the *housing unit method* (Starsinic and Zitter 1968; Smith and Lewis 1980, 1983). The first objective of the method is to estimate the number of occupied housing units for the target year. Starting with the most recent census (e.g., April 1, 1990) and a geographic unit (e.g., a county), an estimate year is chosen (e.g., July 1, 1991). The number of housing units from the 1990 census is adjusted by adding newly constructed units and subtracting demolished units. This construction and demolition information is obtained by examining public records on housing construction and demolition for the period 1990–1991. The number of housing units for July 1, 1991, is the number counted during the April 1, 1990, census plus the net increase in housing units over the time interval. Vacancy rates are also factored in to arrive at the estimated number of occupied housing units. Persons living in group quarters; for example, dormitories, prisons, and rooming houses, are enumerated separately, usually by taking a census of these places.

The second objective of the method is to estimate the population. Once the number of occupied housing units is estimated, the total population (living in housing units) can be estimated by multiplying the number of housing units by the average number of persons per housing unit. The persons per housing unit figure is derived by taking most recent census or estimate data and adjusting that figure for historical change.

The housing unit method has been shown to be an accurate and particularly valuable approach in producing small area estimates at the county or subcounty level. Box 10.3 presents the housing unit method in more detail, while Box 10.4 addresses the issue of customizing the housing unit method.

Box 10.3
The Housing Unit Method in Action

In order to estimate the population of an geographic unit such as a county or census tract, we start with the equation

$$P_t = (HU_t \cdot PPH_t) + GQ_t,$$

Box 10.3 continued

where

P_t = total population at time t

HU_t = occupied housing units at time t

PPH_t = average number of persons per household at time t

GQ_t = group quarters population at time t.

It is assumed that the GQ_t population is accounted for by a census of these institutions. We also assume that time t is a census year, and, in this example, the data are from the 1990 census. The key, then, is to find values for H and PPH for the target year, in this case April 1, 1996. We will need one more equation in this example:

$$H_t = (HU_c + U_t - D_t) \cdot OCC_c \,,$$

where

HU_c = housing units enumerated in most recent census

U_t = utility hookups for housing units between most recent census and time t

D_t = housing units demolished between most recent census and time t

OCC_c = overall occupancy rate observed in most recent census.

We begin with the following data for census tract 110.1 in MSA Y.

Population (P_c)—1990	1,996
Housing Units (HU_c)	557
Utility Hook-ups (U_t) Between Census & April 1, 1996	257
Demolished Units (D_t) Between Census & April 1, 1996	13
Occupancy Rate (OCC_c)—1990	.99
Persons Per Household (PPH_c)—1990	3.62

Local survey data indicate that between April 1, 1990, and April 1, 1996, PPH for this area of town has increased to 3.75 while the occupancy rate has stayed constant.

So: HU_{1996} $= (HU_{1990} + U_{90\text{-}96} - D_{90\text{-}96}) \cdot OCC_{1996}$

$= (557 + 257 - 13) \cdot .99$

$= 801$ occupied housing units,

P_{1996} $= H_{1996\,(OCC)} \cdot PPH_t$

$= 801 \cdot 3.75$

$= 3,004.$

Therefore, the population of tract 110.1 increased from 1,996 to an estimated 3,004 persons between April 1, 1990, and April 1, 1996.

Box 10.4

Customizing the Housing Unit Method

High-quality population estimates are critical for business planning and the housing unit method has been shown to provide reliable estimates for small units of geography. Since most U.S. businesses operate in relatively small market areas, owners and managers should have a working knowledge of methods that can improve the quality of population estimates based on the housing unit methodology.

Recall that the underlying model for the housing unit method is

$$P_{t+1} = (HU_{t+1} \cdot PPH_{t+1}) + P_{GQ} \,,$$

where

P_{t+1}	=	population estimate for postcensal year
HU_{t+1}	=	occupied housing units for postcensal year
PPH_{t+1}	=	average persons per household for postcensal year
P_{GQ}	=	population in group quarters for postcensal year.

P_{GQ} is derived by approaching the owners or managers of the institutions representing group quarters residents and complete counts are obtained. Often, residents of group quarters are considered to be separate from the remainder of a market and are therefore not factored in as business plans are formulated. However, it is possible that those residents (e.g., of nursing homes or college dormitories) *are* in fact the target market, in which case the housing unit method is not needed.

Small-area updates in occupied housing units and persons per household are key to this method. As previously noted, the housing unit count is adjusted from the most recent census to account for new construction and demolitions. Vacancy rates are also updated. The persons per household figure is adjusted by assuming that the number of persons-per-household in the target area rises or falls in constant proportion to the number for a larger unit of geography for which data are available. (Intercensal persons per household figures are usually not available for small geographic units.) For small markets, other "custom" adjustments can be made to improve the quality of data even more.

In small markets, it may be possible to actually conduct a census of housing units. Since it is imperative that an accurate count of housing units per structure (e.g., in apartment complexes) be obtained, driving through residential areas can yield very accurate counts in a relatively short period of time. This is particularly true in new residential developments where most, if not all, units are single family dwellings. While vacancy rates from the previous census should be examined, adjustments to those rates that reflect new, still not inhabited units, are required. A quantitative/qualitative assessment of vacancy levels can be conducted during the drive through. Aerial photography can also produce a housing unit count, but an accurate assessment of which units are occupied would be nearly impossible. Next, a persons-per-household figure must be derived. In areas undergoing rapid change, the figure from the last census may be of little help. Assuming a constant figure almost always means that the estimated persons-per-household figure is too low in areas where there are young, growing

---

Box 10.4 continued

families. One way to address this issue is to examine historical persons-per-household data (e.g., 1990) for neighborhoods that "appear" to have similar demographic composition to the area in question. Once a fit is found, the persons-per-household figure for that neighborhood can be used.

A note of caution: In most instances, traditional housing unit methods are more accurate and efficient than a neighborhood drivethrough. In stable areas where the number of housing units has not changed very much, little adjustment is needed. However, in rapidly growing areas, the historical data available may have very little connection to the current situation and other ways of estimating housing units and persons per household are called for.

Some estimates and projections of demographic characteristics are linked to previously derived population estimates and projections. For example, labor force projections generated by the Bureau of Labor Statistics (BLS) begin with the detailed population projections produced by the U.S. Bureau of the Census. The population projections are then multiplied by labor force participation rates to generate labor force projection figures. Aggregate economic performance is then factored into the general projections by industry, occupation and a combination of industry-occupation factors (U.S. Department of Labor 1994). Estimates and projections for other population characteristics can also be produced by multiplying incidence or prevalence rates by population estimates and projections. In health care, for example, the number of persons engaging in a specific behavior (e.g., drug use) can be estimated by multiplying current age-, sex-, race-specific drug use rates by age-, sex-, and race-specific population projections. Of course, these projections assume that the incidence rates remain constant.

Much of the contemporary research being conducted in the area of population estimates and projections focuses on evaluating the quality of these data and generating confidence intervals for the data (e.g., Schafer, Tayman and Carter 1995; Tayman and Swanson 1995; Smith and Shahidullah 1995; Smith and Sincich 1992). This work is important for two reasons. First, it recognizes what all demographers know: all estimates and projections contain error. It also measures error by comparing historical data to the estimates and projections produced for that historical period. The difference between the historical data and estimates or projections comprises the error. Second, this work uses the past errors to produce confidence intervals around more recent estimates and projections. While much of this work is very recent, its advancement and spread to private sector vendors promises to offer data users a higher level of confidence in the data being purchased. The quality of data products offered will be markedly improved as these newer techniques are adopted by the vendors.

A NOTE OF CAUTION

The promise made by some data vendors to provide virtually any variable for any geographic unit is certainly exciting for anyone who wishes to use demographic data in a business analysis. Clearly, the entry of business planners into the matrix of data users has helped create and direct an industry that did not exist in the past. However, the demand for data is exceeding the vendors' ability to produce quality information across the wide range of geographic units offered. At the same time, this increased demand is taking the production of estimates and projections of demographic data in directions it would not have gone, and at a much faster speed had business users not entered the market. It is clear that the quality of data will improve, albeit slowly, and that for the near future most users would benefit from some demographic consultation in making choices about data purchase and use. The cost of this consultation is reasonable, especially in light of the complex and expensive data systems that are being purchased or leased by many businesses.

Box 10.5 presents a short biography for a demographer who is employed by one of the data vendors.

Box 10.5
Ken Hodges—Demographer for Claritas

I am a demographer at Claritas, Inc., a major supplier of demographic and consumer marketing information. The company is headquartered in Arlington, Virginia, but I work at the Ithaca, New York, office, where most of our demographic work is done. I have a Ph.D. in sociology/demography and an M.A. and B.A. in sociology. I've been with Claritas for three years and have 14 years of experience in the industry.

My work has always focused on small-area data, especially the production of estimates and projections for small areas such as census tracts and block groups. Claritas is one of several companies producing such data nationwide, and it's my job to ensure that our methods and results are as strong as possible. I spend a lot of time evaluating small-area data and testing methods. For example, we recently assessed the ability of small-area methods to produce suitable summations of age/sex composition for larger areas, such as counties and states. Some areas require special attention and, in recent years, we have focused on the impact of events such as military base closings. For the most part, though, small-area estimates are an exercise in demographic mass production, and I work closely with our Demographic Resources staff, which is highly knowledge-able and proficient at translating a complex set of methods into an efficient production process.

The data industry may not have mastered small-area estimation to the extent suggested by its promotional literature, but it is an established product, and there is always pressure to produce something new. Most recently, I've been working on a set of Workplace Population products to meet the demand for what our customers call "daytime demographics." This work has been a challenge and a learning experience because of the scarcity of data coded by place of work, and because workplace population dynamics are so different from those of residential populations.

Box 10.5 continued

Whenever possible, we internally evaluate our work, and my first major assignment at Claritas was to evaluate their 1990 tract-level population estimates against the results of the 1990 census. This evaluation confirmed that, while such estimates are subject to substantial error, they are effective at identifying change and provide considerable improvement over the use of ten-year-old census data. Last year I evaluated the methods used to retrieve data for geometric areas such as circles and polygons. For years, such geographic approximations have been an industry capability and a source of controversy, but no one had ever tested the accuracy of the alternative methods.

Such evaluations enhance our knowledge of our own work and help us provide better customer support. Because of the error and uncertainty involved, knowledgeable and candid support can significantly increase the value of small area estimates to the user. For this reason, I welcome the frequent occasions when my work is interrupted by a sales person with a question or a call from a customer. It's a chance to impart knowledge, and maybe learn something myself.

Providing an informative but readable written description of our methods is critical to the supportive objective, and I am responsible for writing and updating most of our demographic methodology documents. I also write papers summarizing our internal evaluations and maintain an on-line catalog of documents for use in sales and customer support.

Ours is a competitive environment, and sometimes I am called on to help close a sale—supposedly by impressing the prospect with our demographic prowess. This is where things can get interesting, because by the time I get involved, the prospect has probably been pumped up with claims from all sides. Because I will not misrepresent our work, my challenge often is to bring the prospect's expectations back to a realistic level without losing the sale. It can be done, and there is a real exhilaration in pulling it off.

My job also involves serving as a companywide demographic resource and representing us to the professional community. I keep myself and the company involved in professional associations and, when our work is of broad enough interest, I write papers for presentation at professional conferences. Also, because we and our customers rely so heavily on data from the decennial census, I have actively followed the 2000 census planning effort and sought to keep everyone informed of developments and their implications.

The demographic data industry has never employed a large number of demographers, and there was a time when one might have put one's professional reputation at risk by working for a private supplier. It is still a relatively untraveled career path and one that requires a demographer to do seemingly outlandish things. However, it is a path in which one can accomplish serious work, experience the satisfaction of seeing one's work applied, and even maintain a standing in the profession of demography.

REFERENCES

Ahlburg, Dennis A. (1993). "The Census Bureau's New Projections of the U.S. Population." *Population and Development* Review, 19 (1): 159–174.

Ahlburg, Dennis, and J. Vaupel (1990). "Alternative Projections of the U.S. Population." *Demography*, 27 (4): 639–652.

Campbell, Paul C. (1994). "Population Projections for States, by Age, Sex, Race and Hispanic Origin: 1993 to 2000." *Current Population Reports*, Series P-25, No. 1111. Washington, DC: U.S. Government Printing Office.

Edmondson, Brad (1996). "Your Local Future." *American Demographics* (April): 6–7.

Exter, Thomas G. (1996). "Buying Demographics in the Late 1990s." *Business Geographics*, 4 (3): 18.

Pittinger, Donald B. (1977). "Population Forecasting Standards: Some Considerations Concerning Their Necessity and Content." *Demography*, 14 (3): 363–368.

Rives, Norfleet, and William J. Serow (1984). *Applied Demography*. Beverly Hills, CA: Sage Publications.

Schafer, Edward, Jeff Tayman, and Larry Carter (1995). "Forecasting Errors and Confidence Intervals for Small Area Population Forecasts." Paper presented at the Annual Meeting of the Population Association of America, San Francisco, CA.

Shryock, Henry S., and Jacob S. Siegel (1973). *The Methods and Materials of Demography*. Washington, DC: U.S. Government Printing Office.

Smith, Stanley K., and Bart B. Lewis (1980). "Some New Techniques for Applying the Housing Unit Method of Local Population Estimation." *Demography*, 17 (3): 323–339.

Smith, Stanley K., and Bart B. Lewis (1983). "Some New Techniques for Applying the Housing Unit Method of Local Population Estimation: Further Evidence." *Demography*, 20 (3): 407–413.

Smith, Stanley K., and Mohammed Shahidullah (1995). "An Evaluation of Population Projection Errors for Census Tracts." *Journal of the American Statistical Association*, 90 (1): 64–71.

Smith, Stanley K., and Terry Sincich (1992). "Evaluating the Forecast Accuracy and Bias of Alternative Projections for States." *International Journal of Forecasting*, 8 (4): 495–508.

Spar, Edward J. (1996). "Statistics Held Hostage—A Commentary." *Business Geographics*, 4 (3): 20.

Starsinic, Donald E., and Meyer Zitter (1968). "Accuracy of the Housing Unit Method in Preparing Population Estimates for Cities." *Demography*, 5 (4): 475–484.

Tayman, Jeff, and David A. Swanson (1995). "Alternative Measures for Evaluating Population Forecasts: A Comparison of State, and Sub-County Geographic Areas." Paper presented at the Annual Meeting of the Population Association of America, San Francisco, CA.

U.S. Department of Labor (1994). *The American Work Force*. U.S. Bureau of Labor Statistics, Bulletin 2452. Washington, DC: U.S. Government Printing Office.

SUGGESTED READINGS

Murdock, Steve H., and David R. Ellis (1991). *Applied Demography*. Boulder, CO: Westview Press, Chapter 5.

Pittinger, Donald (1976). *Projecting State and Local Population*. Cambridge, MA: Ballinger Publishing Co.

Smith, David P. (1992). *Formal Demography*. New York: Plenum, Chapter 8.

Statistics Canada (1987). *Population Estimation Methods, Canada*. Ottawa: Ministry of Supply and Services.

U.S. Bureau of the Census (1990). "State and Local Agencies Preparing Population and Housing Estimates." *Current Population Reports*, Series P-25, No. 1063. Washington, DC: U.S. Government Printing Office.

Chapter 11

Contemporary Business Demography

INTRODUCTION

The activities of business demographers are driven by the need to make decisions (Swanson, Burch, and Tedrow 1996; Kintner and Pol 1996). Business owners and managers must decide, for example, whether or not to open a new store, how to react to changes in the pricing tactics of a competitor, if, when, and how to respond to changes in market size and composition, and whether or not to initiate a direct mail campaign. Business practitioners have turned to demographic data, perspectives, and methods in an attempt to make better decisions. Demographers, as in-house employees and as consultants, have provided much of the requisite expertise.

Three factors have affected the growth in business demography during the 1990s. First, business analysts have become more aware of and more open to demographic input. Many business environments are complex and a wide range of data and methodologies are required to arrive at a carefully planned strategy. For some businesses, demographic analyses have become part of the standard mix of planning activities. Many database marketing activities, for example, are driven by the demographic characteristics of customers and geographic areas containing potential customers (Hughes 1994).

Second, the increased integration of demographic analysis to business decision making reflects the expectation that decisions will be information driven. These expectations have been shaped largely by data availability. The 1980s and early 1990s have been witness to an incredible increase in the available sources of data, coupled with vast improvements in data accessibility. This rapid expansion of data availability has been accompanied by a growing emphasis on data for small areas, the level at which most business decisions are made. The availability of data for census tracts, block groups, and even irregularly shaped market areas allows medium- and smaller-size businesses to easily perform relatively complex analyses. This analytical capability is further facilitated by the low cost of the data. As a result, the expectation that decisions will be supported by data has reached all levels of business.

Third, the two trends above have been driven by improvements in computer hardware and software technology. Data storage and retrieval problems that were insurmountable just a few years ago are no longer barriers to utilizing large data sets. These large data sets can now be accessed quickly with a minimum of error. Enhanced software has given impetus to data-driven decisions by facilitating the integration of large data sets into even larger data systems. In most industries today, data from a variety of internal and external sources are appended to sales records in order to enhance the value of information that is collected as part of everyday business activities. The use of large data sets has led to a clearer understanding of the relationship between demographic phenomena and business concerns.

Finally, decision making occurs in both small and large business contexts. While it is clear that small businesses have fewer financial and human resources available for day-to-day planning and operations, improved access to data and a reduction in the cost of software and hardware has brought demographic data within reach of even the smallest businesses engaged in strategic planning.

This chapter offers a contemporary view of business demography, first presenting a typology of studies conducted and then offering examples of these studies. The reader is reminded that much of the work being done by business demographers, or persons engaged in business demography, is proprietary and never made available in any public sense. Therefore, the studies discussed here should not be seen as an exhaustive survey of the most recent work in the field. The works cited are typical of those being performed and provide a good "sense" of how demographic analysis is being used to assist decision makers. The applications section is followed by a discussion of demographic methodologies in use in business and public sector applications. These methods represent a variety of approaches for introducing demographic and nondemographic information into the decision-making process. Finally, a discussion on the future of business demography is presented.

DECISION-MAKING CONTEXTS

Demographic analyses are utilized to address business problems as well as to take advantage of opportunities. As discussed in Chapter 1, the areas affected by input from business demography include finance, marketing, management, accounting, law, and production operations. One or more of these concerns usually arises in the context of a specific decision or set of interrelated decisions. For example, a site location decision involves at the very least finance (can an acceptable level of profit be realized?), marketing (can the business compete in this market?), and law (is the location zoned correctly?). Figure 11.1 presents a list of decision-making contexts. The reader should consider the potential complexity of the decision-making contexts outlined below, as well as the fact that multiple decisions may need to be made (e.g., site analysis and human resource planning) in order to develop and implement a strategic plan.

Figure 11.1
Decision-Making Contexts

Site Analyses	Competitive Analysis
Market Analysis	Identification of Customers/Markets
Market Valuations	Target Marketing
Human Resources Planning	

Site Analyses

Site analyses involve two major concerns: the evaluation of conditions surrounding an existing site and/or the selection of a new site in which to locate a business. In both cases, financial analyses are ultimately required to assess profitability (both short and long term) and produce cash flow projections. Marketing issues must be addressed in regard to an existing or proposed site. Management concerns might focus on labor force composition and availability. Some site location analyses are different from others because the decision is made in the context of numerous existing and/or planned locations. For example, the decision concerning a location for a new Wal-Mart product distribution center would be largely influenced by proximity to other Wal-Mart stores, proximity to other distribution centers, and the availability of labor near the proposed site.

Site analyses are needed in most industries, and site selection is currently the decision that most frequently employs demographic analysis (e.g., Morrison and Abrahamse 1996). Site analyses have been conducted, for example, that involve an assessment of the financial viability of a nursing home (Murdock and Hamm 1994), the decision to construct an assisted-living facility (Peete and Godley 1996), and the determination of the eligibility of a proposed obstetrical unit for a certificate of need (Thomas 1994). In all three instances, potential customers/clients for a market area were estimated and projected. The projections were then used to assess the financial viability of the respective business proposals.

Hospitals and other health care providers frequently study patterns of population growth to identify areas where new health facilities are needed. Demographic-based projections have been used to estimate future demand for physician office visits and the level of health care expenditures by seniors (Davenhall 1993). In addition, the same types of analyses are being performed for physician groups and individual practices, entities that infrequently have resources allocated to planning activities. Site location services offered by consultants and hospitals are now available to physicians when they initially open a practice or relocate an existing one. Health care providers incorporate demographic data—the size and composition of the population within reasonable travel distance—into the decision-making matrix.

There are numerous applications in the retail and real estate industries. Demographic analysis, for example, has been used to assess the profitability of a proposed hotel that could only be constructed in one location (Ambrose and Pol 1994) and to conduct a market analysis for a proposed commercial development (Tayman and Pol 1995). In both cases, demographic data were combined with competitor, cost, sales, and other information to arrive at a build-or-not-build decision. Grocery stores examine market-area size and composition to estimate market share and ascertain how the market area may be changing. In the real estate arena, data on driving time, the location of competitors, and population characteristics are merged to decide among competing locations for commercial real estate investments (Cowen 1995).

Marks and Spencer incorporates demographic and other data to produce a gravity model that is used to drive decisions on new store locations (Bryan 1994). The *John Deere* company uses farm location data from the Census of Agriculture to decide where to establish equipment dealerships. *Honda* uses mapped data to make area-specific sales forecasts and to assist in locating new dealers (Hoerning 1996). The *Frito-Lay* company makes use of information on the location of its customers (e.g., grocery stores) to map out routes for drivers who restock the shelves of those businesses.

Site analyses have been conducted in many other settings. Voss (1994) was part of a decision-making team studying whether a Wisconsin bank should open a branch in Florida in response to management's belief that many of its best customers had retired to that state. The decision also included locating a site for the bank. County-to-county migration flow data were used to ascertain the volume of Wisconsin migrants to Florida and their major destinations in that state. The analysis also used data from the Public Use Microdata Sample (PUMS) generated by the Census Bureau to identify economic factors thought to be positively associated with heavy use of the most profitable bank services.

Johnson's (1994) work evaluated alternative sites for motels that would be part of a national motel chain. Using data for existing motels as well as information about the demographic characteristics of their locations, a regression equation was created to predict sales revenues. This equation then was used to assess the profitability of other locations. A long list of potential sites was shortened to the most favorable sites using this analysis, and further evaluations yielded the sites eventually chosen. Similar types of analyses have been performed to choose sites for restaurants such as *Red Lobster, The Olive Garden, McDonald's*, and *Burger King*.

Once the demographic analyses are conducted, financial evaluations can follow. Tayman and Pol (1995) estimated the sales per square foot and the number of financially viable restaurants in a proposed shopping center given projected population increases. A similar analysis was performed for other retail space. Each analysis was linked to a financial assessment, with decisions being made on the basis of projected short- and long-term profits.

Market Analysis

Market analysis is closely related to site analysis. In some site analyses, the market area is either known or can be easily determined. In other studies, appropriate boundaries must first be specified, and significant resources may be required to accomplish this task. In an era of database marketing, customer lists are often available and a simple mapping of these data may serve to delineate the market area. Demographic data are then aggregated to fit the mapped boundaries, and the aggregation of data on population size and composition produces a profile of the population within those boundaries. Trend data on demographic and socioeconomic characteristics can provide information on the nature of change within those boundaries.

The two pieces of data needed to calculate market share are: the number of households in a market area and the number of households that are customers. Longitudinal analysis provides a mechanism for measuring changes in market share and assessing penetration among new households. Financial services corporations have an advantage over other product/service companies because they possess extensive information about their customers. Plotting customer addresses along with the locations of financial transactions (e.g., banks and ATMs) provides an even more complete view of the market area. This information is then used to decide where to locate other ATMs and branch facilities, as well as to direct cross-selling efforts for other financial services.

Other businesses perform the same types of analyses. *Dayton Hudson*, for example, plots customer addresses via buyer exit surveys and appends that information to data on purchase activity. Linking purchase data to the demographic characteristics of the areas in which customers reside enhances customer information and results in improved marketing efforts.

Market Valuations

Once a market area has been identified, a logical analytical extension is the determination of its value. A simple analysis might take the number of households in an area and multiply that number by an average expenditure per household, using a data source such as the *Consumer Expenditure Survey* (profiled in Chapter 3). An existing business can estimate its market share of dollars spent or determine market share based on the percentage of total households that are its customers. Data on market composition (e.g., size of households and median household income) could be factored in if appropriate.

A market analysis can be used to estimate the average cost of obtaining a new customer in that market area versus the revenue likely to be generated from that customer. It can be subsequently determined if adding new customers will result in an acceptable revenue flow. The analysis can be expanded to include a longer-range view of the profits a new customer might generate. Recent studies, in fact, have demonstrated the advantage of viewing customers from a "lifetime value" perspective. Billings and Pol (1994) studied the assumed market value of cellular customers and the manner in which that information drove the valuation of cellular service areas. The method normally used simply involved multiplying the market area population by some global dollar figure (e.g., $150) to arrive at a total market value. Billings and Pol found that compositional factors such as age and occupation had a significant impact on the probability of an area resident becoming a cellular customer. They concluded that the composition of a market significantly affected its perceived market value. Box 11.1 addresses a business response to market area changes.

Box 11.1
A Drycleaner's Response to a Growing Market

A local dry-cleaning business, JT's Cleaners, was considering whether or not to expand its number of locations. JT's already had five stores, and in some ways the market seemed to be saturated with service providers. However, the western part of the county was undergoing rapid residential growth, and there were no dry cleaning locations in this area. JT's was faced with two decisions: (1) should they expand from 5 to 6 or, perhaps 7 locations and (2) if so, where should they locate the new store(s).

To learn more about their customers, JT's decided to plot the addresses of a sample of recent customers for each of their five existing locations. Unlike many other businesses, cleaning service providers have a readily available customer address list. If JT's had wanted, they could have created a more detailed plotting methodology such as one that distinguished customers on the basis of frequency of service usage or dollar amount of sales. A simpler approach, plotting a sample of recent customers, enabled each store manager to easily determine her market area. In addition, the owner was able to determine the demographic characteristics of areas from which customers were drawn by accessing block group and census tract data from the 1990 Census of Population and Housing via CD-ROM. Moreover, JT's was able to study its market areas in the context of highway/road access and traffic flow. Conventional wisdom, supported by some industry studies, indicated that people either lived near their dry cleaners, worked near their dry cleaners, or took their cleaning to outlets located between home and work. The plot of addresses, along with information on traffic flow and some assumptions about customer employment locations, enabled JT's management team to better understand the relationship between customer residence and business location.

Maps depicting the distribution of customer of the five existing market areas also helped JT's determine where opportunities in the market existed. Assumptions regarding the market reach of competitors were overlaid on the known data for the five existing sites and, as expected, several areas in the western part of the country were found to be "underserved." Using assumptions based upon the financial data from the five existing locations, a sixth site was judged to be potentially profitable using JT's criteria for return on investment. The answer to question 1 was yes, so an answer to question 2 was needed.

Using information on the demographic characteristics of areas likely to contain persons/households with a high propensity to consume dry-cleaning services obtained in the market analysis for the five existing sites, a search routine was launched to identify sites having a high concentration of persons/households with similar characteristics. Travel routes and times had to be factored in, and four "candidate" locations were identified. JT's management calculated the estimated costs, revenues,

> **Box 11.1 continued**
>
> and returns for all four sites for one, three, and five years from the start of operations. At years 3 and 5 another assumption was added to the analysis. The management of JT's assumed that a competitor had entered the immediate market at year 3 and was still in business at year 5. One of the four sites generated profit projections that were clearly better than the others and this site was chosen for the sixth outlet.

Human Resources Planning

Human resource applications fall into two general categories. The first involves an assessment of the current and future labor force supply in an area. The second involves an evaluation of the number and composition of the employees of a specific business, sometimes referred to as *organizational demography*. The former requires geographic data for an existing or proposed trade area, while the latter utilizes internal data for current and past employees. Many analyses require data of both types.

An evaluation of the available labor force is an integral part of many site analyses. Most businesses that are being established, relocated, or expanded require a specific number of employees. They also have specific labor force needs with respect to education, training and experience. Communities that do not have the requisite number of well-trained and experienced workers may not receive consideration when relocation or expansion is considered. The cost of importing workers may be seen as unacceptably high, and recruiting a labor force in this manner may be seen as a strategy that is too risky. Cities and MSAs with favorable reputations in terms of worker availability and educational infrastructure receive special consideration, while those with poor reputations may receive no consideration at all. Places with low unemployment rates may raise concerns because of potentially high labor costs, while areas with high unemployment rates may be avoided for other reasons. Labor force size and composition have an impact on the cost of labor will cost in terms of salaries, benefits, and future training costs.

Labor force analysis for factories, retail outlets, and other employment sites is relatively straight forward. First, the level and types of labor force needs, both current and future, must be determined. Second, the area from which the labor force can be drawn must be identified, paying particular attention to unemployment rates and the travel time expectations of the area. On the East Coast, a one-hour, one-way commute may be expected and tolerated. In many areas of the Midwest a one-hour, one-way commute is unacceptable—workers are unwilling to spend that much time in transit. Once the labor force recruitment area is identified, the size and composition of the labor force can be determined. This will involve the use of current and historical census data, supplemented by any available public or private labor force projections. Local chambers of commerce often produce such projections, although the data user should carefully examine both the methodology and the motive underlying their production. The next step involves a comparison of need versus supply, and the final step incorporates labor force cost and productivity considerations.

In assessing the labor force needs of organizations, the factors that will be relevant vary. First, the motives for analysis may differ from situation to situation; for example, one company may wish to "down-size" its labor force while another may be interested in expanding. Second, changes in the products offered or the method of production may indicate that labor force needs are changing. Third, the changing characteristics of the current labor force itself must be considered.

For the most part, labor force assessments focus on internal records and involve a current profile, a history, and some projections of the organization's labor force. This assessment will consider (1) mortality rates, (2) retirement and other attrition considerations, and (3) hiring rates. Difficulties in comparing and merging data sets from different companies have been noted by Kintner and Swanson (1994). The main problem stems from the fact that these data sets are created for a variety of applications other than generating a labor force profile. However, these data problems can be overcome and the current and projected labor force effectively studied.

As stated earlier, these data can be used to plan for and assess the impact of restructuring on an organization. These decisions must be based on additional studies of present and future labor force needs given (1) trends in sales and profits, (2) technological developments relevant to the business in question, and (3) long-term growth plans. Other components of these studies may include assessments of the ability of the future workforce to produce products/deliver services that are competitive in the market place, estimates of the cost of health care and other benefits attached to the labor force and retirees (Kintner and Swanson 1994), and analyses of the impact of company mergers or workforce considerations.

Competitive Analysis

Businesses need to be able to estimate the effect of competition on revenues, profits, and other financial indicators. Competitor impact studies are relatively straightforward. First, a market area must be identified. The number of potential customers, current market share, and other indicators of size and strength in that market are then calculated. (Presumably, profit/loss, return on assets, and return on investment calculations for the present situation have already been performed.) Assumptions with regard to the effect of competitor activities and their impact on the company are used to generate a series of what-if scenarios. The results of these scenarios are converted into revenue and profits projections. The cost of regaining market share, expanding the geographic boundaries of the market, and other possible reactions are estimated and tied back into profitability and return-on-investment estimates. The potential impact of potential actions are measured against company estimates of the implications of taking strategic actions.

Competition may come in the form of stepped-up marketing initiatives from companies already in the market, the entry of new competitors into the market, mergers and acquisitions among competitors, and/or the expansion of product and service lines on the part of competitors. Thomas (1994) looked at the expansion of obstetrical services of a competitor hospital, arguing that a certificate of need should not be granted because the existing and projected market (i.e., the number of births in a given service area) could not support the additional service (i.e., the proposed obstetrical service would not be financially viable). Rives (1994) studied the impact of expansion of a competitor hospital on patient load, market share, and, ultimately, the financial viability of a client hospital. Both of these studies used mainstream demographic analyses, such as fertility analyses and population projections, coupled with assumptions on the implications of competition to arrive at conclusions regarding the impact of planned activities.

Identifying Customers and Markets

There are two situations in which the identification of customers and markets becomes important. The first arises when a business wishes to know more about its existing customer base, including its demographic characteristics. The second occurs when a business already knows something about its customers (e.g., demographic characteristics) and would like to identify additional market areas containing concentrations of persons with similar characteristics. In both situations, internal and external data are required.

There are three methods for gathering demographic information about customers. The first involves the collection of information such as age, marital status, and income from applications completed by customers. Form completion may be required to obtain check cashing privileges or preferred customer cards. Preferred customer cards are gaining popularity and are used as a mechanism to distribute coupons and award discounts. At the same time a customer is receiving a card, the business is building a valuable database. The same approach to data collection is utilized when consumers complete a warranty form on a purchased product.

The second method involves a survey of customers via mail or telephone. A randomly selected sample of customers is chosen, unless the number of customers is small enough to justify surveying everyone. Individuals are questioned concerning product/store preferences and satisfaction with services. Demographic data are gathered to assist in interpreting the responses. Survey research on consumers is expensive, however, and participation by consumers must be justified, since there is no direct reward. Given these two problems, many retailers and other store owners have chosen other mechanisms than survey research for collecting data.

The third method of data collection requires assembling and tracking a "panel" of customers. A panel is assembled when a group of customers agree to be tracked with respect to both their purchasing behavior and changes in their personal/household characteristics (e.g., employment change, increase in income). Panel data expand the value of the demographic data collected by appending purchase records and expanding the scope of the demographic, attitudinal, and behavioral data gathered.

All these methods facilitate the study of the relationships between demographic characteristics and buyer behavior. The results of these studies serve as a basis for advertising media selection, product line development, and customer relations programs. Many grocery stores, discount stores, and other retailers are already engaged in or are planning to invest in the activities required to produce these databases.

If businesses know who their current customers are, they are in a position to recruit new ones. When their basis of knowledge is demographic (e.g., homeowners with a median household income of $60,000 or more), it is possible to identify geographic areas that contain large numbers of households with comparable characteristics. Once the areas containing comparable consumers have been identified, marketing efforts are used to target the areas containing these households.

Targeting Markets

Targeting markets is a logical extension of most of the analyses discussed so far. *Targeting* involves first dividing a large market into relatively homogeneous segments based on demographic, psychographic, or other information linked to purchase behavior. Market segments with high purchase propensities are separated from those with low purchase propensities. Once the segments have been identified, concentrated efforts are made to encourage persons in the higher-propensity segments to buy the products of Company X or to encourage low-propensity segments to change their behavior. The latter strategy is typically the more difficult of the two. In fact, low-propensity segment members are often eliminated from the target market mailing lists in direct mail campaigns because the added expense is not justified by the potential for sales.

The key in such applications is to link demographic characteristics to purchase propensities. In today's world of target marketing, lifestyle clusters and psychographic profiles are often argued to be superior to demographic profiling. However, the reader should note that (1) some researchers continue to make a strong case for demographic segmentation and (2) most of the lifestyle and psychographic methodologies have strong demographic underpinnings. Lifestyle clusters are typically defined in terms of two or more demographic identifiers (e.g., age, income).

Establishing the correlation between demographic characteristics and purchasing potential is a critical step. Once the relationships are found, individuals or areas with the appropriate demographic characteristics can be targeted. Billboards that market everything from cigarettes to real estate are located in areas where targeted customers are most likely to see them. Television and radio programs appealing to persons with certain demographic characteristics are supported by advertising targeted at those same persons.

APPLICATIONS OF DEMOGRAPHIC METHODS

The contribution of demographic methods to business applications should be clearly understood by business decision makers. These methods are part of contemporary business demography and serve to extend demographic data beyond the bounds of traditional use. While demographers use many of the same methods employed in business analysis (e.g., time series analyses and neural networks), some of the methods and techniques are unique to demography. Business analysts should consider adding these to their repertoire of useful methodologies. Some of the applications seen in the next several pages have been developed for the public sector and are included here to provide a broader range of applied examples.

Life Tables

The earliest usages of life table techniques did not focus on the study of mortality, but on the ways the probability of death affected the pricing of annuities (Halley 1693). This is the same methodology utilized in the life insurance industry today. Life expectancy data combined with insurance premium information is used to estimate the dollars accrued over the lifetimes of subscribers (Smith, 1992, pp. 198–205). Given the expected return on investment and adjustments for the present value of money, prices can be set for these products. Appropriate adjustments can subsequently be made to distinguish whole life policies from term policies.

Life table applications go far beyond those seen in financial markets. Life table analyses have been used in health care for chronic disease modeling and in epidemiology to study the effects of treatment on leukemia patients (Cox 1972). Industrial applications have focused on "life testing" to calculate the expected "life" of a product or product part (e.g., Bain 1978; Nelson 1982). Multiple decrement principles have been used to construct school life tables and increment/decrement calculations have been employed to produce working life tables. Other multiple-decrement-based life tables have been produced for disabilities.

More recent applications have used life table analysis in additional ways. Garcia (1994) constructed a school enrollment life table, with l_x representing a new cohort of students, q_x being the proportion of students who enrolled in year x but did not enroll in year x + 1, and e_0 indicating the average number of years enrolled before graduation or leaving without a terminal degree. These calculations can be used to produce a graduation rate, generate an estimate for average-time-to-degree, and assist in producing enrollment projections. Kintner and Swanson (1994) utilized the corporate database of *General Motors* to calculate life expectancies of its salaried workers. These data were linked to hospitalization rates to gain a clearer understanding of the health care cost liabilities represented by the company's salaried and retiree population. The same basic life table principles could be tied to the lifetime customer value calculations used in database marketing.

Cohort Analysis

As noted previously, a cohort is an "aggregate of individuals who experience the same event within the same time interval" (Ryder 1965, p. 845). Cohort analysis refers to a set of analytic tools designed to study these groupings of individuals. Demographers typically use birth, marriage, and/or education cohorts for analytic purposes. The concept also has applications for studies of labor force changes within an organization (e.g., those hired during the same time period), the planning of product adoption (e.g., those buying a product or service at about the same time), and research focusing on sales projections.

Cohort analysis proceeds by first identifying cohorts and then studying the behavior, attitudes, opinions, and other characteristics associated with these cohorts across time. The key is to discern the differential effects of both cohort membership and time on consumer behavior. The analysis is often extended to include age as a variable.

Cohort analysis is seen as a tool in strategic planning (Reynolds and Rentz 1981). In order to better understand the effect of population aging on the consumption of products and services, these authors created a diagram that reflects the hypothetical age-specific consumption of a product for six time intervals (1930–1980). Using Palmore's (1978) triad method, longitudinal differences (age and period effects), cross-sectional differences (age and cohort effects), and time lag differences (period and cohort effects) were identified and differentiated. In this manner, time-related differences (the difference in consumption for the same cohort over two periods of time) were distinguished from the differences among cohorts with respect to product consumption variations. This application involved the simple calculation of absolute and percentage differences, although more sophisticated methodologies are available for this task (Halli and Rao 1992, pp. 49–61).

Rentz, Reynolds, and Stout (1983) utilized multiple regression to study the effects of cohort, age, and period on soft drink consumption between 1950 and 1979. The observed decline in soft drink consumption with age led the researchers to hypothesize that an aging population would experience a reduction in overall soft drink consumption. The authors found the cohort effects to be much stronger than the period effects. This made intuitive sense, they argued, because of the stepped-up marketing efforts by soft drink producers during this time interval. From a strategic perspective, the results supported the contention that aggregate sales would not decrease due to an aging of the population.

While these studies clearly introduce cohort analysis methodologies to nondemographers and offer some examples of how such studies can be conducted, their overall impact on business demographic research to date has been quite small. Despite the clear benefit of cohort analysis demonstrated in these studies, the methodology has not progressed beyond the work performed in the early 1980s, and more recent applications cannot be found in the literature. Marketing researchers typically do not consider cohort analysis to be one of *their* methodological options. This situation is unfortunate because marketers, as well as other researchers, frequently are interested in aggregate purchase patterns and other behavioral trends that occur as the result of both a changing culture (period effects) and changing behaviors within cohorts (cohort effects).

Standardization

Kitagawa's (1964) classic study on the standardization of rates in comparative research generated a new and valuable family of methodological tools for demographic research. Rate comparisons controlling for differences in, for example, age structure were clarified, and the decomposition of indices was facilitated (Halli and Rao 1992, pp. 8–15). The introduction of statistical tests for measuring the difference in rates refined the comparisons (Smith 1992, pp. 62–70), and the extension of the concept of standardized comparisons was further advanced with the application of log linear models (Clogg and Eliason 1988).

Despite the obvious advantages of standardization procedures for the comparison of markets and market segments, few examples of the applications of this technique can be found in the literature. Billings and Pol (1994) applied basic standardization procedures to compare the market potential for cellular telephone adoption in two Florida counties, with the ultimate goal of determining the value of each market. The initial data indicated that the propensity to purchase a cellular phone varied considerably by age. Cellular penetration indices were calculated and adjusted for the substantial differences in age structure. The use of standardization resulted in a revision of estimates of the relative value of cellular sales between the two markets. A similar analysis can be found in Pol and Tymkiw (1991) who compared two markets with respect to beer consumption. The two markets varied in terms of size and age composition, and beer consumption was found to vary considerably by age. The relative strengths of the two markets was found to change when age-standardized beer consumption indices were calculated.

Studies by Pol and Pak (1995) and Pak and Pol (1996) have also utilized *log linear purging*, a type of standardization, to facilitate comparisons across market segments. In the former study (1995), the effects of age and race/ethnicity were purged while making comparisons across three market segments for food-away-from-home purchase (i.e., nonspenders, lowspenders, and highspenders). Comparisons of purged rates across market segments and purged and crude rates within and among segments led to the identification of submarkets that appeared to have potential for expanded sales. In the other study (1996), purging was used to facilitate comparisons across age segments of the senior market (age 50 and above) regarding their self-assessed health status.

THE FUTURE OF BUSINESS DEMOGRAPHY

The contributions of demographic analyses to decision making are greater now than at any time in the past. The underlying reasons for the expanded role of demography were identified earlier in this chapter. We do not, however, want to imply that the future will simply be a linear extension of the past. This section focuses on the future, the forces driving decision making, and the ways in which these forces are creating opportunities for demographic contributions.

Driving Forces

There are four driving forces that will guide demographic contributions to decision making as we approach the end of this century. The first is the continued and, in many cases, stepped-up emphasis on data-supported decisions. In most businesses today, intuition, good business judgment, and an ability to clearly understand the business environment are supported by data. While some critics argue that there is too much data and not enough information in today's business arena, most analysts are able to extract from large data systems the type of information needed for decision making. Decision making strictly on intuition is, for the most part, a modus operandi of the past.

Second, as noted earlier in the chapter, the improved availability of data has facilitated data-based decision making. While the data sets and systems available today are impressive, the data systems of the future will be much better. Businesses are routinizing internal data collection in ways never seen before and have come to appreciate the need for improved data quality. The available data sets now contain much more detail, with the level of detail is being driven by a better understanding of the ultimate use of the data.

The third factor involves likely future improvements in the technological capabilities for data storage and retrieval. Some businesses now plan for "the one billion record data set" that only a short time ago was physically impossible to create and access. Faster processors and better storage media make possible desktop applications involving large data sets and complex analyses (Thomas and Kirchner 1992). The technology also involves improvements in presentation options, particularly, detailed maps where a large number of records can be plotted in order to study the spatial aspects of customers, businesses, and so forth. Mapping software now includes the ability to sum population and sales data across geographic units. Icons placed on maps represent information that can be accessed with a simple mouse click on the icon.

The final force involves the change in organizational culture that emphasizes the sharing of information. In the past, there was "accounting data," "marketing data," and data for other specific uses, with all of these databases remaining under the tight control of the data processing department. Technological developments, including the creation of local-area networks and wide-area networks and the increasing power of personal computers, have facilitated information exchange. Data are moving out of the control of the data processing departments to arrangements where data are "distributed" to create the systems needed to address contemporary business decisions. Organizations have grown tired of the turf battles once fought over data and are more concerned with bringing any and all information to bear on the opportunities or problems at hand.

Opportunities Created

A more global and open-minded view regarding data and decision making has created opportunities for incorporating demographic perspectives, data, and methods into business. Business analyses increasingly take into account the demographic elements of the business environment. Owners and managers are concerned with, for example, how the baby boom/bust cycles have affected the size of customer bases in regional and local markets. Owners and managers are also becoming more familiar with the types of data needed to study the effects of demographic change and they do not hesitate to rely on this information in the formulation of business strategy. The analyses themselves are becoming more sophisticated. For example, the baby boom cohort is recognized as a large and heterogenous group requiring further segmentation analysis for an adequate understanding of purchase behavior.

The growing appreciation of data-driven decisions and improvements in data access have created an environment in many organizations in which demographic analysis has become standard. Site location, for example, no longer involves an examination of competitor locations and cost/benefit analyses alone. Detailed data on population size and composition are merged with information on traffic flows, land use patterns, zoning restrictions, and competitor locations to produce the type of information-based decision expected in today's business environment. The analyses are becoming more detailed and useful as the range of available data expands.

More than ever before, demographers have the opportunity to play a role in the business decision-making process. Their knowledge of data sources and technology along with analytic skills places them in a position to make significant contributions. As a result, a growing number of demographers are involved in an expanding number of business applications. This number should grow considerably in the future, especially if demographers gain the experience and secure the training required to maximize the discipline's contribution. Demographers are frequently limited in the contribution that they make because they do not adequately understand the "big picture." They are often unaware of the business decision that is going to be made and how the demographic analysis may affect that decision. In addition, they may not understand the way in which the factors that drive the decision interact. This situation is changing, albeit slowly, and some demographers are now recognized more for their business acumen than their demographic knowledge.

Finally, the use of demographic data in the formulation of strategy will become a standard "tool" of even the smallest businesses. Increased competition, the decrease in cost of software and hardware needed to store and retrieve data, and the growing understanding of the value of demographic input will foster this development. Box 11.2 describes one demographer's application of these techniques in the insurance industry.

Box 11.2
A Day in the Work Life of Susan H. Mott

I am Director of Marketing for Nationwide Life Insurance Company where I have the responsibility for all of the market planning, development, and research for two of the company's six lines of business. In addition, I am responsible for all primary market research conducted by Nationwide's Life Insurance Company. I have a staff of four marketing planning specialists and four market research analysts.

I have a Ph.D. in sociology/demography and, when I was first hired at Nationwide over 13 years ago, my title was Marketing Demographer. Despite this title, I was primarily involved in were survey research and statistical business analysis projects. I spent less than 20 percent of my time on strictly demographic analysis. At the time I was hired, I possessed excellent research and analytic skills obtained through my graduate training. However, it has taken me many years to learn the business of insurance, and I have found that understanding the industry has been a necessary requirement for career advancement.

During my first five or six years with the company, I was actively involved in the management of research projects. This involved ongoing customer satisfaction surveys; studies of agent critical success factors for agents; pilot evaluations; estimations of market potential; and, occasionally, site location studies. The latter two called on my demographic preparation and the former three on my survey research skills.

Today I sit on the management teams for two lines of business. I represent the Marketing function on these management teams. The other team members represent the sales, actuarial, operations (administration, systems, and customer service), and compliance (legal) functions. These teams manage the lines of business and require consensus votes on all important business decisions. As a management team member, I have been forced to develop skills I did not acquire in my academic training. Aside from a keen understanding of the business, it is very helpful to have good management skills—especially in negotiation and persuasion.

I work at the home office of Nationwide Insurance in Columbus, Ohio. Despite its appellation of "cow town," Columbus is very urban. It has most of the amenities of larger cities (good opera, symphony theater, museums, and restaurants) with less of the hassle (little rush hour traffic and reasonable housing costs). The Nationwide Insurance enterprise is located in three towers in the heart of downtown.

On a typical day, I may spend as much as half of my time in meetings. Management team meetings are usually focused on decisions that need to be made on such issues as agent recruitment, new product development, royalty fees for sponsoring organizations, and customer service enhancements. As the Marketing representative I am expected to bring information collected on customers, competitors, producers, and industry trends to bear on these decisions. Meetings with the marketing staff are concerned with more technical issues. These might include which primary research methodologies are most appropriate for getting needed information about customers, which data collection vendors should be sent requests for proposals, what are the implications of specific research findings, how can we best carry out a benchmark study on a competitor of interest, what tasks need to be accomplished to update our on-line competitor information network for internal clients, to name just a few.

Box 11.2 continued

Part of my day might be spent explaining research findings to "stakeholders" and facilitating the development of an action plan based on these findings. Recently, our ongoing customer surveys uncovered a low awareness of our automated telephone service for financial transactions. This discovery led to the development of a communication plan to increase use of the service, which in turn enabled us to complete transactions more efficiently without compromising our high level of customer satisfaction.

REFERENCES

Ambrose, David, and Louis Pol (1994). "Motel 48: Evaluating the Profitability of a Proposed Business." In Hallie Kintner et al. (eds.), *Demographics: A Casebook for Business and Government*. Boulder, CO: Westview Press, pp. 144–154.

Bain, Lee J. (1978). *Statistical Analysis of Reliability and Life Testing Models*. New York: Dekker.

Billings, George, and Louis Pol (1994). "Improving Cellular Market Area Valuation with Demographic Data." In Hallie Kintner et al. (eds.), *Demographics: A Casebook for Business and Government*. Boulder, CO: Westview Press, pp. 93–108.

Bryan, Nora (1994). "Marks and Spencer Map It Out." *Business Geographics*, 2 (May): 36–37.

Clogg, Clifford, and Scott Eliason (1988). "A Flexible Procedure for Adjusting Rates and Proportions, Including Statistical Methods for Group Comparisons." *American Sociological Review*, 53 (April): 267–283.

Cowen, Dave (1995). "Assessing a Commercial Real Estate Market." *Business Geographics* 3 (June): 38–41.

Cox, David R. (1972). "Regression Models and Life Tables." *Journal of the Royal Statistical Society*, Series B34: 187–202.

Davenhall, William (1993). "Health Care Reform: 1,000 Not-So-Easy Pieces." *Business Geographics*, 1 (November/December): 36–38.

Garcia, Philip (1994). "Predicting College Enrollment Results from a Variant of the Life Table." In Hallie Kintner et al. (eds.), *Demographics: A Casebook for Business and Government*. Boulder, CO: Westview, Press, pp. 307–326.

Halley, Edmund (1693). "An Estimate of the Degrees of the Mortality of Mankind." *Philosophical Transactions*, 17: 596–610.

Halli, Shiva S., and K. Vaninadha Rao (1992). *Advanced Techniques of Population Analysis*. New York: Plenum Publishing Company.

Hoerning, Roxanne (1996). "American Honda Jump-Starts Sales Geographically." *Business Geographics*, 4 (March): 24–26.

Hughes, Arthur (1994). *Strategic Database Marketing*. Chicago: Probus.

Johnson, Kenneth (1994). "Selecting Markets for Corporate Expansion: A Case Study in Applied Demography." In Hallie Kintner et al. (eds.), *Demographics: A Casebook for Business and Government*. Boulder, CO: Westview Press, pp. 129–143.

Kintner, Hallie, and Louis Pol (1996). "Demography and Decision Making." *Population Research and Policy Review* (forthcoming).

Kintner, Hallie and David Swanson (1994). "Estimating Vital Rates from Corporate Databases: How Long Will GM Salaried Retirees Live?" In Hallie Kintner et al. (eds.), *Demographics: A Casebook for Business and Government*. Boulder, CO: Westview Press, pp. 265–297.

Kitagawa, Evelyn (1964). "Standardized Comparisons in Population Research." *Demography*, 1: 296–315.

Morrison, Peter A., and Allan F. Abrahamse (1996). "Applying Demographic Analysis to Store Site Selection." *Population Research and Policy Review* (forthcoming).

Murdock, Steven, and Rita Hamm (1994). "A Demographic Analysis of the Market for a Long-Term Care Facility: A Case Study in Applied Demography." In Hallie Kintner et al. (eds.), *Demographics: A Casebook for Business and Government*. Boulder, CO: Westview Press, pp. 218–246.

Nelson, Wayne B. (1982). *Applied Life Data Analysis*. New York: Wiley.

Pak, Sukgoo, and Louis G. Pol (1996). "Segmenting the Senior Care Market." *Health Marketing Quarterly*, 13 (4): 63–77.

Palmore, Erdman (1978). "When Can Age, Period and Cohort Be Separated?" *Social Forces*, 57 (September): 282–295.

Peete, Cynthia, and Jenny Godley (1996). "Needs Assessment and Feasibility Study for the City of Pleasanton." Paper presented at the annual meeting of the Population Association of America, New Orleans, May 6–8.

Pol, Louis (1988). "Determining the Demographics of a Market Area." In Thomas Merrick and Stephen Tordella, *Demographics: People and Markets. Population Bulletin*, 43, No. 1 Washington, DC: Population Reference Bureau, pp. 43–45..

Pol, Louis G., and Sukgoo Pak (1995). "Consumer Unit Types and Expenditures on Food Away From Home." *Journal of Consumer Affairs*, 29 (2): 403–428.

Pol, Louis, and Douglas Tymkiw (1991). "A Technique to Compare Demographically Different Markets." *Marketing Research* 3 (March): 29–34.

Rentz, Joseph O., and Fred D. Reynolds (1980). "Separating Age, Cohort and Period Effects in Consumer Behavior." *Advances in Consumer Research*, 8: 596–603.

Rentz, Joseph O., Fred D. Reynolds, and Roy G. Stout (1983). "Analyzing Changing Consumption Patterns with Cohort Analysis." *Journal of Marketing Research*, 20 (February): 12–12.

Reynolds, Fred D., and Joseph O. Rentz (1981). "Cohort Analysis: An Aid to Strategic Planning." *Journal of Marketing*, 45 (Summer): 62–70.

Rives, Bill (1994). "Strategic Planning for Hospitals: Demographic Considerations." In Hallie Kintner et al. (eds.), *Demographics: A Casebook for Business and Government*. Boulder, CO: Westview Press, pp. 251–264.

Ryder, Norman B. (1965). "The Cohort as a Concept in the Study of Social Change." *American Sociological Review*, 30 (6): 843–861.

Smith, David P. (1992). *Formal Demography*. New York: Plenum Publishing Company.

Swanson, David, Thomas Burch, and Lucky Tedrow (1996). "What is Applied Demography?" *Population Research and Policy Review* (forthcoming).

Tayman, Jeff, and Louis Pol (1995). "Retail Site Selection and Geographic Information Systems." *Journal of Applied Business Research*, 11 (2): 46–54.

Thomas, Richard (1994). "Using Demographic Analysis in Health Services Planning: A Case Study in Obstetrical Services." In Hallie Kintner et al. (eds.), *Demographics: A Casebook for Business and Government*. Boulder, CO: Westview Press, pp. 159–179.

Thomas, Richard, and Russell Kirchner (1992). *Desktop Marketing*. Ithaca, NY: American Demographics.

Voss, Paul (1994). "Targeting Ex-Wisconsinites in Florida: A Case Study in Applied

Demography." In Hallie Kintner et al. (eds.), *Demographics: A Casebook for Business and Government*. Boulder, CO: Westview Press, pp. 109–128.

Appendix: State Data Center Program Lead Agencies (Includes Business and Industry Data Center Initiative Components)[1]

Alabama

Center for Business and Economic Research
University of Alabama
Box 870221
Tuscaloosa, AL 35487-0221
*Ms. Annette Watters
(205) 348-6191
Fax (205) 348-2951

Alaska

Census & Geographic Information
Network
Research & Analysis
Alaska Department of Labor
P.O. Box 25504
Juneau, AK 99802-5504
*Ms. Kathryn Lizik
(907) 465-2437
Fax (907) 465-2101

Arizona (BIDC)

Arizona Department of Economic

Security
DES 045Z
1789 West Jefferson Street
Phoenix, AZ 85007
*+Ms. Betty Jeffries
(602) 542-5984
Fax (602) 542-6474

Arkansas

State Data Center
University of Arkansas-Little Rock
2801 South University
Little Rock, AR 72204
*Ms. Sarah Breshears
(501) 569-8530
Fax (501) 569-8538

California

State Census Data Center
Department of Finance
915 L Street
Sacramento, CA 95814
*Ms. Linda Gage, Director
(916) 322-4651

---

[1]*Denotes key contact SDC; + denotes key contact BIDC.

Mr. Richard Lovelady
(916) 323-4141
Fax (916) 327-0222

Colorado

Division of Local Government
Colorado Department of Local Affairs
1313 Sherman Street, Room 521
Denver, CO 80203
*Ms. Rebecca Picaso
(303) 866-2156
Fax (303) 866-2803

Connecticut

Office of Policy and Management
Policy Development and Planning
Division
450 Capital Avenue-MS#52ASP
P.O. Box 341441
Hartford, CT 06134-1441
*Mr. Bill Kraynak
(860) 418-6230
Fax (860) 418-6495

Delaware (BIDC)

Delaware Economic Development
Office
99 Kings Highway
P.O. Box 1401
Dover, DE 19903
*+Mr. Mike Mahaffie
(302) 739-4271
Fax (302) 739-5749

District of Columbia

Data Services Division
Mayor's Office of Planning
Room 570, Presidential Building
415 12th Street, N.W.
Washington, DC 20004
*Mr. Herb Bixhorn
(202) 727-6533
Fax (202) 727-6964

Florida (BIDC)

Florida Department of Labor and
Employment Security
Bureau of Labor Market Information
Hartman Building, Suite 200
2012 Capital Circle, S.E.
Tallahassee, FL 32399-2151
*Ms. Pam Schenker
(904) 488-1048
Fax (904) 488-2558

Bureau of Economic Analysis
Flordia Department of Commerce
107 West Gaines Street
315 Collins Building
Tallahassee, FL 32399-2000
+Mr. Nick Leslie
(904) 487-2971
Fax (904) 487-3014

Georgia

Division of Demographic & Statistical
Services
Georgia Office of Planning and Budget
254 Washington Street, S.W.
Room 640
Atlanta, GA 30334
*Ms. Marty Sik
(404) 656-0911
Fax (404) 656-3828

Guam

Guam Department of Commerce
590 South Marine Drive
Suite 601, 6th Floor GITC Building
Tamuning, Guam 96911
*Mr. Art De Oro
(671) 646-5841
Fax (671) 646-7242

Hawaii

Hawaii State Data Center
Department of Business Economic
Development & Tourism
220 South King Street, Suite 400
Honolulu, HI 96813

(Mailing Address)
P.O. Box 2359
Honolulu, HI 96804
*Ms. Jan Nakamoto
(808) 586-2493
Fax (808) 586-8449

Idaho

Idaho Department of Commerce
700 West State Street
Boise, ID 83720
*Mr. Alan Porter
(208) 334-2470
Fax (208) 334-2631

Illinois

Illinois Bureau of the Budget
William Stratton Building, Room 605
400 Springs Street
Springfield, IL 62706
*Ms. Suzanne Ebetsch
(217) 782-1381
Fax (217) 524-4876

Indiana (BIDC)

Indiana State Library
Indiana State Data Center
140 North Senate Avenue
Indianapolis, IN 46204
Mr. Ray Ewick, Director
*Mr. Laurence Hathaway
(317) 232-3733
Fax (317) 232-3728

Indiana Business Research Center
801 West Michigan, B.S. 4015
Indianapolis, IN 46202-5151
+Ms. Carol Rogers
(317) 274-2205
Fax (317) 274-2483

Iowa

State Library of Iowa
East 12th and Grand
Des Moines, IA 50319
*Ms. Beth Henning

(515) 281-4350
Fax (515) 281-3384

Kansas

State Library
Room 343-N
State Capitol Building
Topeka, KA 66612
*Mr. Marc Galbraith
(913) 296-3296
Fax (913) 296-6650

Kentucky (BIDC)

Center for Urban & Economic Research
College of Business & Public
Administration
University of Louisville
Louisville, KY 40292
*+Mr. Vernon Smith
(502) 852-7990
Fax (502) 852-7386

Louisiana

Office of Planning and Budget
Division of Administration
P.O. Box 94095
1051 North 3rd Street
Baton Rouge, LA 70804
*Ms. Karen Paterson
(504) 342-7410
Fax (504) 342-1057

Maine (BIDC)

Division of Economic Analysis and
Research
Maine Department of Labor
20 Union Street
Augusta, ME 04330
Mr. Raynold Fongemie, Director
*+Staff
(207) 287-2271
Fax (207) 287-5292

Maryland (BIDC)

Maryland Department of State Planning

301 West Preston Street
Baltimore, MD 21201
*+Ms. Jane Traynham
(301) 225-4450
Fax (301) 225-4480

Massachusetts (BIDC)

Massachusetts Institute for Social and
Economic Research
128 Thompson Hall
University of Massachusetts
Amherst, MA 01003
*Ms. Valerie Conti
(413) 545-0176
Fax (413) 545-3686

Michigan

Michigan Information Center
Department of Management & Budget
Office of Revenue and Tax Analysis
P.O. Box 30026
Lansing, MI 48909
*Mr. Eric Swanson
(517) 373-7910
Fax (517) 335-1521

Minnesota (BIDC)

State Demographer's Office
Minnesota Planning
300 Centennial Office Building
658 Cedar Street
St. Paul, MN 55155
*Mr. David Birkholz
(612) 296-2557
+Mr. David Rademacher
(612) 297-3255
Fax (612) 296-3698

Mississippi (BIDC)

Center for Population Studies
The University of Mississippi
Bondurant Building, Room 3W
University, MS 38677
Dr. Max Williams, Director
*Ms. Rachel McNeely, Manager

(601) 232-7288
Fax (601) 232-7736

Division of Research and Information
Systems
Department of Economic and
Community Development
1200 Walter Sillas Building
P.O. Box 849
Jackson, MS 39205
+Ms. Deloise Tate
(601) 359-3593
Fax (601) 359-3545

Missouri (BIDC)

Missouri State Library
600 West Main Street
P.O. Box 387
Jefferson City, MO 65102
*Ms. Kate Graf
(314) 751-1823
Fax (314) 526-1142

Missouri Small Business Development
Centers
300 University Place
Columbia, MO 65211
+Terry Maynard
(314) 882-0344
Fax (314) 884-4297

Montana (BIDC)

Census and Economic Information
Center
Montana Department of Commerce
P.O. Box 200501
1424 9th Avenue
Helena, MT 59620-0501
*+Ms. Patricia Roberts
(406) 444-2896
Fax (406) 444-1518

Nebraska

Center for Applied Urban Research
Nebraska State Data Center
Room 203—Annex 26
The University of Nebraska at Omaha

Omaha, NE 68182
*Mr. Jerome Deichert
Tim Himberger
(402) 595-2311
Fax (402) 595-2366

Nevada

Nevada State Library
Capitol Complex
4100 Stewart Street
Carson City, NV 89710
Ms. Joan Kerschner
*Staff
(702) 687-8326
Fax (702) 687-8330

New Hampshire

Office of State Planning
2 1/2 Beacon Street
Concord, NH 03301
*Mr. Tom Duffy
(603) 271-2155
Fax (603) 271-1728

New Jersey (BIDC)

New Jersey Department of Labor
Division of Labor Market and
Demographic Research
CN 388-John Fitch Plaza
Trenton, NJ 08625-0388
*+Doug Moore
(609) 984-2593
Fax (609) 984-6833

New Mexico (BIDC)

Bureau of Business and Economic
Research
University of New Mexico
1920 Lomas N.E.
Albuquerque, NM 87131
*Mr. Kevin Kargacin
(505) 277-6626
+Mr. Bobby Leitch
(505) 277-2216
Fax (505) 277-7066

New York (BIDC)

Division of Policy & Research
Department of Economic Department
1 Commerce Plaza, Room 905
99 Washington Avenue
Albany, NY 12245
Mr. Robert Scardamalia
*+Staff
(518) 474-1141
Fax (518) 473-9748

North Carolina (BIDC)

North Carolina Office of State Planning
116 West Jones Street
Raleigh, NC 27603-8005
*+Ms. Francine Stephenson,
Director of State Data Center
(919) 733-4131
Fax (919) 733-5679

North Dakota

Department of Agricultural Economics
North Dakota State University
Morrill Hall, Room 224
P.O. Box 5636
Fargo, ND 58105
*Dr. Richard Rathge
(701) 231-8621
Fax (701) 231-7400

Northern Mariana Islands

Department of Commerce and Labor
Central Statistics Division
Saipan
Mariana Islands 96950
*Mr. Juan Borja
(670) 322-0874/0876
Fax (670) 322-0880

Ohio (BIDC)

Ohio Data Users Center
Ohio Department of Development
P.O. Box 1001
Columbus, OH 43266-0101
*+Mr. Barry Bennett

(614) 466-2115
Fax (614) 644-5167

Oklahoma (BIDC)

Oklahoma State Data Center
Oklahoma Department of Commerce
6601 Broadway Extension
(Mailing address)
P.O. Box 26980
Oklahoma City, OK 73126-0980
*+Mr. Jeff Wallace
(405) 841-5184
Fax (405) 841-5199

Oregon

Center for Population Research and
Census
Portland State University
P.O. Box 751
Portland, OR 97207-0751
Mr. Ed Shafer
*Mr. George Hough
(503) 725-5159
Fax (503) 725-5199

Pennsylvania (BIDC)

Pennsylvania State Data Center
Institute of State and Regional Affairs
Pennsylvania State University at
Harrisburg
777 West Harrisburg Pike
Middletown, PA 17057
Michael Beheny, Director
*+Ms. Diane Shoop
(717) 948-6336
Fax (717) 948-6306

Puerto Rico

Puerto Rico Planning Board
Minillas Government Center
North Building, Avenida De Diego
P.O. Box 41119
San Juan, PR 00940-9985
*Sra. Lillian Torrez Aquirre
(809) 728-4430
Fax (809) 268-0506

Rhode Island

Department of Administration
Office of Municipal Affairs
One Capitol Hill
Providence, RI 02980-5873
*Mr. Paul Egan
(401) 277-6493
Fax (401) 277-3809

South Carolina

Division of Research and Statistical
Services
South Carolina Budget and Control
Board
Rembert Dennis Building, Room 425
Columbia, SC 29201
Mr. Bobby Bowers
*Mike Macfarlane
(803) 734-3780
Fax (803) 734-3619

South Dakota

Business Research Bureau
School of Business
University of South Dakota
414 East Clark
Vermillion, SD 57069
*Ms. DeVee Dykstra
(605) 677-5287
Fax (605) 677-5427

Tennessee

Tennessee State Planning Office
John Sevier State Office Buliding
500 Charlotte Avenue, Suite 307
Nashville, TN 37243-0001
*Mr. Charles Brown
(615) 741-1676
Fax (615) 741-5829

Texas

Department of Rural Sociology
Texas A & M University System
Special Services Building
College Station, TX 77843-2125

*Dr. Steve Murdock
(409) 845-5115 or 5332
Fax (409) 845-8529

Utah (BIDC)

Office of Planning & Budget
State Capitol, Room 116
Salt Lake City, UT 84114
Ms. Kirin McInnis
(801) 538-1550
*+Ms. Jennifer Taylor
(801) 538-1036
Fax (801) 538-1547

Vermont

Vermont Department of Libraries
109 State Street
Montpelier, VT 05609-0601
*Ms. Sybil McShane
(802) 828-3261
Fax (802) 828-2199

Virginia (BIDC)

Virginia Employment Commission
703 East Main Street
Richmond, VA 23219
+*Mr. Dan Jones
(804) 786-8308
Fax (804) 786-7844

Virgin Islands

University of the Virgin Islands
Eastern Caribbean Center
No. 2 John Brewer's Bay
Charlotte Amalie
St. Thomas, VI 00802
*Dr. Frank Mills
(809) 693-1027
Fax (809) 693-1025

Washington (BIDC)

Forecasting Division
Office of Financial Management
450 Insurance Building, Box 43113
Olympia, WA 98504-3113

*+Ms. Yi Zhao
(206) 586-2504
Fax (206) 664-8941

West Virginia (BIDC)

Community Development Division
Governor's Office of Community and
Industrial Development
Capitol Complex
Building 6, Room 553
Charleston, WV 25305
*Ms. Mary C. Harless
(304) 558-4010
Fax (304) 558-3248

The Center for Economic Research
West Virginia University
323 Business and Economic Building
Morgantown, WV 26506-6025
Dr. Tom Witt, Director
+Mr. Randy Childs
(304) 293-7832
Fax (304) 293-7061

Wisconsin (BIDC)

Demographic Services Center
101 E. Wilson Street, 6th Floor
P.O. Box 7868
Madison, WI 53707-7868
Ms. Nadene Roenspies
*Mr. Robert Naylor
(608) 266-1927
Fax (608) 267-6931

Applied Population Laboratory
Department of Rural Sociology
University of Wisconsin
1450 Linden Drive, Room 316
Madison, WI 53706
+Mr. Ed Wallander
(608) 262-3097
Fax (608) 262-6022

Wyoming

Department of Administration and
Information
Economic Analysis Division

Emerson Building 327E
Cheyenne, WY 82002-0060
Mr. Steve Furtney
*Mr. Wenlin Liu
(307) 777-7504
Fax (307) 777-5852

Index

About the Authors

LOUIS G. POL is Peter Kiewit Distinguished Professor of Marketing at the University of Nebraska, Omaha. He has conducted research and lectured in a number of countries in Europe and the former Soviet Union. This book is an extension of his first Quorum book, *Business Demography* (1987). He is also coauthor with Dr. Thomas of three other books on the intersection of demography research methods and health care.

RICHARD K. THOMAS is a partner in the Memphis firm Medical Services Research Group. A highly experienced health services researcher, marketer, and planner, with a Ph.D. from Vanderbilt University, Dr. Thomas has published widely on topics in health and health care and is well known as a speaker at medical services conferences. He served on the faculty of the University of Memphis for more than twenty years and is now an adjunct professor for two other health professional training programs.